Evaluating
WELFARE REFORM
in an Era of Transition

Panel on Data and Methods for Measuring the Effects of Changes in Social Welfare Programs

Robert A. Moffitt and Michele Ver Ploeg, *Editors*

Committee on National Statistics

Division of Behavioral and Social Sciences and Education

National Research Council

NATIONAL ACADEMY PRESS
Washington, DC

NATIONAL ACADEMY PRESS • 2101 Constitution Avenue, N.W. • Washington, DC 20418

NOTICE: The project that is the subject of this report was approved by the Governing Board of the National Research Council, whose members are drawn from the councils of the National Academy of Sciences, the National Academy of Engineering, and the Institute of Medicine. The members of the committee responsible for the report were chosen for their special competences and with regard for appropriate balance.

This study was supported by Contract No. HHS-100-98-0011 between the National Academy of Sciences and the U.S. Department of Health and Human Services. Support of the work of the Committee on National Statistics is provided by a consortium of federal agencies through a grant from the National Science Foundation (Number SBR-9709489). Any opinions, findings, conclusions, or recommendations expressed in this publication are those of the author(s) and do not necessarily reflect the views of the organizations or agencies that provided support for the project.

Library of Congress Cataloging-in-Publication Data

Evaluating welfare reform in an era of transition / Panel on Data and
Methods for Measuring the Effects of Changes in Social Welfare Programs
; Robert A. Moffitt and Michele Ver Ploeg, editors.
    p. cm.
"Committee on National Statistics, Division of Behavioral and Social
Sciences and Education, National Research Council."
Includes bibliographical references and index.
  ISBN 0-309-07274-3 (hardcover)
  1. Public welfare—United States—Evaluation. 2. Public welfare
administration—United States—Evaluation. 3. Social surveys—United
States—Evaluation. I. Moffitt, Robert. II. Ver Ploeg, Michele. III.
National Research Council (U.S.). Panel on Data and Methods for
Measuring the Effects of Changes in Social Welfare Programs.
  HV95 .E958 2001
  361.973—dc21

                          2001002534

Additional copies of this report are available from National Academy Press, 2101 Constitution Avenue, N.W., Lockbox 285, Washington, D.C. 20055; (800) 624-6242 or (202) 334-3313 (in the Washington metropolitan area); Internet, http://www.nap.edu

Suggested citation: National Research Council (2001) *Evaluating Welfare Reform in an Era of Transition.* Panel on Data and Methods for Measuring the Effects of Changes in Social Welfare Programs, Robert A. Moffitt and Michele Ver Ploeg, Editors. Committee on National Statistics, Division of Behavioral and Social Sciences and Education. Washington, DC: National Academy Press.

THE NATIONAL ACADEMIES

National Academy of Sciences
National Academy of Engineering
Institute of Medicine
National Research Council

The **National Academy of Sciences** is a private, nonprofit, self-perpetuating society of distinguished scholars engaged in scientific and engineering research, dedicated to the furtherance of science and technology and to their use for the general welfare. Upon the authority of the charter granted to it by the Congress in 1863, the Academy has a mandate that requires it to advise the federal government on scientific and technical matters. Dr. Bruce M. Alberts is president of the National Academy of Sciences.

The **National Academy of Engineering** was established in 1964, under the charter of the National Academy of Sciences, as a parallel organization of outstanding engineers. It is autonomous in its administration and in the selection of its members, sharing with the National Academy of Sciences the responsibility for advising the federal government. The National Academy of Engineering also sponsors engineering programs aimed at meeting national needs, encourages education and research, and recognizes the superior achievements of engineers. Dr. William A. Wulf is president of the National Academy of Engineering.

The **Institute of Medicine** was established in 1970 by the National Academy of Sciences to secure the services of eminent members of appropriate professions in the examination of policy matters pertaining to the health of the public. The Institute acts under the responsibility given to the National Academy of Sciences by its congressional charter to be an adviser to the federal government and, upon its own initiative, to identify issues of medical care, research, and education. Dr. Kenneth I. Shine is president of the Institute of Medicine.

The **National Research Council** was organized by the National Academy of Sciences in 1916 to associate the broad community of science and technology with the Academy's purposes of furthering knowledge and advising the federal government. Functioning in accordance with general policies determined by the Academy, the Council has become the principal operating agency of both the National Academy of Sciences and the National Academy of Engineering in providing services to the government, the public, and the scientific and engineering communities. The Council is administered jointly by both Academies and the Institute of Medicine. Dr. Bruce M. Alberts and Dr. William A. Wulf are chairman and vice chairman, respectively, of the National Research Council.

Acknowledgments

The Panel on Data and Methods for Measuring the Effects of Changes in Social Welfare Programs wishes to thank the many people who contributed to the preparation of this report.

The study was sponsored by the Office of the Assistant Secretary for Planning and Evaluation in the U.S. Department of Health and Human Services (ASPE-DHHS) through a congressional appropriation. Throughout the study, the panel was assisted by the dedicated staff of the agency. In particular, we thank Patricia Ruggles, Susan Hauan, Julie Isaacs, and Don Oellerich for briefing the panel and providing background information. The panel also thanks Howard Rolston of the Administration for Children and Families (ACF) in DHHS and his staff for meeting with panel members to discuss the reporting requirement data for the Temporary Assistance for Needy Family (TANF) program and efforts to catalogue state welfare programs.

The panel is greatly indebted to those who presented and discussed papers at the Workshop on Data Collection for Low-Income and Welfare Populations sponsored by the panel. The papers comprehensively discussed the current state of knowledge for surveying low-income populations; preparation and use of and access to welfare program-relevant administrative data systems; and measuring important outcomes for welfare studies. The panel would also like to acknowledge Kristin Moore of Child Trends, Inc., and Janet Norwood of the Urban Institute for their remarks at the workshop. The panel is also grateful to Greg Acs and Pamela Loprest of the Urban Institute, who prepared a paper summarizing welfare leavers studies and to Leyla Mohadjer and Hussain Choudhry of Westat, who prepared a paper on adjusting for missing data on surveys. These papers will appear in the panel's companion volume entitled "Data Collection and Research Issues for Studies of Welfare Populations" to be published later this year.

Many other individuals participated in panel meetings or briefed the panel on data and methodological issues that provided background information for the panel's deliberations. Kenneth Bryson, Patricia Doyle, Enrique Llamas, Stephanie Shipp, and Edward Welniak, of the Census Bureau, briefed the panel on the Bureau's low income and welfare related data sets. The panel is also grateful to participants of the panel's Seminar on Evaluation Methods: Burt Barnow of Johns Hopkins University, Randy Brown of Mathematica Policy Research, Gary Burtless of the Brookings Institution, Robert LaLonde of the University of Chicago, Charles Metcalf of Mathematica Policy Research, Bruce Meyer of Northwestern University, Charles Michalopoulos of the Manpower Demonstration Research Corporation, and Robert Schoeni of RAND. The panel also thanks David Stevens of the University of Baltimore for preparing and presenting a paper and a follow-up memorandum on the composition of the Maryland caseload. We thank Sheila Zedlewski and Linda Giannarelli of the Urban Institute for preparing a paper on microsimulation methods and for briefing panel members and staff on the Welfare Rules Database. The panel also thanks Gary Cyphers and Kathleen Kinsella of the American Public Human Services Association for meeting with panel members and staff to discuss state efforts to develop administrative databases for use in welfare program research. Finally, we thank the Institute for Research on Poverty and its former director, Barbara Wolfe, for providing hospitality to Michele Ver Ploeg to conduct a study of Wisconsin welfare leavers.

The panel is indebted to the efforts of the National Research Council (NRC) staff in the work of the panel and in the preparation of this report. Michele Ver Ploeg, the study director for the panel and coeditor of this report, provided essential support throughout the life of the panel and in drafting the report. She organized the panel's discussions into coherent topics, identified issues and formulated questions and conclusions, and supervised the general activities of the panel by organizing meetings, gathering materials and interviewing outside experts, and serving as liaison to the sponsor and other outside groups. She also assisted the panel by drafting major sections of this report and by supervising the redrafting process as part of the NRC internal review process. Shelly also conducted an independent study of welfare leavers at the same time, which is included in the panel's companion volume. Constance Citro, senior project officer, provided experienced and wise counsel throughout the life of the panel and on this report, and contributed important insights in panel discussions. Miron Straf, former Director of the Committee on National Statistics under whose auspices the panel operated, is acknowledged for his assistance in organizing the panel and working out the charge of the panel with the sponsor. The panel is very appreciative of the work of Jamie Casey, senior project assistant, for arranging the logistics of panel meetings and for her excellent work on the production of this manuscript. We also thank Eugenia Grohman, associate director for reports of the Division of Behavioral and Social Sciences and Education, for her careful and thorough technical editing, her commentary on report drafts, and for overseeing the review process.

This report has been reviewed in draft form by individuals chosen for their diverse perspectives and technical expertise, in accordance with procedures approved by the NRC's Report Review Committee. The purpose of this independent review is to provide candid and critical comments that will assist the institution in making the published report as sound as possible and to ensure that the report meets institutional standards for objectivity, evidence, and responsiveness to the study charge. The review comments and draft manuscript remain confidential to protect the integrity of the deliberative process.

We thank the following individuals for their participation in the review of this report: Kenneth Arrow, Department of Economics, Stanford University; Greg J. Duncan, Institute for Policy Research and School of Education and Social Policy, Northwestern University; David Illig, California Health and Human Services Agency, Sacramento; Michael Pergamit, National Opinion Research Center, Washington, DC; Frank Samaniego, Department of Statistics, University of California, Davis; Fritz Scheuren, Urban Institute, Washington, DC; and Deanna Schexnayder, Lyndon B. Johnson School of Public Affairs, University of Texas, Austin.

Although the reviewers listed above have provided many constructive comments and suggestions, they were not asked to endorse the conclusions or recommendations nor did they see the final draft of the report before its release. The review of this report was overseen by John Bailar, Department of Health Studies, University of Chicago (emeritus), and Robert Michael, Harris Graduate School of Public Policy, University of Chicago. Appointed by the National Research Council, they were responsible for making certain that an independent examination of this report was carried out in accordance with institutional procedures and that all review comments were carefully considered. Responsibility for the final content of this report rests entirely with the authoring panel and the institution.

Finally, I thank my fellow panel members for giving their time and expertise so generously towards the completion of this report. Every member of the panel brought a critical perspective and expertise to the discussions, without which the report would have been missing important elements. Their hard work and selfless dedication in the service of a public benefit was exemplary.

Robert Moffitt, *Chair*
Panel on Data and Methods for
Measuring the Effects of Changes in
Social Welfare Programs

Contents

Evaluating
WELFARE REFORM

Executive Summary

With the passing of the Personal Responsibility and Work Opportunity Reconciliation Act (PRWORA) of 1996, the United States embarked on a major social experiment with its social welfare and safety net programs for the poor. The most far-reaching reform of the cash welfare system for single mothers since 1935, PRWORA replaced the federal entitlement program for low-income families and children (Aid to Families with Dependent Children, AFDC) with a state-administered block grant program, the Temporary Assistance for Needy Families (TANF). Determining the consequences of this experiment is of great importance. Has welfare reform "worked?" What were the effects of the reforms on families and individuals? What reforms worked for whom and why? In looking toward the development of new policies to aid low-income families, which elements of the new welfare system need to be changed and which left as is?

For these fundamental questions to be answered adequately, two issues need to be addressed. First, how should one go about answering these questions—what methods should be used and what types of studies should be conducted in order to determine the effects of welfare reform? Second, what types of data are needed to measure the effects of welfare reform? Are federal and state data sources currently available sufficient to carry out needed evaluations, and, if not, what investments in that infrastructure are needed?

These two issues are the subject of this report.

THE PANEL

To answer these questions, the Committee on National Statistics of the National Research Council formed the Panel on Data and Methods for Measuring the Effects of Changes in Social Welfare Programs. This panel is sponsored by the Office of the Assistant Secretary for Planning and Evaluation (ASPE) of the U.S. Department of Health and Human Services (DHHS) through a congressional appropriation. The charge to the panel is to review methods and data needed to evaluate the outcomes of changes in social welfare programs on families and individuals. The panel is specifically charged with assisting the department in (1) identifying how best to measure and track program eligibility, participation, child well-being, and other outcomes; (2) evaluating data, research designs, and methods for the study of welfare reform outcomes; and (3) identifying needed areas and topics of research. In doing so, the panel was asked to consider alternative federal and state data sources, the limitations of currently available data, appropriate evaluation designs and methods for analysis, and findings from previous research and evaluation. The panel is also specifically charged with reviewing data needs and methods for tracking and assessing the effects of program changes on families who stop receiving cash assistance—i.e., welfare leavers.

FINDINGS

The set of welfare reform projects that have been completed or are now under way is impressive in scope, volume, and diversity. The volume of research is unprecedented in comparison with any prior era of welfare reform. A large number of capable researchers in the private and public sectors are devoting major efforts to welfare reform research and have been producing a number of valuable and informative studies. Both ASPE and the Administration for Children and Families (ACF) in DHHS have substantial agendas for welfare reform research and have supported much high quality work, as have private foundations.

The panel finds that studies of welfare reform to date have done a reasonable job of monitoring the progress of the low-income and welfare populations—that is, tracking the well-being of these populations over time, although usually only after reform. More useful studies of this type are under way. However, monitoring studies are only the first step in assessing the effects of welfare reform. The second, more critical step is to evaluate the effects of welfare reform—that is, how it has changed the outcomes for families and individuals relative to what would have happened in the absence of reform. The panel finds that the evaluation studies that have been done are only able to address a small number of questions. There are many important questions that have not been addressed at all or not adequately addressed. Little is known about the effects of specific individual reform strategies, for example, a human capital approach versus a work-first approach or a set of relatively strict work requirements versus a set of less strict work requirements. Evaluations of other questions have been limited by weaknesses in data. These weaknesses are particularly limiting for studies that have assessed the overall effect of welfare reform and for national-level studies of broad components of the reform, such as any time limit versus no time limit or work requirements versus no work requirements. Consequently, many important evaluation questions have not been adequately answered.

The panel also finds that the nation's data infrastructure currently has serious limitations and weaknesses for the study of welfare reform, at both the national and state levels. These limitations have implications for both monitoring and evaluation studies. National-level survey data sets are of limited sample size, have significant problems of nonresponse, and are not readily able to adjust the content of questions on welfare program participation to the devolved structure of programs. Moreover, serious delays in producing key data sets have limited publicly available data for the post-PRWORA period, making it very difficult to examine TANF outcomes. Data on program characteristics and rules in the various states have only lately been developed. State-level administrative data have considerable potential but vary greatly in quality and quantity and lack comparability across the states. Matching different state-level administrative data sets across different programs would be of great value, but confidentiality and access rules limit the degree to which matches of data sets can be made. Finally, state-level surveys are in their infancy and have only provided limited data for monitoring and evaluation.

On an even more basic level, the panel finds that no overarching research agenda for evaluating the changes in welfare program policy has been established. There has been no concerted effort to outline which questions about the effects of the reforms need to be answered in order to assess whether the reforms were a success, or more generally, what set of outcomes the research and evaluation community should be examining. Existing welfare reform research consists of a large number of studies, funded by a wide and diverse set of public and private organizations, that, taken as a whole, are unfocused and uncoordinated and leave some questions unaddressed. Some types of studies have been overemphasized and have received disproportionate attention—those focusing on families who have left welfare, for example—while others have been underemphasized–for example, those that evaluate the effects of broad and specific components of reforms on families and individuals. Overall, the panel finds that the nation has largely failed in one of the most important goals of a mature and advanced society, namely, to be able to measure the effects of the policies it enacts so that these policies can be improved in the future.

KEY QUESTIONS OF INTEREST

Finding no systematic assessment of important questions that need to be addressed to evaluate welfare policy reforms, the panel took up the task of identifying the key questions of interest itself. The panel considered three separate issues in this respect: What are the populations of interest? What outcomes are of most interest? What formal evaluation questions should be answered?

Populations of Interest

For a reform as fundamental as that which has occurred under PRWORA, virtually all families in the low-income population may be affected, as the effects of reforms of particular welfare programs reverberate through all families in low income communities. Low-income families should, therefore, be the first and foremost population of interest for welfare reform evaluations. For the TANF program in particular, the population of all low income single mothers and their children is a broad population of interest, for virtually all have been affected by reform. A broad perspective has not been taken in most existing studies of the recent reforms, which have, rather, focused on fairly narrowly defined subgroups.

Within this broad population, many subgroups are indeed of interest. Those families who once were on welfare but subsequently left are one subgroup of interest, for example. Studies of welfare leavers have, in fact, constituted the major focus of research on the effects of welfare reform. However, leavers are only a small portion of the population of interest, for this group is not only just a subset of those families in the low-income population who are affected by welfare reform, but also only a subset of those who might be defined as the welfare population. Other important groups include families who are still receiving benefits—so-called "stayers"—and those who are not receiving benefits because they have been diverted, rejected, or discouraged from applying as a consequence of welfare reform. In addition, subgroups with special needs, such as those with mental or physical health problems, substance abuse problems, or other problems that may make their transition to employment and self-sufficiency more difficult, the "hard-to-serve" welfare population, should also be the subject of evaluation studies on specific groups within the low-income population. There have been some studies on these special need groups but much more is needed.

Outcomes of Interest

The welfare reform act of 1996 had many goals, ranging from increasing work and self-sufficiency for poor families, to reducing out-of-wedlock births and promoting marriage, to reducing welfare caseloads, and to giving states more flexibility and control over their own programs. Not surprisingly, different audiences—national legislators and administrative officials, state legislators and program administrators, and the general public—are interested in different outcomes.

The panel concludes that the set of outcomes of interest for measuring the effects of welfare reform should be defined broadly and should include outcomes of interest to all of these different audiences. Broadly defined, these outcomes include:

> traditional measures of well-being for adults and families (including income, poverty rates, consumption of food, clothing, housing and other goods, employment, education and health);

traditional measures of child well-being (physical, cognitive, and behavioral);

measures of family structure and family formation (marriage, childbearing, out-of-wedlock birth, and living arrangements);

outcomes for governments themselves such as sizes of caseloads and expenditures on programs; and

changes in organizational structures for administering programs.

This list is not exhaustive of all the possible outcomes, but it covers the categories of outcomes that must be included in a complete assessment of the effects of welfare reform. Measures of well-being should be conceptually broad and cover all dimensions of adult, child, and family well-being—including health, economic, social, and safety—and should be operationally measured according to current scientific standards. How each of the specific outcomes are defined and operationally measured is a very important and difficult issue, but not one that the panel addresses in this report.

The body of welfare reform research conducted to date has been reasonably complete in addressing most of these outcomes in one place or another. There are certain areas that are understudied, such as the effects of welfare reform on family structure and on children, perhaps at least partially because these outcomes may not change as rapidly as some economic outcomes like employment. Nevertheless, the main limitations in studying different outcomes have been related to gaps in methods and data availability, not lack of interest in the outcomes themselves.

Research Questions of Interest

In outlining a broad research agenda for understanding the effects of welfare reform and for future assessments of reform, the panel has identified three types of questions of interest for understanding welfare reform: monitoring questions, which concern trends in the well-being of the low income population and its subgroups; questions about what rules govern recipients and how welfare reform has affected state and local welfare systems themselves; and formal evaluation questions, which assess the effect of welfare reform on individuals and families relative to what would have happened in its absence. The panel concludes that the key set of questions of interest for a comprehensive research agenda are as follows:

Conclusion 3.5 The monitoring questions of interest are the following: How has the well-being of the low-income population and key subgroups evolved subsequent to welfare reform? Which subgroups are doing well and which are doing less well? Which subgroups are in greatest need and deserve the attention of policy makers?

**Conclusion 3.6 The descriptive questions of interest regarding pro-
gram policy and implementation are the following: What policies,
programs, and administrative practices have states and localities
actually implemented as part of welfare reform? How wide is the
variation across states and even within states in policy? How has
implementation differed from officially described policy? How has
the non-TANF programmatic environment changed?**

**Conclusion 3.7 The impact evaluation questions of interest are the
following: What are the overall effects of the complete bundle of
changes in policies, programs, and practices on the well-being of the
low-income population, including the effects on both adults and children and on specific subpopulations of interest? What are the effects of the individual broad components of welfare reform on the
well-being of the low-income population and subpopulations of interest? What are the effects of specific detailed strategies within
each of the broad program components on the well-being of the low
income population and the subpopulations of interest—what works
and for whom?**

The greatest weakness in the identification of the key questions of interest
has been a lack of public articulation of the questions, and consequently, a failure
to systematically ensure that all questions are addressed with appropriate emphasis. Ideally, a research framework that outlines the populations, outcomes, and
research questions of interest, like the type the panel has composed, would have
been established early in the post-PRWORA period. Because it has not, there are
major gaps in what is known about the effects of reform. For future waves of
welfare reform, this comprehensive listing of questions, populations, and outcomes is the responsibility of the federal government and should be conducted by
an agency that is capable of taking a leadership role in guiding research on
welfare reform. The most appropriate agency for that role, in the view of the
panel, is ASPE.

**Recommendation 3.1 The panel recommends that ASPE take pri-
mary responsibility for publicly defining the questions of interest
for welfare reform research and evaluation, identifying emerging
issues for social welfare programs, and defining alternative detailed
strategies and policies that address the what-works-and-for-whom
questions. In doing so, ASPE should expand its current activities in
seeking input from states, private foundations, and other stakeholders on emerging policy and evaluation issues.**

EVALUATION METHODS FOR THE QUESTIONS OF INTEREST

In its examination of evaluation methods for welfare reform, the panel asked what evaluation methods are best for addressing each of the three types of evaluation questions identified in Conclusion 3.7 above. Different methods are preferable for different questions and, therefore, each of the three evaluation questions must be approached with different methodological considerations. The most promising methods for addressing the first question, the overall effect of welfare reform, are nonexperimental methods such as time-series, caseload, and econometric modeling. However, these methods require good across-area data on programs, area characteristics, and individual characteristics and outcomes, for across-area variation is the primary means by which effects of welfare reform are inferred. Data limitations have constrained the ability of these studies to credibly estimate overall impacts, although there have been several good studies of this type.

The second question, concerning the effects of broad welfare reform components (e.g., time limits, work requirements, sanctions, or family caps) within a fixed overall reform environment, is best addressed with a combination of experimental methods and nonexperimental methods. However, the experiments that have been conducted to date have not been designed to estimate the impact of broad components, and nonexperimental methods have not been successful in doing so as well because of data limitations. Consequently, there have been virtually no credible studies of the effects of broad components.

The third question, concerning the impact of detailed welfare reform strategies (for example, a human capital versus a work first approach, or a 2-year time limit versus a 5-year time limit) are best addressed with experimental methods. There have been several experiments designed to assess the effects of detailed strategies in welfare reforms, but they have been significantly weakened by design problems that threaten their validity. However, there is considerable promise for the use of experiments for this purpose in the future.

Conclusion 4.2 Experimental methods could not have been used for evaluating the overall effects of PRWORA and are, in general, not appropriate for evaluating the overall effects of large-scale, system-wide changes in social programs.

Conclusion 4.3 Experimental methods are a powerful tool for evaluating the effects of broad components and detailed strategies within a fixed overall reform environment and for evaluating incremental changes in welfare programs. However, experimental methods have limitations and should be complemented with nonexperimental analyses to obtain a complete picture of the effects of reform.

Conclusion 4.4 Nonexperimental methods, primarily time-series, and comparative group methods, are best suited for gauging the

overall effect of welfare reform and least suited for gauging the effects of detailed reform strategies, and as important as experiments for the evaluation of broad individual components. However, nonexperimental methods require good cross-area data on programs, area characteristics, and individual characteristics and outcomes.

DATA FOR MONITORING AND EVALUATING SOCIAL WELFARE PROGRAMS

Addressing the research questions of interest for welfare reform require data from multiple sources (survey, administrative, qualitative, and program description data) and across multiple levels (national, state, and local). Although the current data infrastructure contains many excellent sources, limitations in the infrastructure are sufficiently severe that important questions concerning the effects of PRWORA and other welfare reforms have been, and will continue to be, very difficult, if not impossible, to answer. As a consequence, much work needs to be done to make them useful for research.

The report contains many recommendations for improvements in the current data infrastructure, both for national-level data sets and for state- and local-level data sets. These recommendations are geared toward addressing specific limitations of currently available data. However, limitations in the current data infrastructure for human service and social welfare program research are partly the result of inadequate governmental structures to support the collection and maintenance of data on these programs. Current responsibilities and functions for collection of such data are spread across several different agencies, none of whose primary purpose is the maintenance and development of data.

Within the DHHS, both the ACF and ASPE are responsible for components of the entire data collection system. ACF is primarily a programmatic department charged with administering social welfare programs aimed at families and children. It is also responsible for collecting administrative data on TANF and related programs from the states, but these data are collected to assess state performance and compliance with federal mandates; they are not collected with the primary purpose of research or program evaluation. ASPE is responsible for strategic planning, policy development, and evaluation of all health and human service programs. It has supported many data collection activities in the past and currently is supporting data collection for welfare leaver and diversion study grants. However, data collection is not part of its specific charge, and ASPE does not have the resources to fully address the extensive data needs. DHHS has a number of other agencies that collect data covering health topics and health programs, but none of these is charged with collecting data for social welfare programs. Other federal departments, such as the U.S. Department of Labor, U.S. Department of Education, and U.S. Department of Justice have agencies that are charged with collecting data needed to administer and evaluate programs and to carry out the missions of their larger agencies; DHHS does not contain such an agency for carrying out data collection for social welfare programs.

Conclusion 6.1 No agency within DHHS has distinct administrative authority and responsibility for the collection and development of data relevant to social welfare and human service policies and programs. This administrative gap is a major reason for many of the inadequacies in the data infrastructure for monitoring and evaluating welfare policies.

The need for methodological leadership, increased capacity for data collection and analysis, technical assistance to states for developing their own surveys and administrative data, leadership in addressing data confidentiality issues, and guidance in the development of data archives dedicated to social program data leads the panel to recommend that alternative administrative mechanisms be considered. Consideration should be given to several alternatives. For example, the functions that the panel believes need to be performed could be placed within an existing statistical agency in DHHS, such as the National Center for Health Statistics. Alternatively, a new statistical agency within DHHS could be created to handle social welfare program data. Another option would be to expand one of the other agencies within DHHS with increased statistical staff and to assign that agency the responsibility for working with both federal agencies and states in developing and maintaining data. What option is chosen will require careful consideration and joint discussions between all the relevant agencies and departments. Reassignment of functions from one agency to another would be required, and departments and agencies outside DHHS would have to be involved because they have authority over other welfare programs (e.g., the Department of Labor, Department of Agriculture, and Department of Education, to name only three).

Recommendation 6.2 The panel recommends that an organizational entity be identified or created within DHHS, and that this entity be assigned direct administrative responsibility and authority for carrying out statistical functions and data collection in the area of social welfare programs and the populations they serve. The entity would also coordinate data collection and analysis activities between states and the federal government.

However the entity is achieved, it is critical that it is separate and independent from other programmatic and policy agencies within DHHS, which is important for ensuring that data collected will have credibility with both data suppliers and users.

Because devolution has made states responsible for TANF and other related programs, state data collection and coordination functions must necessarily be a part of the responsibilities to be assigned. Coordination of data collection activities will require strong cooperation between the states and DHHS, an effort that the panel concludes will be most effectively conducted if the federal government takes the lead. Such a federal-state program would probably require the creation of state agencies to work with the federal government and to ensure that state-level data relevant to social welfare programs are available. Cooperatively developing data programs is necessary, as the DHHS entity should provide both technical assistance and some funding for states to develop their data collection systems.

The panel does not offer a specific blueprint for administrative arrangements, but we are specific about the types of functions that should be carried out. These functions fall under the topics of national surveys, administrative data, technical assistance, reports, and a data archive.

National Surveys   The organizational entity that is assigned responsibility would be the primary sponsor of the national surveys used to monitor and evaluate human service and social welfare programs and, in general, content related to the low income population. It would contract with the Census Bureau or with private survey organizations to conduct these surveys. These include the Survey of Income and Program Participation and the Survey of Program Dynamics, and perhaps parts of other surveys, like the topical modules in the Current Population Survey that cover social welfare program topics. As the entity with lead responsibility for content and design of these surveys, it would also work with other agencies that have interests in these surveys. It would also explore the linkage of national-level administrative data to the national survey data that address social welfare program topics.

Administrative Data   The development and management of a cooperative welfare and social statistics data and information effort with the states would also be a needed function. Existing or new state statistical agencies should be full partners in this effort. Funding or financial incentives for the states to provide data to the federal agency and determining the form and content of the data submission should also be part of the responsibilities of the federal authority. Periodic reporting would be part of this program. Benefits Reporting Areas should be considered.

The development of standards for the use of administrative data for research purposes is an additional needed function. These standards should include definitions of services and benefit units, recipients and case members, data formats, and processes for documenting administrative data files.

In order to promote sharing of data resources for welfare and social statistics research and evaluation, coordination with other federal and state data collection agencies would also be required.

Leadership in advancing the use of and accessibility to all data provided by the states to DHHS for monitoring and social welfare program evaluation purposes is another important function.

Technical Assistance Another need is the provision of technical assistance to states on the use of administrative data and on the development, conduct, and analysis of surveys. The technical assistance could be used as a tool to promote the goals of comparability, improved data quality, data linkages, and data security and access.

Reports The federal entity should have responsibility for producing periodic reports on topics related to social welfare program utilization and the well-being of those who utilize these programs. One set of reports would be based on the data submitted by the states through the cooperative data collection effort mentioned above. It should also collect and publish social welfare program rules and policies, particularly for TANF and related separate state programs, for every state and every sub-state area where appropriate.

Data Archive for Continuing Research Needs A leadership role is needed in developing data archives on particular topics for use in social welfare program evaluation and research. Archives may include state surveys and administrative data, for which the agency would be responsible for preparing the surveys or administrative data for use by researchers. Maintaining an archive of welfare policies and programs description data throughout the states, and where relevant, in local areas, should also be a responsibility.

Carrying out these functions of the proposed data collection system will require strong leadership and sustained support at both the federal and state levels. If welfare programs continue to be operated in a devolved system, the need for and benefits from such a federal-state system will continue to grow.

1

Introduction

With the passage of the Personal Responsibility and Work Opportunity Reconciliation Act (PRWORA) of 1996, the United States embarked on a major policy change to its social welfare and safety net programs for the poor. The most fundamental and far-reaching reform of the traditional cash welfare system for single mothers since 1935, PRWORA replaced the federal entitlement program for low-income families and children (Aid to Families with Dependent Children, AFDC) with a program financed by state-administered block grants, the Temporary Assistance for Needy Families (TANF) program.

PRWORA furthered a trend started earlier in the decade under so-called "waiver" programs—state experiments with different program rules—toward devolution of the design and control of social welfare programs from the federal government to state governments. The legislation imposed several new major requirements on state programs—lifetime time limits on receipt of benefits paid out of federal funds, minimum work requirements, and minimum sanction requirements, for example—but otherwise allowed states to reconfigure their programs as they wish. Taking advantage of this new flexibility, states have made and continue to make major changes in the nature of their welfare programs. Changes made by some states emphasized immediate work and job placement, strengthening sanctions (i.e., benefit penalties) for failure to comply with regulations, and limiting or eliminating extra benefits for additional children. Some states have broadened the scope of services they provide to low-income families by implementing programs that provide noncash assistance, such as child care assistance, job search assistance, or transportation assistance. The aim of the reforms was to "end welfare as we know it," and most observers have agreed that the former AFDC system has been fundamentally transformed.

Determining the consequences of this experiment is of great importance to the public as well as legislators and federal and state officials. Has welfare reform "worked?" Has it been a success or a failure, however those terms are defined? If the effects have varied across families, for which types of families has it been beneficial and for which types harmful? In addition to these questions about the past, there are questions about the future. Should the welfare system be pushed further in the same direction or pulled back? Which elements of the new welfare system need to be changed and which left as is? What works and what doesn't in aiding former welfare recipients to leave the rolls and become self-sufficient?

For these fundamental questions to be answered adequately, two issues need to be addressed. The first concerns how these questions can be answered: What methods can and should be used to determine the effects of welfare reform? Simply tracking families from before the reforms to after the reforms is not sufficient because other things have happened simultaneously, most notably the improvement in the economy. In the four years since PRWORA was passed, a large number of evaluation efforts have been initiated: Have those studies used the appropriate evaluation methods? If not, what evaluation methods should be used, and what steps should be taken to promote their use?

A second key issue concerns what types of data are needed to measure and evaluate the effects of welfare reform. Are the data sources currently available to evaluators at the federal and state levels adequate for assessing the effects of reform? In the many welfare reform studies that have been initiated since 1996, have the best data been used? Have the studies been handicapped by inadequate or unavailable data? If so, what steps should be taken to improve the quantity and quality of data needed to evaluate welfare reform?

These two issues are the subject of this report.

THE PANEL

To answer questions about the methods and data needed to assess the consequences of welfare reform, the Committee on National Statistics of the National Research Council formed the Panel on Data and Methods for Measuring the Effects of Changes in Social Welfare Programs. This panel is sponsored by the Office of the Assistant Secretary for Planning and Evaluation (ASPE) of the U.S. Department of Health and Human Services through a congressional appropriation. The same congressional appropriation provided funding to ASPE for data collection and evaluation of the effects of welfare reform on families who have left welfare, commonly called "welfare leavers." Language accompanying the appropriation requested that the panel provide guidance on the ASPE research plan for tracking former welfare recipients and suggest directions for future welfare-related research.

The charge to the panel is to review methods and data needed to evaluate the outcomes of changes in social welfare programs on families and individuals. The panel is specifically charged with assisting the department in (1) identifying how best to measure and track program eligibility, participation, child well-being, and other outcomes; (2) evaluating data, research designs, and methods for the study of welfare reform outcomes; and (3) identifying needed areas and topics of research. In doing so, the panel was asked to consider alternative federal and state data sources, the limitations of currently available data, appropriate evaluation design and methods for analysis and inference, and, finally, findings from previous research and evaluation. The panel is also specifically charged with reviewing data needs and methods for tracking and assessing the effects of program changes on families who stop receiving cash assistance.

The membership of the panel was constituted in the summer of 1998 and the panel issued an interim report in the summer of 1999 (National Research Council, 1999). The interim report summarized the general principles of good evaluation, gave an initial assessment of the data infrastructure for welfare reform evaluation, specifically discussed studies of welfare leavers, and gave the panel's short-run recommendations for improving the data infrastructure needed to measure the effects of changes in the cash assistance program. In this final report, the panel considers broader and more long-run data and methodological needs for evaluating welfare reform.

In carrying out its work, the panel quickly realized that assessing which methods and data are most appropriate for evaluating welfare reform requires that the key evaluation questions and outcomes of most interest have to be specified first because the methods and data needed must be oriented around specific questions and outcomes. The panel therefore focused its attention on determining the research questions and outcomes of most interest for measuring the effects of welfare reform, as well as the appropriate methods for answering these questions and the data needed to carry out these evaluations. These three topics defined the structure of the panel's work.

In addition to the discussions and detailed investigations carried out by the panel members and staff, the panel also sponsored many other activities and enlisted the advice of numerous other experts. The panel commissioned several papers on issues concerning data collection, most of which were presented at the Workshop on Data Collection for Low Income and Welfare populations held in December 1999. These papers were revised and will be published as a companion volume to this report (National Research Council, 2001a). The panel also held a seminar on evaluation methods for measuring the effects of welfare reform. This seminar brought together experts in social program evaluation to discuss the appropriateness of different evaluation methods for measuring the effects of changes in welfare policies. The panel also invited representatives of the U.S. Census Bureau to a meeting to discuss four major surveys relevant to evaluations of welfare reform: the Current Population Survey, the Survey of Income and Program Participation, the Survey of Program Dynamics, and the American Community Survey. In addition, the panel consulted a wide variety of private researchers and government officials involved in welfare reform research and commissioned a number of expert studies on welfare reform methods and data, which are included in the panel's companion volume (National Research Council, 2001a). The panel also had continued discussions with ASPE officials on the agency's research agenda on welfare reform.

POLICY BACKGROUND

The modern constellation of means-tested transfer programs in the United States originated in 1935 with the creation of the Aid to Families with Dependent Children (AFDC) Program. Intended to provide cash support to low-income widows with children, the program grew slowly through the 1940s and 1950s and then began growing rapidly in the 1960s. At the same time, the nature of the caseload changed, as more recipient families were divorced women with children rather than widows. The "welfare explosion" of the late 1960s and early 1970s was a defining moment in the history of the program. While there had been controversies prior to that time, the big growth in the number of recipients generated widespread public discussion of the program. Legislative interest also grew during this time, and reforms of the program became a high priority on the government's agenda.

As shown in Figure 1-1 the growth in the late 1960s and early 1970s was followed by very little growth in the late 1970s and early 1980s. However, growth again accelerated in the late 1980s, leading to concern by state governments about the cost of welfare. In addition, the nature of the caseload changed as the fraction of recipients who were unmarried single mothers grew relative to the number who were divorced or separated; see Figure 1-2. Over time, the early concentration of widows in the program in the 1940s was followed by a dominance of divorced and separated women in the 1960s and 1970s, and finally the growth and predominance of never-married women in the 1980s and 1990s. This development changed public attitudes toward the program and led to concerns over the implicit support of nonmarital childbearing that the program seemed to provide.

Table 1-1 lists the major pieces of legislation in the history of the program. After its creation in 1935, the program remained essentially unchanged until 1961, when eligibility was extended to two-parent families in which the primary earner is unemployed (AFDC-UP). The 1967 Social Security Amendments were the first to directly address the issue of work by AFDC recipients, creating financial incentives by lowering the benefit reduction rate and by creating a work

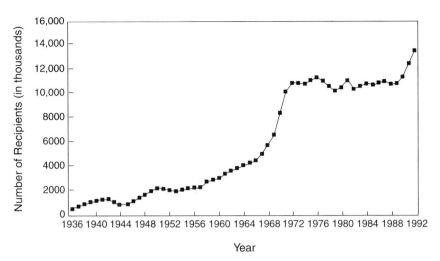

FIGURE 1-1 Total Number of Cash Assistance (AFDC) Recipients, 1936-1992.

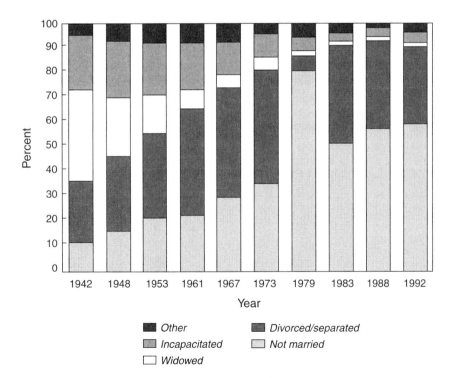

FIGURE 1-2 Basis of AFDC Eligibility, 1942-1992.

TABLE 1-1 Major Legislation in the AFDC and TANF Programs

Date	Title	Main Provisions
1935	Social Security Act	Created the AFDC program for low-income children without a parent present in household
1961	Amendments to the Social Security Act	Created the AFDC-UP program for children in two-parent families whose primary earner is unemployed
1967	Amendments to the Social Security Act	Lowered the benefit reduction rate to two-thirds; created the Work Incentive (WIN) Program
1981	Omnibus Budget Reconciliation Act of 1981	Increased the benefit reduction rate to one; imposed a gross income limit; counted income of stepparents; allowed waiver authority
1988	Family Support Act of 1988	Created the JOBS program for education, skills training, job search assistance, and other work activities; created transitional child care and Medicaid programs; mandated AFDC-UP in all states
1996	Personal Responsibility and Work Reconciliation Act	Abolished the AFDC program and created the TANF program

program called WIN, the Work Incentive Program. Raising the financial incentive for working was not successful in increasing employment to any significant degree and was eliminated in the 1981 Omnibus Budget Reconciliation Act, which effectively increased the benefit reduction rate back to 100 percent of net earnings. The WIN program remained small and provided little training to the majority of AFDC recipients. However, an emphasis on work continued to grow during the 1970s and 1980s, with most initiatives proposing work programs with a strong focus on education and training. This trend culminated in the 1988 Family Support Act, which created the Job Opportunities and Basic Skills Training (JOBS) program to encourage skills training. This trend was reversed in the welfare reform movement of the 1990s, which eschewed expensive and arguably low-return education and training programs in favor of more immediate job placement and employment programs. The PRWORA legislation reflected this change in philosophy toward employment by backing up a "work first" approach with strong sanctions for noncompliance with work requirements.

Another significant trend in reform has been an increasing focus on child support enforcement. Strengthening child support enforcement has been a part of every welfare reform law since 1974, when the federal-state child support enforcement system was established. The Family Support Act of 1988, as well as PRWORA, followed in this tradition by increasing efforts to obtain payments from noncustodial parents, usually fathers. The most recent laws have established routine withholding of child support obligations, statewide registries of obligations, reporting of new hires, seizure of assets and forfeiture of driver's licenses and professional licenses, mandatory blood and genetic testing, and in-hospital voluntary paternity establishment programs. These laws have made it more difficult and costly for fathers of children receiving welfare to avoid paying child support.

The current era of welfare reform has been characterized by major structural changes in the system and by drastically falling caseloads. Beginning in the late 1980s and early 1990s, states began to request waivers from federal law in order to experiment with different rules in their AFDC programs. The variations ranged from the imposition of time limits on welfare receipt to new and strengthened work requirements for recipients, stricter financial sanctions for violations of rules and noncompliance with work requirements, family caps that limit benefit increases for women who had additional children while on the welfare rolls, and other provisions. These waiver programs initially tested the new provisions on small numbers of recipients but became more comprehensive over time as they were increasingly applied to all recipients in the state.[1] Another important change during this period was an increasing tendency of states to test multiple sets of new rules simultaneously, comprising a "package" or "bundle" of reforms, rather than introducing each separate reform component sequentially. Both of these trends reflected a growing desire on the part of states to change their AFDC systems in a fundamental way and to enact a basic restructuring of the entire state's caseload, often with the goal of changing the "culture" of welfare. By the summer of 1996, more than 40 states had requested and been granted statewide waivers.

The passage of the Personal Responsibility and Work Opportunity Recon-ciliation Act in August 1996 incorporated the spirit of these waivers in federal law. States are required to impose a 5-year lifetime limit on benefit receipt by adults (at least those paid for out of federal funds). States are also required to impose work requirements for a large portion of their caseloads, and a narrower range of activities satisfy these work requirements than was the case under prior law. Equally if not more important, states were freed from other federal regula-tory authority, and funding was switched from matching grants to block grants, thereby freeing states to set benefit levels, eligibility requirements, and financial incentives, and to enact sanction, diversion, and other types of rules and programs as they wished. The program was also renamed and is now called Temporary Assistance for Needy Families.

States have used the TANF provisions to completely redesign their pro-grams. Several states have imposed even more stringent time limits than required by TANF, and some states have imposed stricter sanction policies than required by federal law, with the result that sanctions have become a commonplace occur-rence in the lives of welfare recipients. Other changes include Work First Pro-

---

[1]Usually, a small number of families in each state remained on the old AFDC program for com-parison purposes. This approach is discussed further below.

grams, which attempt to move recipients into employment (rather than training or education) as quickly as possible and numerous diversion, family cap, and other provisions governing and limiting benefit receipt. The overall goal of most new state programs, at least in the initial period, has been to move recipients from welfare to employment. Some states have also attempted to move recipients to employment while still on welfare through more liberal earnings disregards, which encourage recipients to combine welfare and work. This goal has been reinforced by changes in the nature of local welfare offices, as they attempt to change from mere eligibility-determining and cash-dispensing agencies to agencies whose primary mission is to assist recipients in moving from welfare to employment. This kind of fundamental restructuring of the welfare system cannot happen quickly, and at this writing, 4 years after the passage of the law, states are still developing their welfare programs and experimenting, often by trial-and-error, with different strategies for achieving employment, caseload-reduction and other program goals.

This period of welfare reform has been accompanied by a drastic reduction in the caseload in the AFDC program, as illustrated in Figure 1-3. Over the 1993-1999 period, the AFDC caseload has fallen by 49 percent, an historically unprecedented reduction that has decreased the program caseload to its level in 1970. Some states have experienced much more drastic declines: Wisconsin leads the nation with a 86 percent decline between its peak caseload in January 1992 and June 1998 (U.S. Department of Health and Human Services, 1998). Poverty rates have also declined, as shown in Figure 1-4.

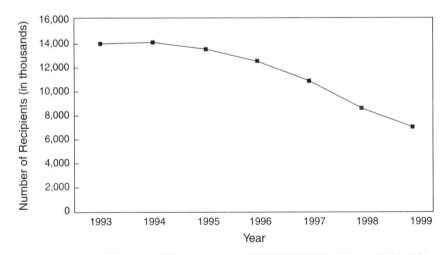

FIGURE 1-3 Total Number of Cash Assistance (AFDC/TANF) Recipients, 1993-1999.

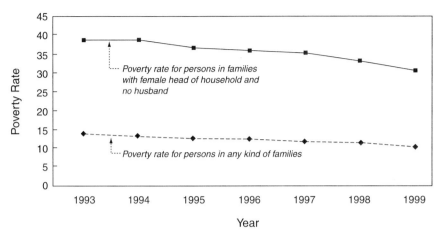

FIGURE 1-4 Poverty Rates in the United States, 1993-1999. NOTE: Poverty rate is defined as the percentage of families with children under age 18 and incomes below the federal poverty level for family size. Family is defined by the CPS as a group of two or more (one of whom is the head of household) people related by birth, marriage, or adoption and residing together; all such people are considered members of one family. SOURCE: Data from U.S. Census Bureau, Current Population Survey (CPS).

Although it is natural to associate the decline in the caseload with the nature of the welfare reforms, other forces have been at work and could have contributed to the decline in caseloads.[2] An equally historic occurrence is the unprecedented period of economic growth and falling unemployment rates the nation has experienced in the 1990s, which has lifted employment rates to all-time highs and has reached deeply into the low-skill labor market. Major policy shifts have also occurred: the Earned Income Tax Credit (EITC) has been expanded, providing major new income support for families off welfare, and Medicaid has expanded its coverage for nonwelfare low-income families and children. A major research and evaluation issue has been how to parcel out the relative contributions of welfare reform, the economy, and the other policy developments to the decline in the caseload over this period. Most analysts attribute a sizable fraction of the decline in welfare recipients to welfare reforms, although methodological problems and data limitations create some uncertainty about this conclusion, an issue we discuss in Chapter 4.

Welfare reform is a moving target for evaluation because the strategies and policies practiced by states are still evolving. There is some evidence that states,

---

[2]A recent compilation of papers studied explanations for recent trends in welfare caseloads (W.E. Upjohn Institute for Employment Research, 1999). Previous studies have also discussed the increases in caseloads in the late 60s and early 70s (Michel, 1980; Moffitt, 1992).

having largely accomplished their caseload-reducing goals, are now turning their attention to the provision of services to poor families, in general, and to women and families who are not receiving welfare. Provision of work supports, such as child care, as well as services meant to address other problems and barriers women experience in attempting to reach self-sufficiency, are widely discussed. Welfare reform is a continuing, dynamic process as states gradually confront new problems and face new challenges. The energy in this evolution is an indication of a system that is constantly trying to improve itself, which is clearly desirable, but it makes the problem of evaluation quite difficult. Estimates of the effect of welfare reform to date are not necessarily applicable to the future, when the nature of the reform may have changed. Moreover, from an evaluation point of view, it can be argued that the highest priority now should be to set up data and evaluation mechanisms that are capable of monitoring relevant populations and evaluating the impact of the new and ongoing strategies constantly being adopted.

Although there is much concern about the effects of the landmark welfare reforms of the 1990s, especially the effects of the fundamental AFDC-TANF Program change, this program is only one of the nation's set of means-tested transfer programs. Other programs have changed, too. The growth of Medicaid, food stamps, supplemental security income (SSI), and EITC spending over the past 30 years has been much more rapid than that for AFDC, and all four programs now have much greater expenditure levels than TANF—and all of them except EITC had greater expenditures even prior to PRWORA.[3] Moreover, PRWORA had some provisions relating to programs other than TANF: immigrants were barred from Food Stamp receipt and strict time limits were imposed on some able-bodied program recipients without dependents; states were required to continue Medicaid eligibility for families that would have been eligible under the provisions of the pre-PRWORA AFDC program; and eligibility for SSI was restricted, with new income tests imposed and with certain types of child disabilities restricted. The result is that there is still major support for the low-income population even without considering TANF.[4]

However, many of the transfers in the other major programs go to more families than those headed by poor unmarried mothers. Despite the growth of noncash and non-AFDC programs, AFDC provided a major source of financial support to disadvantaged single mothers prior to 1996 and that level of that support has been greatly reduced. Moreover, the symbolic importance of PRWORA in signaling a new approach to welfare reform in general cannot be underestimated. The publicity and attention that this wave of welfare reform has

---

[3]In addition, new programs continue to be initiated, for example, the state Children's Health Insurance Program (S-CHIP), was enacted in 1997 to fund states to expand health insurance coverage for poor children.

[4]PRWORA also significantly increased child support enforcement federal directives and assistance to the states.

received has been extensive. It is fair to say that the U.S. welfare system is in an era of major transition to a new system that is considerably different from that which existed 10 years ago.

STRUCTURE OF THE REPORT

The attention that this transition has received is reflected in a major stream of research, evaluation, and monitoring activity among private researchers and in federal and state governmental agencies. Chapter 2 summarizes the major projects and provides a picture of the current landscape of welfare reform research. Before turning to a discussion of methods and data, Chapter 3 identifies the broad and specific populations of interest for measuring the effects of welfare reform and the specific research questions that need to be addressed to assess the impact of welfare reform and to inform future policy debates. It also assesses how well existing research has addressed the questions. Chapter 4 discusses alternative evaluation methods and considers which are best suited for the questions of interest identified in Chapter 3. Chapter 5 characterizes the data needed to address the questions of interest and presents the panel's findings on the various national and state level data sources currently available. Chapter 6 presents and discusses the panel's recommendation for a centralization and reorganization of administrative authority and responsibility for federal and state data collection on social welfare programs and populations.

2

Welfare Reform Monitoring and Evaluation: The Current Landscape

This chapter describes the landscape of studies on welfare reform about four years after the passage of PRWORA. It includes both completed studies as well as a larger number that are under way or even in the planning stages. We provide short summaries of each study and describe its goals, evaluation methods, and the data sets used.

The types of studies under way are very diverse. We have found it useful to develop a classification of these studies into categories according to their type and nature—the questions asked, the methodologies used to achieve those goals, and the scope of inquiry. In our schema, studies can be classified as either; (i) descriptive and monitoring studies; (ii) studies of welfare leavers and related groups; (iii) randomized experiments; (iv) caseload and other econometric modeling efforts; (v) process, implementation, and qualitative studies; (vi) other welfare reform studies; and (vii) a variety of studies which do not focus on welfare reform per se but on related policy issues or low-income groups. Table 2-1 summarizes these types. Appendix Table B-1 contains a comprehensive list of the studies under way. In the next few sections we describe each of these types of studies. We withhold any critical evaluation of them until Chapter 4.

Our review of studies–and indeed, our entire report—is primarily focused on the Temporary Assistance for Needy Families (TANF) program. Studies of the Food Stamp, Medicaid, or related programs for the low-income population are not discussed in any detail. The focus on TANF is a partial result of PRWORA itself, which primarily reformed the Aid for Families with Dependent Children (AFDC) program and a partial result of the mission of our sponsoring agency, the Office of the Assistant Secretary for Planning and Evaluation (ASPE) in the

TABLE 2-1 Types of Welfare Reform Projects Currently Under Way

Type of Study	Description
Monitoring and Descriptive	Studies that examine adults and children by following families over time, documenting trends in well-being
Welfare Leavers and Related Groups	Studies that document the outcomes for individuals and families who have left welfare
Randomized Experiments	Evaluations using randomized experimental and control groups to estimate impact of a specific reform program or feature
Caseload and Other Econometric Models	Analyses using econometric methods to estimate the effects of welfare reform on caseloads and other outcomes
Process, Implementation, and Qualitative Studies	Studies using qualitative methods to examine and document implementation of welfare reform, state program rules, or detailed pictures of individuals and families
Other Welfare Reform Studies	Studies of special populations, the child welfare system, and data collection projects
Studies on Topics Related to Welfare Reform	Studies of child support enforcement, absent fathers, low-income neighborhoods, low-income children, and other topics

Department of Health and Human Services. However, virtually all of our findings on methods and data extend to evaluation efforts for food stamps and Medicaid as well.

Before describing the studies, we briefly note who the major supporting funders are and how the types of funders of current welfare reform research differ from those in past eras.

Major Supporting Funders

The most active federal governmental agencies supporting research on welfare reform are ASPE and the Administration for Children and Families (ACF), both in the U.S. Department of Health and Human Services (DHHS). Both agencies have extensive and detailed research agendas on welfare reform, ranging from broad overview studies to data collection activities to evaluation efforts of specific programs and population groups. They are supporting dozens of research and evaluation activities around the country, both private-sector researchers and state government agencies conducting studies of their own state programs. The breadth of their activities is considerable; Appendix Tables A-1 and A-2 show the research projects currently supported by or being carried out internally at ASPE and ACF.

However, unlike some past periods of reform evaluation, many other federal agencies are actively involved as well. These include the Food and Nutrition Service and Economic Research Service of the U.S. Department of Agriculture; the U.S. Department of Labor; the Office of Research and Statistics in the Social Security Administration; various health and housing agencies; and several other agencies. The U.S. Census Bureau is also heavily involved in welfare reform because of its responsibility for the Survey of Program Dynamics, which is specifically aimed at providing information for welfare reform evaluation (and is discussed later in this report). The National Institutes of Health is also newly engaged in welfare policy evaluation and is sponsoring several large-budget studies, most of which focus on children and families.

State governments are also now heavily involved in sponsoring welfare reform studies, which is a natural result of the devolution of authority over the TANF program to the states. Almost every state in the country has some type of evaluation under way, sometimes conducted in-house and sometimes contracted out. Many of these projects are solely funded by the state; others are partially funded by the federal government or by private foundations.

Even newer to the current evaluation funding environment is the active involvement of foundations in support of welfare reform studies. Many large national foundations, as well as many smaller foundations with interests in specific cities or states, have devoted funds to a wide variety of studies. Although there are no figures on the total amount of these foundation funds, the amounts are unquestionably large and often rival those of federal government agencies.

DESCRIPTIVE AND MONITORING STUDIES

As we noted in our interim report (National Research Council, 1999), descriptive and monitoring studies play an important role in studies of social policies in general and have assumed an important role in the study of welfare reform as well. A monitoring study follows a population of families or individuals over time and tracks their well-being, as measured by economic status and other indicators. However, monitoring studies do not attempt to make formal assessments of the effects of a reform relative to what would have happened in its absence. Monitoring studies are important because they signal whether the well-being of the target population is improving, deteriorating, or remaining the same. They are also useful in identifying specific subgroups that are doing particularly poorly, and may therefore, be in need of additional assistance, regardless of what might have caused that condition.

Some "monitoring" studies track families before and after a reform and attempt to make an assessment of the effect of the reform by comparing outcomes before and after. If such an assessment is made, the study is then actually an evaluation study. Tracking families can be valuable from a monitoring point of view, but it is a weak evaluation tool because such before-and-after evaluations cannot generally separate the effects of welfare reform from other simultaneously occurring events, such as the improvement in the economy.

Although most monitoring studies have focused on individual states and local areas, a few have a national focus. The latter group describes the course of the disadvantaged population over time for the nation as a whole or for major portions of it, sometimes both before and after PRWORA. National-level studies depend, necessarily, on the availability of data that are representative of the country as a whole and so are most easily classified by the data set used. Some studies, for example, have used multiple waves of the March Current Population Survey (CPS) (e.g., Primus et al., 1999) to track the well-being of the low-income population. The Survey of Program Dynamics (SPD) is expected to be used for monitoring as well, but has thus far not been used very much for this purpose. Other national-level studies include baseline and continuing reports on welfare dependency, reports on the development of child indicators by states, general reports on trends in the well-being of children and youth, reports on trends in the economic well-being of low-income Americans, and reports on poverty dynamics and contingent employment. These reports typically also use the CPS, though they are sometimes supplemented by SIPP or other data sets as well.

There are three major monitoring studies at a somewhat more localized level: the National Survey of America's Families (NSAF), the Project on Devolution and Urban Change, and the Three-City Study. The NSAF consists, to date, of two waves of a telephone survey of almost 50,000 families in 13 states plus a small sample of families in the rest of the country. Low-income families and children are oversampled. The families in the two waves are not the same, so the survey essentially gives snapshots of the population at two points in time, in mid-1997 and in 1999. Both survey waves took place after the passage of PRWORA; NSAF thus monitors the population subsequent but not prior to PRWORA. Columbia University is also conducting a study of welfare reform in New York City based on a repeated survey of a population cross-section, the Social Indicators Survey, that closely parallels the NSAF.

The Urban Change Study and the Three-City Study involve four urban counties and three cities respectively. Both studies have longitudinal, in-person surveys as a central element, and both have an ethnographic component as well; the Urban Change Study also has an implementation component and a neighborhood indicators component. In the survey components, information is collected on both adult and child well-being, although the Three-City Study has perhaps the most intensive focus on children and includes a special supplemental survey and assessment of a subsample of parents and children. The first wave of the Urban Change Study survey was fielded in 1998, after PRWORA; the first wave of the Three-City Study survey was fielded in 1999, also after PRWORA. The two surveys differ in their sampled populations: the Urban Change Study is drawn from families on TANF at several times, both before and after PRWORA, and both survey and administrative data are being collected on these families; the

Three City Study drew its sample from the general population of low-income families in the three cities, both those on and off TANF, and is based only on survey data.

There are also a large number of monitoring and descriptive studies that are narrower in their geographic and substantive focus than those we have mentioned, usually focused on a particular state or area and sometimes on only some groups of interest. Typically, these studies use administrative data to track certain groups of the low-income or recipient population. These studies, many of which are listed on the web site of the Research Forum on Children, Families, and the New Federalism, are generally more limited in scope (see http://www.researchforum.org).

STUDIES OF WELFARE LEAVERS AND RELATED GROUPS

There have been several dozen state-level studies of women who have left welfare subsequent to PRWORA. Indeed, studies of these welfare leavers constitute by far the most common type of welfare reform study conducted since 1996. Most of these studies are specific to a particular state or area within a state, and most to date have only measured employment and earnings outcomes of leavers from administrative data; a few, especially ASPE-sponsored studies, have conducted short telephone or in-person interviews as well.[1] The goal of these studies is, simply, to track the well-being of women who have left welfare.

Existing leaver studies are implicitly designed as monitoring studies, for they do not attempt to determine what the outcomes of leavers would have been if welfare reform had not occurred—or even if those families would have left welfare. They do not assess the effects of the reforms nor explain whether or how much the improving economy has led to exits from welfare. They cannot give a full picture of the effects of policy changes because they focus only on those receiving welfare at a given time, not the entire population that might be affected. Nevertheless, like the more general monitoring studies discussed in the previous section, leaver studies can be very useful in tracking and documenting the well-being of one particular subpopulation—welfare leavers—and determining how well they are doing, even if the cause of those outcomes is not known. Like other monitoring studies, leaver studies can also be useful in identifying specific subgroups of those who have left welfare who have not done well or who have particular special needs that require additional assistance.

As we noted in our interim report (National Research Council, 1999), many of the early leaver studies were scientifically low in quality because of data

---

[1]For a review of data, methods, and findings of state welfare leaver studies, see Parrott (1998), Tweedie and Reichert (1998), Brauner and Loprest (1999), Cancian et al. (1999), Tweedie et al. (1999), U.S. General Accounting Office (1999a), Isaacs and Lyon (2000), and Acs and Loprest (2001).

constraints. Many did not collect survey data, and of those that did, nonresponse rates were often very high. More commonly, leaver studies used administrative data and usually only from a narrow set of sources; consequently, they had only limited information on well-being after leaving welfare, often only employment and earnings from records of the unemployment insurance system. Also, different states used different definitions of leavers and examined different groups, so that the results of the studies are not comparable across states.

In fiscal 1998, ASPE funded 14 states and areas to conduct new leaver studies. These studies use a set of definitions that are uniform in some respects and are therefore more likely to be comparable across states. They also collect survey and administrative data on a wider variety of adult and child outcomes (see National Research Council, 1999:Tables A-1, A-2). Most of these ASPE-sponsored studies were designed to examine leaver outcomes for two cohorts of recipients as well—a pre-PRWORA, AFDC cohort and a post-PRWORA, TANF cohort. These two cohorts were to be compared to assess whether rates of leaving and leaver outcomes were different after PRWORA than before, thereby addressing the issue of whether leaver outcomes have indeed changed over time. In fiscal 1999, ASPE funded seven more states to expand significantly on the scope of the leaver studies to examine applicants as well as leavers, diverted applicants as well as other applicants, and eligible nonapplicants. These projects are based on the recognition that welfare reform can affect the rate of entry to welfare as well as the rate of exit, as families who might otherwise have opted to go on welfare chose to attempt self-sufficiency instead. In addition, diversion programs, or programs that seek to dissuade potential recipients or applicants from enrolling in the cash assistance program, directly affect the entry rate. Unfortunately, at this writing very few multiple cohort studies or studies of entry have been completed.[2] ASPE has also commissioned a review and synthesis of its leaver studies, which should be completed soon.

While most studies of leavers have been conducted at the state level, a few have used national-level data. These studies use cross-sectional surveys, such as the Urban Institute's new National Survey of America's Families (Loprest, 1999); the National Longitudinal Survey of Youth (Cancian and Meyer, 2000; Meyer

---

[2]Multiple cohort studies have been completed for Arizona, Illinois, South Carolina, Washington, and Wisconsin (Cancian et al., 2000; Institute for Public Affairs and School of Social Work, 2000; Isaacs and Lyon, 2000; South Carolina Department of Social Services, 2000; Ahn et al., 2000). All of the cohorts in these studies were post-PRWORA except for the Wisconsin study, which included a 1995 cohort (when Wisconsin was operating under waiver authority in 1995) and Washington. No state-level entry-rate or diversion studies have been completed except for a recent study (Mueser et al., 2000), which examined the employment rates of entrants to AFDC-TANF in five urban areas from 1990 to 1997, controlling for business-cycle effects. A Wisconsin study of applicants to TANF in Milwaukee is under way but has not been completed.

and Cancian, 1998); and the Panel Study of Income Dynamics (Hofferth et al., 2000).[3]

There are also a few studies that examine "stayers," or women who remain on welfare, although these studies are not as prevalent as leaver studies. Some have compared characteristics of leavers to stayers (Cancian et al., 2000; Fogarty and Kraley, 2000; Institute for Public Affairs and School of Social Work, 2000; Loprest and Zedlewski, 1999); others have focused on the characteristics of stayers per se, particularly whether they have barriers or obstacles to employment (Danziger et al., 2000; Zedlewski, 1999).[4] There are also a number of projects that are tracking the characteristics of welfare recipients over time with administrative data (e.g., the Illinois Panel Study of Recipients, and a recently funded ASPE project on the California caseload).

RANDOMIZED EXPERIMENTS

Randomized experiments have been a major evaluation method in welfare reform since the 1980s when a number of small-scale experiments of state-level welfare innovations were tested. A larger number of experiments were begun in the early 1990s as states were awarded waivers from the federal government to conduct experiments of various alterations of their AFDC programs, alterations that were related to those later enacted in PRWORA. However, most of these waiver experiments were discontinued after PRWORA. The Administration for Children and Families has continued to fund nine of the waiver experiments in those states that chose to continue to operate their waiver programs (rather than convert immediately to TANF); five of them are funded to measure child outcomes in the experimental and control groups as well. These continuing waiver experiments constitute the bulk of experiments that attempt to directly test packages of reforms that resemble those adopted after PRWORA.

A number of experiments that study different aspects of welfare reform are also under way, have been completed, or are in the planning stages. The Post-Employment Services Demonstration was an experiment testing alternative strategies for increasing the rate at which welfare recipients keep jobs once they have obtained them. The Employment Retention and Advancement Project, sponsored by ACF, followed up on this demonstration with a large and more comprehensive experimental test of alternative strategies to assist welfare recipients and welfare leavers in retaining jobs. The evaluation of the Labor Department's

---

[3]Either panel data or a cross-sectional database with a retrospective history for several years is needed to conduct a leaver study, so the Current Population Survey, for example, cannot be used for this purpose.

[4]The Danziger et al. (2000) study includes both leavers and stayers combined and pooled into one sample.

Welfare to Work Program contains experimental components in some sites and tests the effect of the Welfare to Work Program legislation. The Los Angeles Jobs First-GAIN experiment is also testing work-first versus education-based assistance strategies. The Wisconsin Works Child Support Waiver Demonstration tests the effects of Wisconsin's changes to the child support system and rules in the state. The National Evaluation of Welfare-to-Work Strategies (NEWWS) is an experiment in a different category, for it began in 1989 as an evaluation of the JOBS component of the Family Support Act of 1988 and hence predates PRWORA and the waiver reforms of the early 1990s. It has been continued, however, because it does test alternative employment strategies—namely, a work-first strategy versus an education-training strategy—and this issue is still relevant to welfare reform after PRWORA. Finally, a number of states are also testing small-scale program features with experimental methods.

There are a number of other ongoing or completed experimental evaluations of welfare-related programs that test particular types of welfare reforms other than those enacted by PRWORA. The evaluation of the pilot phase of the Minnesota Family Investment Program, for example, tested a package of reforms containing more generous earnings disregards and some new work requirements.[5] The New Hope evaluation and the Canadian Self-Sufficiency Program evaluation both test programs that have a few of the features of post-PRWORA programs, but both differ from welfare reform policies significantly in many important respects and are generally quite different in philosophy, particularly in their heavy emphasis on earnings subsidies. The results from these experiments will be useful if the particular reforms they test arise in future policy discussions in Congress, but they are not directly relevant to the effects of PRWORA.

CASELOAD AND OTHER ECONOMETRIC MODELS

There have been a number of econometric evaluations of the effects of pre-PRWORA waiver programs and a few of the effects of PRWORA itself. Most of these evaluations have aimed to estimate the effect of welfare reform on welfare caseloads, while a few have examined the effects on earnings, income and other measures of well-being of the low-income population. Most have been nationwide in scope, although in a few cases only a single or small number of states have been examined (e.g., Hill and Main, 1998; Mueser et al., 2000). The majority of pre-PRWORA waiver evaluations used variation across states in the timing of when waiver programs were enacted in each state, as well as the type of program that was adopted, to explain subsequent rates of caseload decline (Council of Economic Advisers, 1997; Figlio and Ziliak, 1999; Moffitt, 1999; Wallace

---

[5]Interestingly, the later post-PRWORA package adopted in Minnesota was quite different.

and Blank, 1999; Ziliak et al., 1997). The small number of studies that have used post-PRWORA data (Council of Economic Advisers, 1999; Ellwood, 2000; Schoeni and Blank, 2000) have estimated effects of PRWORA either by comparing states that implemented PRWORA later than other states; by simply comparing state outcomes after PRWORA to state outcomes before (i.e., a before-and-after, or pure time-series design); or by comparing trend changes in the outcomes of single mothers before and after PRWORA to trend changes in outcomes for other groups (married women, men, etc.) that presumably were not affected by PRWORA. Most of the studies examining the effect of welfare reform on caseloads have used state-level aggregated caseload totals as their primary data base, while those examining individual and family outcomes have used survey data, most often the Current Population Survey (CPS), which is available annually for many years prior to PRWORA.

Probably the most notable feature of the econometric evaluations of welfare reform is that they have attempted to control for the state of the economy—most often using the unemployment rate in a state as a proxy—on caseload and other outcomes in order to estimate the net effect of welfare reform. Because the unemployment rate declined at the same time welfare reform occurred, disentangling their relative influences has been a major challenge. The econometric evaluations are the only type of study that has attempted to estimate these relative influences. They have a number of other strengths as well, though also some weaknesses, which we discuss in Chapter 4. ACF has commissioned a project to synthesize the results of the econometric evaluations.

A number of the monitoring and leaver studies already mentioned have some type of implicit econometric evaluation components as well. The most common type of evaluation design is what we termed a cohort comparison study in our interim report (National Research Council, 1999): the Urban Change Study, the Three-City Study, and the NSAF all have plans for this type of analysis, as do some of the leaver studies. In addition, these and other studies will be developing comparison groups within their designs to estimate some effects of welfare reform, but these plans have not been developed to date.

Indeed, any study that seeks to estimate the effects of policy alternatives with nonexperimental methods is, in a sense, conducting an econometric study if that term is defined broadly. For example, the Rural Welfare Reform Project sponsored by ACF aims to gauge the effects of welfare reform strategies in rural areas with nonexperimental means. A number of other projects sponsored by ACF in individual states are doing the same. ASPE has funded a number of relatively small research grants that use nonexperimental methods to evaluate the effect of welfare reform. Many nonexperimental studies using various observational designs are funded primarily at the state or local level, such as a large evaluation in California of the CALWORKS program, an evaluation of welfare reform in Los Angeles County, and the large New York State comprehensive welfare reform evaluation.

PROCESS, IMPLEMENTATION, AND QUALITATIVE STUDIES

A major study of implementation of welfare reform in 20 states, the State Capacity Study, is currently being conducted at the Rockefeller Institute of Government, for example. The project aims to describe changing state management systems for social service programs, to describe their goals, and to make recommendations on different management strategies. The Urban Institute, as part of its Assessing the New Federalism Project, is studying implementation and policy choices in the same 13 states that are covered in NSAF, described above. The Urban Change Study has an implementation component that involves studying the implementation of welfare reform in the same four areas where the individual-level data are being collected. In addition, virtually all the waiver experiments have a process analysis component, as have virtually all large-scale experiments conducted in the last 10 years. There are also a large number of implementation studies that have been, and continue to be, conducted in individual states and local areas examining how PRWORA or various welfare services are being provided in the era after PRWORA; they are funded either by state and local governments or by the federal government. Process and implementation analysis, therefore, is thriving in the current welfare reform research scene.

Efforts to document state program rules in the aftermath of PRWORA are also under way. Unlike the situation under AFDC, a federally regulated program, all the precise rules that states have adopted no longer need to be reported to the federal government. The Urban Institute, as part of its Assessing the New Federalism initiative, has developed a Welfare Rules Database that contains descriptions of each state's (and the District of Columbia's) TANF rules from 1996 to 1999 (the 1996 data include AFDC rules). The 2000 update (funded by ACF) is now being produced. Current plans call for further updates in 2001 and 2002, also funded by ACF. The Center for Law and Social Policy (CLASP) and the Center for Budget and Policy Priorities (CBPP) are jointly collecting information on state TANF and Medicaid policies as part of the State Policy Documentation Project. This information was collected for legislation enacted before and updated through 1999. A joint effort between the U.S. Department of Health and Human Services (DHHS), the Welfare Information Network (WIN), the American Public Human Services Association, and the National Governors Association is summarizing state plans provided to DHHS as part of the final reporting rules of April 1999 (*Federal Register*, 1999) of PRWORA. These summaries will be entered into a database and made public on the Internet. This information is also being supplemented with information collected through the Urban Institute's Welfare Rules Database and the State Policy Documentation Project of CLASP and CBPP. The database will be updated every time new state plans are submitted. Finally, the Congressional Research Service has also used state TANF plans reported to DHHS and ACF to produce reports summarizing state program rules on different topics.

Finally, there have been a number of qualitative studies of welfare or non-welfare poor families. Most of these studies collect participant-observation or related types of in-depth information on families through an intensive personal contact process, although some conduct shorter unstructured interviews with families. The Urban Change Study conducted an ethnographic investigation of approximately 40 welfare-reliant families in each of its four areas to explore how families coped with the new rules and policies (Quint et al., 1999). The Three-City Study has a similarly large ethnographic project in its three cities to portray welfare reform from the point of view of the affected families. Other ethnographic studies have been a part of the New Hope Project, the Iowa Benefit Plan Project, the Wisconsin Child Support Demonstration Evaluation, and many others. The presence of a fairly large number of ethnographic and qualitative studies is a feature of welfare reform research in the 1990s that was rarely present in earlier periods of research.

OTHER WELFARE REFORM STUDIES

A variety of other ongoing welfare reform studies do not fall neatly into any of the above categories. One large group of studies of specific populations examine welfare recipients or leavers with problems of substance abuse, domestic violence, mental or physical health, or English-language difficulties. Others focus on specific populations, such as Native Americans or immigrants. Sometimes these studies are purely monitoring in nature, and sometimes they involve an assessment of the effects of particular new policies that apply to the group in question. A second group of studies consists primarily of data collection projects, most often collection of administrative data. These include a national survey of women and children in the child welfare system, as well as data assembly projects at UC-Data in California, a six-city consortium led by the University of Baltimore, and a multiple-state study using confidential data on business firms collected by the Census Bureau. ASPE is also funding a variety of studies to support data collection, including projects to assist states in establishing administrative and survey data bases on welfare recipients and the low-income population, to match federal data bases on employees and welfare recipients, and to use Social Security earnings records in the evaluation of welfare reform.

STUDIES ON TOPICS RELATED TO WELFARE REFORM

There are many other studies that do not bear directly on reform of the TANF or related welfare programs but rather on other programs that serve some of the same populations. We do not have the space to detail all of them, but we do mention a few of the major ones here. ASPE is funding studies on child support enforcement, child care, abstinence education programs, and child welfare, for example, all of which serve groups heavily overlapping with TANF population.

ASPE and ACF are jointly sponsoring a project to encourage the measurement of child outcomes in state-level studies, particularly those involving waiver experiments. ASPE is also sponsoring studies of specific groups such as, child-only cases, those with disabilities, and victims of domestic violence. ACF has funded state evaluations of employment retention initiatives and rural welfare reform strategies. Both the Urban Change and Los Angeles Survey of Families and Communities studies have components that study neighborhoods in low-income communities in the aftermath of welfare reform. Yet another ongoing project related to welfare reform is the Fragile Families Study, which is studying the relationship between fathers and mothers of unwed children, as well as the children of such relationships, in 20 cities.

3

Research Questions
and Populations of Interest

The vast number of important questions about the effects of welfare reform on different populations is enough to keep evaluators in business for many years. Because resources for evaluation are limited, however, there is a crucial need to set priorities for which questions are addressed, which population groups are examined, and which outcomes are to be measured. This chapter describes the monitoring and evaluation priorities the panel believes must be pursued in order to understand the effects of welfare reform. Special circumstances and new developments may require future additions to this list, but the needs discussed here are likely to be long-standing.

We begin by first discussing what groups in the population are of interest, emphasizing that welfare recipients are too narrow a group for focus. We also provide a brief discussion of the types of outcomes that should be studied in welfare reform projects. Next, we provide a categorization of different types of welfare reform effects and, in so doing, outline the set of important research and evaluation questions that should be addressed. Because different individuals— those in policy-making positions and those in the outside research community, those in the federal government and those in the state government, and the public—sometimes are interested in different questions because of their own responsibilities and vantage points, we cast our net widely to include questions that are of interest to these different individuals. Finally, we assess whether the existing monitoring and evaluation efforts summarized in Chapter 2 adequately cover all the important groups and outcomes of interest for welfare programs and whether these efforts adequately address the priority research questions of interest.

POPULATIONS OF INTEREST

At the broadest possible level, the group of most concern to welfare reform is the low-income population in the United States. The welfare system exists to provide assistance to families, children, and individuals in this population and to help them raise their incomes, escape poverty, and avoid the negative consequences of poverty and low incomes. Thus, the landscape of evaluation efforts in the wake of PRWORA should include assessments of the effects of welfare reform on this broadly defined population.[1]

Virtually all low-income groups are covered by one type of program or another historically; however, particular subgroups have been given more attention by Congress and the public. Single mothers with children have received perhaps the greatest amount of programmatic assistance, although married couples with children have also been the recipients of major new programs in recent years (the Earned Income Tax Credit [EITC], Medicaid expansions, etc.). However, single individuals without children are also the targets of some programs, such as food stamps. Children have also been the focus of much recent policy attention, as in the expansions of the Medicaid program and the creation of the State Children's Health Insurance Program (S-CHIP) and Early Head Start programs; children have also been the focus of more long-standing programs, such as Social Security Insurance and Head Start.

Recent welfare reform was primarily directed at changing the old AFDC program into the new TANF program. Although both the new and old programs served other subpopulations, both are concerned primarily with poor single mothers and their children. Consequently, trends in the well-being of that group are clearly a primary concern. However, the spirit of welfare reform in the 1990s, as embodied in the PRWORA legislation, works toward a broader focus. As the emphasis on leaving welfare continues, and as more families attempt to gain self-sufficiency without welfare, attention tends to shift to those families off welfare who are still having difficulties and need assistance. Consequently, policy discussions are shifting towards a focus on the nonwelfare poor population (the "working poor"), as well as the welfare population, or sometimes on the population in transition between welfare and nonwelfare. Programs that provide employment supports in the form of child care, job training, and transportation, for example, tend to be aimed at the nonwelfare population rather than the welfare population. In addition, much of the welfare reform debate over PRWORA and just prior to it focused more on low rates of marriage and high rates of nonmarital

---

[1]We do not specifically define the "low-income" population but only suggest that it be considered broadly. Identifying exactly what low-income means is more complicated than just considering income because income does not capture all resources that may be available to individuals and families (see National Research Council, 1995).

childbearing, to a degree greater than in past decades. This, in turn, has led to an increased policy interest to discourage nonmarital childbearing by providing assistance to working, married families with children, a group that has also not traditionally been a focus of attention in welfare discussions.

To date, this shift toward a broader focus is only slight, for most attention continues to be given to families who are on welfare or who have had contact with the welfare system. These families have been the major group studied in most of the welfare reform projects conducted to date.

Even within the narrower population of those currently on welfare, however, groups of special interest can still be identified. One obvious group includes those women and children classified as welfare leavers, by some definition of that term, which have been the subject of the greatest number of recent welfare studies. However, as we detailed in our interim report, other groups of interest include those still on welfare ("stayers"), as well as those who are not on welfare but who have either applied and been diverted or rejected or who might have been discouraged from applying. Because these groups are also affected by welfare reform, their well-being should also be assessed.

Welfare stayers are usually presumed to be more disadvantaged than welfare leavers because they have been unsuccessful in leaving welfare. This expectation may be incorrect, however, because welfare sanctions lead to a considerable number of welfare exits. Those sanctions tend to affect the least educated and most disadvantaged families on welfare. Consequently, welfare leavers tend to be either quite well off or quite badly off in comparison to stayers.

Welfare reform also sought to raise the employment levels of those on welfare. Families who are not on welfare but who are potential applicants are normally less disadvantaged than those on welfare, but they often experience job loss or other events that may cause them to seek assistance from time to time. Like welfare leavers, they may be more likely now than previously to turn to nonwelfare sources of support or return to employment. In addition, like welfare leavers, as they explore alternative sources of support, they are likely to have very diverse experiences. These three groups—leavers, stayers, and those who have not received welfare—together make up the total population eligible for welfare. A complete picture of the effects of welfare reform on the welfare-eligible population requires a study of the outcomes of all three groups.

Finally, there are many special-need subgroups within the low-income population that require special programmatic assistance. Families in particularly poor physical or mental health; the disabled; individuals with a history of substance abuse; women and men who experience domestic violence; men with a criminal history who have difficulty reintegrating into society, families with troubled adolescents; children with special physical, cognitive, or behavioral problems; and abused and neglected children are examples of groups with such special problems. Programmatically-defined groups, such as child-only cases, two-parent family cases, and poor but ineligible immigrants, should also be of interest in welfare reform studies. Teenage mothers, who are at risk of not obtaining enough education or other adverse outcomes, are another group that many believe should be targeted for special attention. The subgroups of interest are likely to vary across areas, too, as states and localities may have specific populations that have specific service needs. These subgroups with special needs are important populations for monitoring and evaluation as agencies that serve them need to plan and devise programs to address their needs.

Conclusion 3.1 The primary population of interest for measuring the effects of changes in social welfare programs is the low-income population. The primary group of interest to the TANF program is the population of low-income mothers and their children.

Conclusion 3.2 Within the low-income population, those groups who have been on welfare or who are eligible for welfare are of particular interest. Within the population of welfare eligibles, there are four separate subgroups, each of which is of special interest for welfare reform studies: those who leave welfare, those who stay on welfare, those who are formally diverted from welfare through diversion programs, and those who are poor but have not applied for benefits or who have applied but been rejected.

Conclusion 3.3 The specific service needs of some low-income individuals and families also define subpopulations of interest for welfare reform research. First among these are families with special circumstances or characteristics that make the transition to employment and self-sufficiency difficult. Other subgroups of the low-income population have special needs that require assistance independent of their effects on employment, including: families with poor physical or mental health, substance abuse problems, or problems of domestic violence, as well as families with troubled adolescents or children with special physical, cognitive, or behavioral problems.

OUTCOMES OF INTEREST

A comprehensive list of all the outcomes of interest in welfare evaluations would be quite long and is not appropriate for this report. However, several distinctions among outcomes are worth making because these distinctions effect the evaluation methods and data needs that we discuss in subsequent chapters. How the specific outcomes are defined and operationally measured is a very important issue, but one that is beyond the scope of the panel's charge. Many outcomes we discuss are measures of individual and family well-being. Well-being is a broad concept with many different dimensions, including health, safety, economic, and social. Defining well-being, both conceptually and operationally, along these multiple dimensions is not easy, and the panel does not attempt to do so. Our discussion does not prescribe exact measurement of these concepts, only that they be measured according to current scientific standards.

The most important point to note is that there are a variety of different consumers of research and evaluation studies who are interested in different types of outcomes. The public and their elected representatives are, in part, interested in the well-being of the general low-income population as measured by many traditional outcomes: income levels; poverty rates; standard of living; and level of food, housing, and clothing consumption; as well as measures of health status and educational attainment, and traditional measures of child well-being, in terms of both educational attainment and health, and cognitive and affective competence. In a somewhat different category is employment, which might be considered an outcome of interest only inasmuch as it is an indirect indication of such outcomes as income, consumption, and a higher standard of living. However, employment is also important in itself in terms of traditional American values and hence it is legitimately included as an outcome of interest.

A rather different group in society, mostly government officials but also the public as taxpayers, is concerned with program expenditures and welfare caseloads. Welfare reform discussions have made it clear that many elected officials and a large segment of the public prefer that the well-being of families and children be achieved outside public programs. This is a long-standing public preference for independence from welfare through work and earnings. While some people believe that the government should limit its assistance for welfare and other programs, others believe that government should provide assistance outside welfare through more universal programs, such as EITC, child support enforcement, and universal health insurance. Others take a position between these. For all these groups, the sizes of caseloads and expenditures are themselves outcomes of interest.

A still different group of policy makers is interested in the administrative effects of welfare reform and how the agencies that provide welfare services have reorganized to better provide services. Because PRWORA has resulted in a greatly devolved administrative structure, there is now more room for differential implementation of programs across states and localities. Reorganizations of program administrative structures have been common throughout the country. For example, to offer a wider variety of services under TANF and related programs, many local welfare offices have merged with other social and economic program offices and now use front-line caseworkers as gatekeepers to these services. The way administrative systems have been reorganized to be more synchronized with the new TANF program is, thus, another outcome of interest to state and local officials.

Family structure and family formation outcomes have become more prominent and of direct interest in policy discussions than they once were (the preamble to PRWORA explicitly discusses these, unlike prior welfare legislation). The emphasis on marriage and on childbearing within marriage reflects long-standing American values. Many reforms have been implemented specifically to discourage nonmarital childbearing (e.g., family caps, sanctions for not cooperating with paternity establishment, abstinence education programs, requirements that teenage parents live with their parents, etc.). PRWORA has also given an incentive to states to focus on nonmarital childbearing outcomes by implementing an illegitimacy bonus that will be given to the five states whose out-of-wedlock birth and abortion rates decrease the most over 2-year periods. As a consequence, family structure and family formation outcomes, such as marriage and divorce, out-of-wedlock birth, paternity establishment, and teenage pregnancy also belong on the list of outcomes of interest.

Thus, there is a broad range of outcomes that should be the focus of welfare reform evaluation and monitoring. Each of these broadly defined outcomes discussed here—individual adult and family well-being outcomes, such as income, poverty, consumption, employment, education and health; traditional measures of children's physical, cognitive, emotional and behavioral well-being; family structure and family formation outcomes, such as marriage and divorce, childbearing, teenage pregnancy and out-of-wedlock births; and outcomes of governments themselves, such as expenditures, caseloads, and administrative structures—should be studied as part of a comprehensive welfare program research agenda.

Conclusion 3.4 The set of outcomes of interest for studies of welfare reform should be defined broadly to include all the outcomes that the different audiences of studies of welfare reform—the public, Congress and state legislators, and other governmental officials and program administrators—are concerned about.

QUESTIONS OF INTEREST

The number of important questions about the effects of changes in social welfare programs on the various populations of interest is virtually limitless. Thus, priorities have to be set in order to assess the needs for services among the low-income population, to make an assessment of whether PRWORA should be reauthorized, and to assess what future programmatic reforms may be needed. This section describes the questions that the panel believes are most important and should be used to guide evaluations and data collection efforts.

As was the case in detailing the diversity of audiences interested in different outcomes, there is diversity of audiences interested in different questions. It is important to realize that there are many different questions of interest and not all audiences are interested in all questions. The panel has taken a broad approach by considering the types of major questions in which significant segments of the public and government have an interest.

We classify the questions of interest into three general areas: (1) monitoring and describing trends in the well-being of the populations and subpopulations of interest; (2) determining the types of programs that states and localities have chosen and how the programs have been implemented and administered; and (3) conducting formal evaluations to assess how reform has changed outcomes relative to what they would have been in the absence of reform, and how future reforms will change outcomes relative to what they would be without further reform.

The questions of interest identified are both retrospective and prospective in nature. Some questions of interest concern the effects of the most recent changes in welfare policy, which is necessarily a retrospective question. Assessing the overall effect of PRWORA is necessarily a retrospective question, although we argue that the answers to this question may have implications for future system-wide changes. Questions of the effects of broad components and detailed strategies are retrospective in that they assess the effects of policies already in place. However, as we argue below, what is learned from these evaluations may have implications for the kinds of policy changes that are made in the near future within PRWORA's overall, devolved framework. It is in this sense that they are also prospective. It is difficult to predict specific questions that will be of future policy interest. For example, policy priorities may change if there is a severe economic recession, perhaps causing a change in focus to job training for welfare recipients instead of immediate employment. Instead of trying to predict specific questions of interest for the future, and the methodological and data needs for answering these questions, we instead define the questions of interest broadly and, accordingly, keep our discussion of methods and data needed to answer these questions in later chapters at a more general level as well.

Monitoring the Well-Being of the Low-Income Population

As we have already noted at several points in this report, monitoring the well-being of the low-income population is, in and of itself, an important task that is essential to a complete and satisfactory study of major welfare policy changes for several reasons.

First and foremost, the well-being of the low-income population is just one part of a much broader effort to monitor the well-being of the nation's population as a whole over a wide range of domains (e.g., poverty, educational attainment, unemployment, and health status) and over a range of subpopulations (e.g., children, the elderly, minorities, workers). Such monitoring is crucial in order to understand trends in the population and its well-being so that both private and public entities can gear production or policies to meet the nation's needs. Understanding the well-being of the low-income population is part of this endeavor.

Second, monitoring studies can provide valuable information to guide the design and targeting of future program changes. Many federal programs are targeted at the low-income population, and high-quality and consistent statistics can detect needs for service or policy change, early responses to changes in these programs, and responses to changes in macroeconomic conditions that might affect participation in these programs. For example, tracking program participation rates among poor families can help detect lack of use, changes in use, or critical gaps in coverage of programs. Monitoring efforts might also reveal subpopulations within a state that are doing especially well or especially poorly in comparison to the well-being of the larger population. This knowledge could be useful in helping to identify the types of services that the subpopulation uses or is in need of, which is important for budgetary planning purposes and for developing and planning future policy changes. Monitoring the well-being of the population can also be helpful in identifying areas where further policy evaluation and general behavioral research are needed.

State legislators and agency officials also benefit from knowledge of early responses to changes in policy and macroeconomic conditions in their states. Thus, it is valuable to monitor the well-being of the low-income population within each state. This is especially true as services for the low-income populations are increasingly blended together and caseworkers increasingly act as gatekeepers to an array of services. Agencies also benefit from knowing the service needs of their clients, such as needs for child care or needs for substance abuse or domestic violence counseling.

Monitoring also is important in directing research and evaluation activity. Research should focus on improving understanding of those groups in the population who are most in distress and most in need of assistance. Identifying those groups and characterizing the nature of their needs is a key function that monitoring can serve and that is therefore a necessary first step to effective evaluation and research.

Characterizing and Tracking Policies, Programs, and Administrative Practices

The need to understand policies, programs, and administrative practices in the TANF program is as great after devolution as it was before, but the task has grown enormously in size and complexity because of the need to cover a much larger number and range of programs. Under AFDC, there was some variation in benefit levels and a few other program characteristics across the states, but, there was considerable uniformity in the basic nature of the program nationwide. Under TANF, program authority has devolved to the states, who now have the discretion to devise programs of their own choosing (subject to a few requirements in the PRWORA legislation). States have responded by developing programs that differ in myriad ways, and the reporting requirements under PRWORA do not require the states to specifically describe all the details of their program features to the federal government, thus there is no automatic mechanism for knowing many details of state programs in the new era of welfare reform.

Documenting the nature of state programs is complicated by several additional factors. The PRWORA legislation and the regulations that have been issued by DHHS give the states the ability to develop noncash programs for TANF recipients as well as cash programs (e.g., transportation assistance).[2] Noncash, service programs are more difficult to track than traditional cash programs. As states move toward greater provision of noncash services of multiple types, this problem will increase. Another factor is that states have in many cases given considerable discretion to the local offices in their states to implement variations on a common model, which results in even more variation in programs. Yet another aspect of this issue is that the way programs are administered and implemented may vary in significant ways from the way they are understood to operate from a formal description of the policy, which also creates the need for detailed descriptions. Finally, all of these developments pertain only to TANF. States are free, however, to develop non-TANF programs with their own funds or from other federal funds. These programs may serve either TANF recipients or, perhaps more often, those who have left the TANF program or been diverted from TANF, but who still need assistance. It is the entire programmatic environment in a state that has changed by welfare reform, and this total environment needs to be tracked and characterized.

Knowing what states and localities are actually doing—and making collection of this information a major research question in need of directed and focused investigation—is important for a variety of reasons. First, it is of interest in and of itself, because the flowering of different program types across different states and localities was one of the intentional outcomes of changing the program structure to a block-grant system. Indeed, PRWORA was not really designed to institute a new set of policies. Rather, it was designed to allow devolution of policy-setting to the states, under the belief that states know the needs of their populations better than the federal government and could better design programs to meet those needs. Evaluation of the PRWORA legislation, in this sense, necessarily requires knowing what types of programs actually exist. During the debate over PRWORA, many people were also concerned that some states, when freed from federal requirements, would adopt policies or program features that were inconsistent with the national interest in assisting the poor. A related concern at the onset of PRWORA was that states would limit the benefits they offered to recipients in a "race to the bottom," fearing that if a state was relatively more generous, welfare recipients would migrate to that state from states that were relatively less generous. Determining the variation in programs that has resulted from the legislation is needed to address these concerns. Thus, once again,

---

[2]These programs can be financed out of federal block grant dollars or state maintenance-of-effort funds. States are required to continue to spend their own funds on social welfare programs at a level that is a fraction of what each state's spending was before PRWORA.

tracking and monitoring state policies is an intrinsic and critical outcome of welfare reform and needs to be documented. This includes tracking and documenting how different state and local program agencies have been restructured.

Second, the U.S. federal structure has often been touted for its ability to create knowledge by allowing states to undertake variation in public policies and then to learn from each other (states as "laboratories of democracy" in Justice Brandeis's famous phrase). These spillover and learning features require that states know what other states are doing. To some degree this has already occurred. States currently do consult with one another, and there are informal networks across states that communicate ideas and strategies. Nevertheless, a reasonable nationwide policy tracking system is needed to provide states with a more complete set of information.

Third, determining what states and localities are doing is a necessary intermediate step in evaluating outcomes, which is a main goal of formal evaluation. Policy evaluation that makes use of the program variation across areas is handicapped if only broad and superficial descriptors of policies are available. Evaluations of welfare reform would not be very useful if it were not clear what welfare reform actually is and what is actually being evaluated. The proliferation of different policies engendered by PRWORA was initially seen by evaluators as a potential benefit because it was presumed that it would allow many informative comparisons across areas. This view is the evaluator's counterpart to the laboratories-of-democracy argument used in policy circles. However, capturing that benefit of policy variation requires that the policies be documented in sufficient detail for accurate characterization when conducting a formal evaluation analysis.

Formally Evaluating the Impact of Welfare Reform

A critical set of questions concerns the formal evaluation of the effects of welfare reform, where by formal evaluation we mean a rigorous assessment of the effects of a change in policy on outcomes relative to what would happen in the absence of that change. Forming the questions of interest for evaluating welfare reform in the 1990s and after PRWORA is difficult because of the structural change created by the reform. Unlike the incremental changes in the AFDC program that resulted from policy changes in 1967, 1981, and 1988, for example (see Chapter 2)—all of which changed a broad component of the program but not its fundamental character—welfare reform in the 1990s changed the entire system. The consequences of this type of systematic reform are many and influence all the conclusions drawn in this report in subsequent chapters on evaluation methods and data collection.

For defining the sets of evaluation questions that need to be addressed, systematic reform implies that there are several different levels at which the effects of reform need to be assessed. We have classified the questions in three general categories, which are ordered with increasing specificity, in relation to outcomes:

- What is the overall impact of welfare reform, taken as a whole and with all individual components bundled together?
- What are the impacts of the individual, but still broad, components of welfare reform (work requirements, sanctions, time limits, family caps, etc.) on outcomes?
- What are the impacts of individual, detailed strategies within each of the broad components (type of work strategy, specific cash assistance level, nature of sanction policy, etc.)?

This three-tier classification of the questions that need to be asked is useful because each type of question requires a different evaluation strategy and some-what different data, as discussed in the next two chapters, and because there are different audiences for each of the three questions.

The overall effect takes into account not just the immediate effects on wel-fare recipients, but also the multiple systemic changes that result, such as changes in the nature of the welfare system, in the expectations that the individuals and the families in the low-income population (including current nonrecipients) have of the system, in their behavior, in the way the program is organized and admin-istered locally, and in the types of assistance provided by other agencies. The overall effect can be measured at the national level or in individual states or localities.

The overall effect of welfare reform is of interest to many groups, including members of the public and members of Congress. Answering the question re-quires separating the effects of the economy and of other policy developments from the effects of welfare reform and requires estimating how outcomes in the low-income population (and in specific subgroups) would have differed in the absence of welfare reform. As we discuss in the next two chapters, answering this question has proven to be very difficult with existing evaluation methods and with the available data.

One reason for the interest in the overall effect of PRWORA stems from the fact that changes relative to the AFDC program were profound. PRWORA was one of the most important pieces of legislation affecting the AFDC program since 1935, and was surrounded by a great deal of public interest and media attention. A second reason for an interest in the overall effect is that the PRWORA legisla-tion and the waiver reforms that preceded it were based on the presumption that changing many of the individual components of the program simultaneously—to enact an entire "bundle" of individual reforms—would have a synergistic effect that would equal more than the sum of its parts. In other words, the impact of the entire bundle would be greater than the cumulative impact of individual compo-nents had they been enacted separately. Welfare reform in the 1990s was intended to change the culture of the welfare system and to change the basic expectations for the role that welfare plays in the lives of poor families, both the expectations held by families and those held by caseworkers and agency personnel. Separate estimations of the effect of individual components cannot capture this synergistic effect. A third reason for interest in determining the overall effect of welfare reform is to identify the evaluation and data needs required to answer this type of question should major, systemwide welfare reform take place in the future. Lessons can be learned from the attempt to answer this question that may be usefully applied to future rounds of reform, although there is little expectation of major change in welfare policy in the near future.

The question of the overall effect is of far less interest to many policy makers, particularly those at the state and local levels, who take the new welfare structure as given and are more interested in prospective questions concerning the incremental effects of future policy changes. As noted above, many states are actively considering how to assist low-income families in greatest need, including those not on welfare, and how to do so with noncash as well as cash assistance. These policymakers do not want to return to the AFDC system as it existed in the 1980s and, consequently, are not especially interested in what outcomes would have been today under that system, because it is no longer an interesting policy option. For this audience, the effects of broad components and detailed strategies (discussed below) are of more interest because they are more relevant to what future reforms might be—that is, incremental adjustments under the basic structure as it now exists. Nevertheless, even for this audience, determining the overall effect of welfare reform could be useful if it illuminated differential effects among subgroups of the population. Such evaluations could identify the subgroups toward whom new policies could be addressed.

The second category of question that many audiences find interesting is the effect of individual, broad components of welfare reform, such as family caps, time limits, work sanctions, and special provisions applicable to teenage parents. For example, one may ask how the introduction of time limits of any particular type has affected outcomes relative to not having any time limits.

As with the question of the overall effect, questions of the effects of individual, broad components has both a retrospective and a prospective formulation. One may ask what outcomes would have been under the old AFDC system had one component of welfare reform (e.g., family caps) been enacted while all the others had not been, for example. Or, one may ask what outcomes would be like in the future if that component were eliminated or modified and all other components were retained in their present form. The answers to these two questions are likely to be quite different, because the base policy from which the individual component is added or subtracted is different, and the base policy structure is likely to influence the effect of each component taken individually. Evaluations of the effects of individual program components is more likely to be of interest to policy makers interested in incremental reform from the current structure, especially if effects are considered prospectively. However, the evaluation and data problems that arise are the same whether the question takes a retrospective or prospective form, as we discuss in the next two chapters.

Currently, there is considerable dispute about the effects of individual broad components, which confirms that these questions are indeed of interest to many. For example, there is considerable disagreement on the effects of the time-limit policies that were contained in PRWORA and in many pre-PRWORA waiver plans. Some analysts have argued that time limits have not had the substantial effect that many anticipated, or feared (especially given that time limits were probably the most controversial feature of welfare reform). The evidence from states that set short time limits does not indicate that their effects on exit rates have been very big, on average, and the effects on post-welfare employment are unclear as well (Bloom, 1999). Whether this result is because states have used extensions and exemptions to avoid the time limits, because most recipients leave long before the limits are reached, because the work requirements have more effect, or for some other reason, is not clear. It may also be the case that not enough time has passed to assess the full effects that time limits will eventually have. Nevertheless, the importance that many give to determining the incremental contribution of time limits to the effect of welfare reform illustrates the policy importance of questions surrounding the effects of broad program components.

The third category of evaluation questions concerns the effects of detailed strategies and detailed programs and approaches within the broad components. The specific requirements for work activities, the relative effects of time limits of 2 years and 5 years, the relative emphasis on immediate work and job placement in comparison with training, the way in which sanctions are applied, strategies to encourage job retention among those who have already found work, the magnitude of family cap penalties, and the specific teenage parent requirements or programs to discourage teenagers from becoming pregnant are all examples of detailed strategies whose effect on outcomes is of interest. Many very detailed strategies are also administrative in nature. One concerns case management strategies, for which the issue is how best to guide families with particular needs to the programs and services that will best address those needs. A related issue is whether to house multiple programs in a one-stop shopping facility or parcel them out to different agencies. Indeed, the list of such detailed strategies is almost limitless.

While these examples are all easily distinguished from the broad components that we just mentioned—time limits, work requirements, and sanctions, for example—the distinction can be overdrawn because there are many policies that fit in a gray area between broad components and detailed strategies. There is, in truth, a continuum of policies ranging from the broadest archetype to the narrowest and most specific. Nevertheless, we make this distinction between different types of questions because the audience differs as one moves across the spectrum, and because, as we discuss in Chapter 4, the most desirable evaluation methods change as one moves across that spectrum. Policy makers at the state and local level and at the federal level who are most actively involved in searching for incremental improvements within the existing welfare structure constitute the primary audience for answers to questions about detailed strategies. They are of critical importance and are also large in number. Priorities in isolating the most important issues and the most important alternative policies among the many that might be imagined must be established. The overall question is "what works, to what degree, and for whom."

> **Conclusion 3.5 The monitoring questions of interest are the following: How has the well-being of the low-income population and key subgroups evolved subsequent to welfare reform? Which subgroups are doing well and which are doing less well? Which subgroups are in greatest need and deserve the attention of policy makers?**

> **Conclusion 3.6   The descriptive questions of interest regarding program policy and implementation are the following: What policies, programs, and administrative practices have states and localities actually implemented as part of welfare reform? How wide is the variation across states and even within states in policy? How has implementation differed from officially described policy? How has the non-TANF programmatic environment changed?**

> **Conclusion 3.7 The impact evaluation questions of interest are the following: What are the overall effects of the complete bundle of changes in policies, programs, and practices on the well-being of the low-income population, including the effects on both adults and children and on specific subpopulations of interest? What are the effects of the individual broad components of welfare reform on the well-being of the low income population and subpopulations of interest? What are the effects of specific detailed strategies within each of the broad program components on the well-being of the low-income population and the subpopulations of interest—what works and for whom?**

NATIONWIDE VERSUS INDIVIDUAL STATE ASSESSMENTS

A final issue in formulating the questions of interest concerns whether an overall nationwide assessment of the effect of welfare reform is needed or whether a set of state-specific results, perhaps not even for a complete set of all the states, would be sufficient. Although an overall nationwide estimate of a major piece of legislation is usually appropriate, the devolution inherent in current welfare reform and the proliferation of different types of reform programs across the states and localities makes a nationwide estimate of somewhat lesser interest than usual, because such an estimate does not represent the effect of any one type of program and so is not very instructive for what policies work best and which do not. However, to the extent that PRWORA is not so much a law leading to specific policies but a law giving states freedom to formulate the programs they desire, the effect at the national level is of interest. Estimating the effect at the national level does answer the question of the effects of devolution in that it answers questions about the effects of the many programs that states have implemented with their new discretion over program design. A nationwide estimate of the effect of welfare reform (either overall or broad components) is therefore of interest, even if it is not particularly helpful for assessing what to do next.

Conclusion 3.8   The effect of welfare reform is a question of interest for the nation as a whole as well as for individual states.

ASSESSMENT

The set of welfare reform projects under way at the present time is impressive in its scope, volume, and diversity. The number of projects is unprecedented compared to any prior era of welfare reform evaluation—such as, for example, the evaluation efforts following the landmark 1981 and 1988 legislation referred to in Chapter 1. A large number of capable researchers in the private and public sectors are devoting major efforts toward welfare reform research and have been producing a great number of valuable and informative studies. Both ASPE and the Administration for Children and Families (ACF) have substantial agendas for welfare reform research and have supported much high quality work. The role of private foundations is also notable for its scope and magnitude of funding to support high-quality welfare reform research. The knowledge and information base that has been established and continues to develop is broad and deep.

Taken as a whole, the studies have been reasonably successful in addressing the correct populations, outcomes, and questions of interest. However, we find that there are still gaps and areas of overemphasis and underemphasis. This section assesses the projects described in Chapter 2 in light of the populations and questions of interests discussed in this chapter.

Several studies and a number of government agencies have focused on monitoring the general well-being of adults and children in the low-income population over time. ASPE has sponsored and conducted many studies that extensively document trends in the low-income population, both adults and children, and in the welfare recipient population. These are perhaps the best and most comprehensive examples of monitoring studies. These studies should be continued and expanded. The other monitoring studies described in Chapter 2 are also addressing the key monitoring questions of interest for the low-income population, even if only for localized areas.

However, while most of the important monitoring questions are being addressed in one place or another, we find considerable imbalance in the amount of attention paid to different groups. As noted in Chapter 2, the current landscape of research overemphasizes welfare leaver studies and underemphasizes studies of stayers, applicants, divertees, and discouraged nonapplicants. Leaver studies serve a valuable monitoring function in documenting the outcomes of leavers, identifying what types of leavers are doing well and what type are not, and assessing the degree to which self-sufficiency has been attained after leaving the rolls. But the other groups deserve equal attention because they are also affected by welfare reform. A complete picture of the trends in well-being of the welfare-eligible population as a whole is needed for a satisfactory monitoring effort. Such a picture has not been completed to date, 4 years after the passage of PRWORA. ASPE has made a start in the right direction in its funding of state studies of divertees and applicants, but much more needs to be done.

While monitoring questions are being addressed with reasonable frequency, questions concerning the determination of what states and localities have actually been doing has until recently received much less attention and fewer resources than they deserve. As a consequence, there are large gaps in knowledge about what governments have done in the wake of PRWORA. Documentation of welfare rules at the Urban Institute, at the Center for Law and Social Policy (CLASP) and the Center for Budget and Policy Priorities (CBPP), and at other organizations are laudable, but represent only a small fraction of what needs to be done. These documentation efforts do not cover all programs and still lack much important detail about local implementation. They are also coming at a very late date after the passage of PRWORA. Studies of process and implementation at the Rockefeller Institute, the Urban Institute, at the Manpower Demonstration Research Corporation as part of the Urban Change Project, and in other evaluation projects, are valuable and will provide useful information in the future. But more process and implementation studies need to be conducted at the local level and in a more comprehensive set of areas around the country. We return to these issues in our discussion of data needs in Chapter 5.

With respect to the evaluation questions of interest, most are being addressed by one or more research studies in the set we discussed in Chapter 2. The overall effects of PRWORA and welfare reform have been addressed in the caseload and econometric modeling literature, in which the effects of individual broad components have also been studied. The ACF waiver experiments also seek to determine the impacts of entire bundles of reforms, albeit in a pre-PRWORA environment. While we have findings and recommendations in Chapter 4 on the strength of the particular evaluation methods used in these studies, and in Chapter 5 on the strength of the data bases used, the questions themselves, as we have posed them, have been addressed in at least some studies. Likewise, studies of detailed strategies have begun, particularly at ASPE and ACF, although most are in their beginning stages and few results are yet available. These efforts should be greatly expanded and strengthened.

Although most of the evaluation questions are being addressed in one study or another in the total constellation of projects under way, future efforts should invest more in identifying emerging issues of importance, defining the key questions of interest, and in providing a framework for welfare reform studies that the evaluation community can follow. Our review of existing studies shows a large number of studies funded by different public or private organizations, addressing a wide variety of questions, but in an unfocused and uncoordinated fashion. A clear delineation of populations, outcomes, and evaluation questions of interest as we have laid them out in this chapter has not been made. The panel has concluded, therefore, that there is a need for some organization to take a leadership role in defining the questions and populations of interest for the welfare research community as a whole and in setting the agenda for what types of research is needed. Setting that agenda should involve consultation with a broad set of groups, including the states, private foundations supporting research on welfare programs, and others. Research conferences like the ones ASPE and ACF have previously held are a possible venue for such consultation. We view such an agenda-setting task as appropriately a federal responsibility because a full view of the effects of reform across the nation is needed and because no one state will be able to do this on their own. Because ASPE is the branch of DHHS with the specific mission to advise the secretary of DHHS on policy research and evaluation, economic analysis and more generally, policy development, it is the most appropriate agency to provide that leadership. We recommend therefore that ASPE take a more proactive and public role in this regard.

Recommendation 3.1 The panel recommends that ASPE take primary responsibility for publicly defining the questions of interest for welfare reform research and evaluation, identifying emerging issues for social welfare programs, and defining alternative detailed strategies and policies that address the what-works-and-for-whom questions. In doing so, ASPE should expand its current activities in seeking input from states, private foundations, and other stakeholders on emerging policy and evaluation issues.

Finally, the panel believes that defining the questions of interest is sufficiently important that they should be subject to congressional and public review. The best way for this review to take place is for ASPE to document its list of important questions in the form of an annual report to Congress. Such an annual report should also review the degree to which existing welfare reform studies, both those funded by ASPE and those funded by other government agencies and private entities, are addressing the necessary questions. The annual report should relate its own agenda of research to those questions, and should place itself in the constellation of welfare reform research and discuss how it sees its own role. In doing so, it will need to coordinate with ACF and other programmatic branches in DHHS that administer and evaluate specific welfare programs. In subsequent chapters, we suggest other topics for inclusion in such an annual report.

Recommendation 3.2   ASPE should produce an annual report to Congress that, among other things, presents a comprehensive list of the important questions to be addressed in welfare reform research, describes how those questions are being addressed in the overall landscape of welfare reform studies, and explains how its own research agenda relates to those questions and to other studies under way.

4

Evaluation Methods and Issues

Chapter 3 identified three types of questions: monitoring the well-being of the low-income population, tracking and documenting what types of programs states and localities have actually implemented, and formally evaluating the effects of welfare reform relative to a counterfactual. In this chapter we consider only the last of these types of questions. The proper methods for conducting monitoring studies and for determining what policies have actually been implemented are primarily data collection issues; there is no evaluation methodology component to these questions. They are discussed in Chapter 5 in connection with data issues.

This chapter has five sections. In the first, we provide an overview of evaluation methodologies (discussed in more detail in our interim report [National Research Council, 1999] and in evaluation texts). The second section discusses the relative advantages and disadvantages of alternative evaluation methods in relation to each of the different evaluation questions of interest identified in Chapter 3. The third part of the chapter discusses several specific evaluation methodology issues in more detail: the reliability of nonexperimental evaluation methods, statistical power in nonexperimental methods, generalizability, process and qualitative research methods to complement formal evaluation analyses, and the importance of welfare dynamics for evaluation. The fourth part assesses the evaluation projects currently under way (discussed in Chapter 2) in light of the findings that have been presented on the different evaluation methods. The final part of the chapter briefly considers ways in which federal and state agencies can improve evaluations of welfare reform.

We note that recommendations of appropriate evaluation methodologies are sometimes influenced by data availability, for the two are necessarily intertwined.

Chapter 5 presents our major discussion of data issues and data needs; it follows this chapter because data needs should be dictated by what is needed for evaluation. However, a discussion of the strengths and weaknesses of evaluation methods is inevitably influenced by the types of data currently available, likely to be available, or remotely possible to collect; in that context, data issues do arise in this chapter.

OVERVIEW OF EVALUATION METHODS

Formal evaluation studies are those that attempt to estimate the "effect" of a policy change, or the impact of the change on those outcomes which are of interest. By common usage of the word "effect," this implies that it must be determined what would have happened to those outcomes if the policy change had not occurred. Thus, a formal evaluation study requires the estimation of two quantities: the outcomes that have actually occurred following a policy change, and those that would have occurred if the policy had not changed. The latter is called the "counterfactual." The basic difficulty in all evaluation studies is that the counterfactual is not naturally or directly observed—it is impossible to know with certainty what would have happened if a policy change had not occurred.[1] All evaluation methodologies attempt, implicitly or explicitly, in one way or the other, to estimate those counterfactual outcomes. In experimental methods, the outcomes are estimated by means of a control group to which individuals have been randomly assigned. In nonexperimental methods, the outcomes are estimated by means of a comparison group, a group of individuals that are not randomly assigned to a comparison group, but who are considered to be similar to those who received the policy.

The different types of policy alternatives of interest to different audiences all fit within the counterfactual conceptual framework. Comparing PRWORA in its entirety to its precursor, AFDC, constitutes one pair of policy alternatives, for example, that we concluded would be of interest to many observers. Comparing PRWORA in its present form to a modified PRWORA that might result if its components were altered or improved in some way, constitutes another pair of alternatives in which many policy makers and others are interested. Sometimes, three alternatives are considered, such as the case when the goal is to compare (say) two alternatives (Policy A and Policy B) to current policy. Most of the general issues we discuss for different evaluation methods are the same regardless of which of these policy comparisons is of interest.

---

[1] A recent discussion of the counterfactual approach can be found in Dawid (2000), with several commentaries to this article in the June 2000 issue of the *Journal of the American Statistical Association*.

Experimental Methods

Randomized experiments have a long history in welfare reform evaluation and have produced some of the most influential results in past reform eras. The strength of the experimental method is that it has a high degree of credibility because randomization assures that those who do experience the policy change (the experimental group) are alike, in all important ways, to those who do not experience it (the control group), except for the difference in treatment (the policy) itself. In evaluation terminology, well-run and well-conducted experiments have strong "internal validity" because they have considerable credibility in generating correct estimates of the true effect of the policy tested in the location and on the population of individuals enrolled in the experiment. The experimental method is also influential because it is simple and easy to understand by policy makers.[2]

Despite these strengths, the experimental method has weaknesses as well (see Burtless [1995] and Heckman and Smith [1995] for discussions of these issues). A common weakness is that the results of the experiment may not generalize to types of individuals other than those enrolled in the experiment, or to different areas with different economic and programmatic environments, or to policies that differ slightly from those tested in the experiment. In evaluation terminology this is the "external validity" problem. The severity of this problem can be reduced if a large number of experiments are conducted in multiple sites, on different populations, and with different policy features. The expense of doing so is generally prohibitive. A related problem is that experiments are ill suited to estimating the effects of large-scale policy changes which are intended to change the entire culture of a welfare system. If the program is only tested on a small group of individuals in a few cities, the culture will not be affected. However, if the program is enacted nationwide with only a small group of individuals still subject to the old program as a control group, the cultural effects will occur but they will also affect the control group. The experimental method is also not well positioned to estimate so-called "entry effects," effects that occur because a policy change affects the likelihood of becoming a welfare recipient in the first place. This problem may occur because most welfare experiments draw their experimental and control samples from welfare recipients and not from individuals who are not currently receiving welfare, but who may later do so. A somewhat related problem with experiments is that they usually take a relatively long time to design and implement, so that the policy change tested in the experi-

---

[2]Of course, experiments can be conducted badly by incorrectly conducting the randomization, erroneously assigning treatment status, allowing some of the control members to receive the treatment, by high nonresponse rates or missing data that biases the results, or a number of other problems in implementation. See Gordon et al. (1996) for a study that found that many of the pre-PRWORA waiver experiments suffered from inadequate sample sizes, and cross-overs, contamination, and control group exposure, for example.

ment may not be of interest to policy makers by the time the results are completed. Finally, experiments often have practical difficulties when they are conducted in real-world environments with on-going programs and when they require the cooperation and effort of agencies engaged in running current programs.

Despite these weaknesses, the strengths of experiments for answering some types of questions cannot be overemphasized. Even if they may not be completely generalizable and even if they do not always capture all the relevant effects of the program, they provide more credible evidence than other methods for the effects of the programs in one location and on one population. In a policy environment where little credible evaluation research is available, even a small number of experimental results can contribute a great deal to knowledge.

Nonexperimental Methods

Nonexperimental methods are more diverse and heterogeneous than experimental methods, which is one of the reasons that there is often confusion about their nature and value. In all cases, however, nonexperimental methods require that the outcomes experienced by a group of individuals after a policy change be compared with the outcomes that occur for some other group—the comparison group that did not experience the policy change.

A key difference between experimental methods and nonexperimental methods is that an experiment implements a particular policy or program and therefore ensures that it is exactly the one of interest (although, as noted, the time lag in obtaining results may significantly reduce this advantage, and, like nonexperimental studies, the exact policy of interest may not actually be implemented as intended). Nonexperimental methods are necessarily more passive—they can only estimate the effects of programs and policy changes that have actually been implemented, which may not be those of greatest interest. This approach can be advantageous, however, if a wide variety of policy changes have been implemented in different areas, in different environments, and at different times, because a wider range of policies can be studied and generalization is easier. In evaluation terms, nonexperimental evaluations, if they make use of this range, have a greater potential for external validity than do experiments. This potential for external validity must be balanced against the weaker internal validity of nonexperimental methods—that is, the risk that the comparison group is not comparable to the group receiving the policy or program so the correct effects are not estimated.

There are several generic types of nonexperimental evaluations used in welfare evaluations. Perhaps the most traditional is a "cross-area" comparison, which compares outcomes of similar individuals in different geographical areas where different types of policies have been implemented and attributes differences in their outcomes to the differences in policy. A variation on this approach, which is still essentially cross-area in nature, follows individuals over time in different areas where policy is changing in different ways and observes the outcomes across areas. All these methods can be formulated as econometric models in which individual differences in characteristics are controlled for statistically. This method is not available if all areas are affected by the same policy changes at the same time. In addition, even when there is cross-area variation, there is some danger that not all relevant differences in states' outcomes, either at a given time or over time, are controlled for; omitted state differences may be correlated with policy choices, either by chance or by design.[3]

Another, cruder evaluation method is a pure time-series analysis—also called an interrupted time series or before-and-after method—which examines the pattern of outcomes for a group of individuals before and after a policy change. For this method, the "comparison group" is simply the population prior to the policy change. This approach can be implemented either with aggregate data or with micro data—that is, data at the level of the individual or family. In the latter case, the data follow the individuals or families over time before and after a policy change to see how outcomes change. These are among the weakest nonexperimental methods because outcomes change over time for many reasons other than the policy change (for example, changes in the economy and in other policies) which are difficult to control for fully. Outcomes may also change for a given cohort of individuals simply because those individuals age. However, the cohort comparison method (or simply the use of aggregate data, which implicitly uses different cohorts) circumvents this problem by examining a population at the same age at each point in time.

The cohort comparison method examines the outcomes over time of multiple groups of individuals (cohorts) who experience different policies because policy is changing over time.[4] If the analysis is conducted in only one area, or in the nation as a whole, the method is essentially a time series. It differs from pure time-series analysis only inasmuch as the cohorts are assumed to be alike in other respects because they are of the same age or are on welfare at the same time. The cohort comparison method can be combined with the cross-area method by comparing changes for different cohorts in different areas where policy has been changing, leading to a cross-area cohort comparison method.

An issue in the cohort comparison method when applied to welfare reform concerns how the cohorts should be defined. If two cohorts are drawn from the welfare rolls at different times—say, one cohort before the legislation and one after—there is a danger that the two cohorts are noncomparable. Noncompara-

---

[3]The latter is a case of what is known as "policy endogeneity" and occurs when different policies are chosen by different states on the basis of the populations and their outcomes in the state—the same outcomes that are examined to assess the effects of policies.

[4]Cohort comparison methods were used in the evaluation of the 1981 AFDC reforms (Research Triangle Institute, 1983; U.S. General Accounting Office, 1984); both studies examined the exit rates and outcomes of a pre-1981 cohort and a post-1981 cohort.

bility can arise if (for example) the caseload is falling and those still receiving welfare after the legislation goes into effect are different—for example, more disadvantaged—than those in the first cohort. The exit rate of the second, more disadvantaged cohort is likely to be lower than the first cohort. This lower exit rate is not due to a policy change, but rather because the cohort of welfare recipients has itself changed. This difference can make it difficult to distinguish "true" effects of the legislation on exit rates—that is, whether it really does cause a given recipient to leave welfare sooner than she would have otherwise—from spurious "selection" effects, which arise if the exit rate in the second cohort differs from the first solely because of differences in the make-up of the caseloads.

Another set of nonexperimental methods enjoying some popularity are "difference-in-difference" methods. This method compares the evolution of outcomes over time for different individuals in the same area where a single policy change has occurred, but for which some individuals are in a position to be affected by the change while others are not (Meyer, 1995). Those assumed not to be affected by the policy change constitute the comparison group. In most implementations of the method in welfare reform evaluations, the comparison group is chosen to be a group of individuals ineligible for welfare, or at least ineligible for the policy change in question. Common comparison groups are single women without children, married women with or without children, and men, groups that are mostly ineligible for AFDC or TANF. Sometimes single mothers who are more educated and hence of higher income are used as a comparison group for low-income single mothers because the former group is generally ineligible for welfare. The key assumption in the method is that the evolution of outcomes of the group affected by the policy change (e.g., single mothers) would be the same as that of the comparison group in the absence of the policy change. The major threat to the credibility of this method is that the two groups are sufficiently different in their observed and unobserved characteristics (although observed characteristics can be controlled for) that these differences, and not the policy difference, account for the differences in outcomes.

Another nonexperimental evaluation method that is quite similar to the difference-in-difference method, but that is implemented quite differently and actually predates it, is the method of matching.[5] In this method, comparisons are made within given areas between those who are directly affected by a new reform and a comparison group of individuals (or sometimes populations) who are, for one reason or another, not directly affected. Although in principle the types of individuals used to construct a comparison group could be quite similar to those just mentioned for the difference-in-difference method, in practice the method of

---

[5]Although matching has a long history in program evaluation, a variant that has received attention more recently is that of the propensity score, which bases the match only on the predicted probability of participation. See Rosenbaum and Rubin (1983) for the initial article and see Hahn (1998) and Heckman et al. (1997, 1998) for recent contributions in the econometrics literature on this method.

matching follows the exact opposite strategy of seeking a comparison group that is as similar in observed characteristics to the affected group as possible. Typically, the group will be drawn from the population of eligibles (usually those not participating in the program) rather than the population of ineligibles, as in the difference-in-difference method. The two groups are matched on observable characteristics (age, education, earnings and welfare history, geographic location, etc.) to eliminate differences resulting from those factors. Like the difference-in-difference method, this method can be implemented in a single area with a single policy change, and does not require cross-area or over-time variation in policy in order to estimate effects.

Also like the difference-in-difference method, the major threat to the matching method is that there are unmeasured characteristics that differ between the two groups and related to the reason that one group was subjected to the policy and the other was not. Because there is no policy variation per se—all individuals reside in the same area, under a single policy—comparison groups have to be constructed from individuals who are, for example, not on welfare, or who are on welfare but are exempted from the new reform by reason of some characteristic they possess (e.g., very young children). Learning whether the members of the comparison group are really comparable to those who were made subject to the new policy—in the sense of having the same outcomes as they would have had in the absence of the policy—is difficult.

The major disadvantage of nonexperimental methods in that it is difficult to assess the degree of bias in the estimates of a policy's or a program's effects because of threats to internal validity from the choice of a comparison group. This problem has been given extensive attention in the research literature on nonexperimental evaluation methods. The most convincing approach is simply to conduct formal sensitivity analyses that reveal how different degrees of bias that are thought to be present, on a priori grounds or on the basis of other information, affect the estimates of program effects.[6]

The magnitude of the effect of a policy change is also important because any given amount of bias is less likely to affect the sign (positive or negative) and policy importance of the estimate if the magnitude is large. This truism underlies the common supposition that nonexperimental methods have greater credibility in cases in which a large effect of the program under study is expected and less credibility in cases when a small effect is likely, for in the latter case it is more likely that any bias in the estimate will swamp the true effect.

---

[6]Some practitioners have proposed that program effects could be estimated using more than one of the available nonexperimental methods and then compared across methods. The presumption is that if similar estimates are obtained across each method, then the estimates are credible. Unfortunately, there is no scientific basis for this approach because the threats to internal validity for each method are different.

Despite the threats to internal validity in all nonexperimental methods, they can be very useful when carefully implemented. Pure time-series methods, the crudest of the nonexperimental approaches, are useful as a descriptive piece of evaluation showing whether, given the other changes over time that can be controlled for, a policy change is correlated with a deviation from the trend in outcomes. Cross-area methods have credibility when the groups of individuals examined in each area are strongly affected by policy, when the policy measures in each area are adequately measured, and when there is a reasonable judgment that the existence of different policy changes is not correlated with outcomes. Difference-in-difference methods have some credibility, particularly for large systemwide changes. Only matching methods suffer from an inherent inability to judge credibility, because they depend on untestable assumptions about unobserved characteristics (we discuss some methods for testing the validity of the matching method below). For all nonexperimental methods, credibility is increased if the expected magnitude of the effects is large. The major advantage of nonexperimental methods is that they have greater generalizability, across a great diversity of areas and population groups, than experiments. These methods can also be used to capture entry effects. Nonexperimental methods are, therefore, a necessary part of welfare reform evaluation.

Process Analysis and Qualitative Methods

Implementation and process analyses collect information on the implementation of policy changes; how those changes are operationalized within agencies, often at the local level; what kinds of services actually get delivered and how they get delivered; and, sometimes, how clients perceive the services. They can be used in conjunction with either experimental or nonexperimental analyses, although analysts disagree about their role in formal evaluations. At one level, they can be seen merely as providing a more accurate description of what is being evaluated: in evaluation language, they provide a more precise description of the policy treatment. This is, indeed, the way many process and implementation evaluations are used.[7]

A more ambitious role for process and implementation analyses is to assess the effects of experimentally varied or nonexperimentally observed differences in policy implementations. For example, one could have a randomized trial in which the actual policy or program treatment offered is the same for both experimental and control groups, but for which the implementation differs. Or, in a nonexperimental analysis that correlates program variation with outcomes across a number of areas, measures of implementation might be used to characterize each area's program, in addition to the formal program descriptions. The effects

---

[7]See Corbett and Lennon (forthcoming).

of implementation differences could then be estimated. This more ambitious goal has not been attempted in any systematic way in welfare reform evaluations thus far, partly because of the difficulty in constructing measures of implementation that are comparable across areas (see below).[8]

Implementation and process analysis can also play an important informal role in interpreting the estimated effects from analysis of the official treatment. Implementation and process analysis can reveal features of a program that have been carried out successfully—in the way the program designers intended and expected them to be carried out—and it can also reveal features that are not carried out successfully. If difficulties or failures of implementation are found, these can be used to consider why the estimated effect of a program was larger or smaller than anticipated or even why the program had no apparent effect. This interpretative, hypothesis-generating function of implementation and process analysis can be quite valuable when formal effect estimates come out differently than expected.[9]

More broadly, qualitative methods can be used not only as a method of collecting information for process and implementation analyses, but also to study the behavior of individuals and families. Qualitative methods may involve collecting data through focus groups, semi-structured interviews (sometimes longitudinally with the same individuals or families over time), open-ended questions in surveys, and ethnographic observations of individuals (Newman, 2001). A process study may also use one of these methods to collect data on how caseworkers are implementing a particular policy.

Qualitative methods used to collect information on individuals and families can serve multiple roles in evaluation settings and in a different dimension than process and implementation analysis. To some extent, such data may simply provide a better measure of outcomes than data collected through formal survey or administrative data outcome measurements because they provide much more in-depth information on how individuals and families are affected. In principle, it is possible that formal evaluations of different programs could yield similar estimates of outcomes but that quite different outcomes would be found with the qualitative analysis. This provides a valuable insight into how seemingly similar program effects are not the same. In addition, like implementation and process analysis, qualitative data can also provide insights into the precise mechanism by which policy affects individuals' lives (or, perhaps more commonly, fails to

---

[8]Although this approach has not been formalized, many process evaluations interpret their results in a causal way, that is, they argue implicitly that the outcomes generated by the program would have been different if implementation had been different. However, without the types of formal comparisons described here, such inferences do not have a strong basis.

[9]In addition, the discoveries concerning the reasons for program outcomes obtained in this way can lead to new program innovations which can subsequently be tested with evaluations that again contain qualitative components, leading to a cycle of evaluation and discovery.

affect those lives). Just as implementation and process analyses can discover what works or does not in the delivery of program services, qualitative data can reveal the mechanisms and processes by which program services or offers of services are translated or incorporated into the lives of individual families. Formal survey and administrative data outcomes typically are too crude to ascertain the details of that mechanism. By studying the complexity of individual experiences, qualitative data can both illuminate more clearly how successful programs achieved their successes or illuminate why some programs have been unsuccessful or have had unexpected outcomes. This information can then be used to design improved programs or programs that are differently configured so as to avoid the undesirable outcomes. (In Chapter 5, we discuss how qualitative and ethnographic studies can also be used to enhance survey data collection.)

EVALUATION METHODS FOR THE QUESTIONS OF INTEREST

In Chapter 3 we delineated three formal evaluation questions of interest:

- What are the overall effects of structural welfare reform?
- What are the effects of individual, broad components of a welfare reform?
- What are the effects of alternative detailed strategies of welfare reform within each of the broad components?

In this section, we discuss the evaluation methods that are appropriate to answer each of these questions. We begin with a key conclusion.

Conclusion 4.1   Different questions of interest require different evaluation methods. Many questions are best addressed through the use of multiple methods. No single evaluation method can effectively and credibly address all the questions of interest for the evaluation of welfare reform.

Table 4-1 gives a summary of how this conclusion plays out for the questions of interest and evaluation methods available.

Estimating the Overall Effects of Structural Welfare Reform

Estimating the overall effects of structural welfare reform of the type that has occurred in the 1990s—that is, a reform that bundles together a number of significant changes in the program whose joint impact is to change the basic nature of the welfare program(s) involved—is perhaps the most challenging question for evaluators. Structural reform affects the entire programmatic environment, from the top policy level to the way that local welfare offices operate. In a structural reform, families and individuals in low-income communities (both those on and

TABLE 4-1 Alternative Evaluation Methodologies for Different Questions of Interest

	Questions of Interest		
Evaluation Methods	Overall Effects	Effects of Individual Broad Components	Effect of Detailed Strategies
Experimental	Poorly suited	Moderately well suited	Well suited
	Problems: contamination of control group; macro and feedback effects; entry effects; generalizability from only a few areas	Need to be complemented with nonexperimental analyses for entry effects and generalizability	Need to be complemented with nonexperimental analyses for generalizability and, possibly, entry effects
Nonexperimental	Moderately well suited	Moderately well suited	Poorly suited
	Time-series modeling and comparison group designs using ineligibles are the most promising	Cross-area comparison designs, followed over time, are the most promising	Within-area matching designs may be the most appropriate, followed by cross-area comparison designs
	Problems: lack of cross-area program variation; data limitations	Problems: lack of cross-area program variation; measurement of policies; data limitations	Problems: extreme data limitations and lack of statistical power; uncertainty of matching reliability

off welfare) change their expectations about welfare programs; the level of community and neighborhood resources are affected; governments involved in the program (federal, state, and local) alter their spending and taxation levels and the types of services they offer; and other agencies and private organizations that serve the low-income population change, often restructuring themselves to meet new demands for their services.

In such a changed environment, neither experimental methods nor most traditional nonexperimental methods can provide reliable estimates of what would have happened to individuals and families in the absence of the reform having taken place. As noted previously in our discussion of the drawbacks to experimentation when cultural effects are part of the outcome, a control group in a randomized experiment that has been chosen just prior to the initiation of the reform will almost surely be affected by the broad effects created by the reform, thereby contaminating their outcomes as representing those that would occur in the absence of reform. This makes experimental comparisons subject to unknown bias. Nonexperimental methods that rely on cross-area variation are also generally inadequate because the welfare systems in all areas are changed simultaneously: there is no "no change" area with which the "change" areas can be compared. Similarly, within-area matching methods that compare welfare-eligible nonrecipients to welfare recipients and attempt to control for differences through matching are also unlikely to be reliable because the nonrecipients are almost surely affected by the overall reform.

There are only two possible methods of evaluation in this circumstance, both of which have problematic aspects. One is a pure time-series analysis or its cousin, the cohort comparison method. The second method is the difference-in-difference method.

The time series and cohort comparison methods would be used in combination with either aggregate data or individual data on outcomes before and after the reform and attribute the change in outcomes to the reform. Individual data are generally preferred because individual and family characteristics can be controlled for in the analysis or used to stratify the analysis into different types of individuals and families. At the individual level, panel data that follow individuals over time (from pre- to post-reform) are suitable for this type of analysis. Repeated cohorts of different individuals before and after the reform are also suitable. In either case, it is necessary to estimate the trends in outcomes that occurred over the preform period, and to implicitly or explicitly extrapolate those outcomes to the postreform period—in other words, to estimate what the course of outcomes would have been in the absence of reform. Then, those extrapolated outcomes are compared with the actual outcomes.

The time-series method requires that changes in the economy and other changes in policy that occur simultaneously with the welfare reform be explicitly controlled for and that their influence be estimated indirectly in one way or another. Thus, for example, the influence of the business cycle must be controlled by econometric methods that use data from past business cycles to estimate their effects and to project what outcomes would have been during the period of reform if only the business cycle had changed. Effects of other reforms, such as Medicaid expansions and the Earned Income Tax Credit must be estimated and controlled for as well. General trends in outcomes, including those that may be different for different types of individuals and families (e.g., trends in the demand for labor for people with modest job skills or extremely limited job skills) must also be controlled.

This type of exercise has been attempted, with limited success, in the econometric modeling literature.[10] It is very difficult to control adequately for all the changes in the social and economic environment and in policies, and to estimate their effects accurately. It can also be difficult to assess exactly when a policy was implemented in different areas to make a pre- and post-policy change dis-

---

[10]Schoeni and Blank (2000) show time-series estimates but argue that differences-in-differences methods are preferred.

tinction and it can be difficult to distinguish any lagged effects of previous policy changes from the effects of the current policy change of interest. Despite these heavy qualifications, time-series models can be of considerable value in providing "ballpark" estimates of the overall effect of a welfare reform. In part, this is because the expected magnitude is usually large so that the biases in nonexperimental methods are outweighed by the magnitude of effects. If the estimates are interpreted as approximate effects rather than precise ones and if they are treated as having a possibly significant margin of error, they can be quite informative, particularly if large effects are detected.

The second method that can be used in this context is the difference-in-difference method, which requires the availability of a comparison group that, with reasonable assurance, has not been affected by the reform. The comparison group serves as the counterfactual to the group affected by reforms, and its outcomes are presumed to be comparable with what the outcomes of the group affected by the policy change would have been in the absence of reform. Studies that have used this method typically compare the changes in prereform to postreform outcomes of one group with those for a comparison group for which the policy did not change. For example, changes in outcomes for single mothers have been compared with those for married women (either with or without children), with those of single women without children, or with those for men (married or unmarried, with or without children) or changes in outcomes for less educated single mothers are compared with those for more educated single mothers or more educated women as a whole (Ellwood, 2000; Meyer and Rosenbaum, 1999, 2000; Schoeni and Blank, 2000). Because the various comparison groups are by and large ineligible for, and therefore presumably unaffected by AFDC or TANF, the trends in their outcomes may be a reasonable indication of the trends in outcomes that single mothers would experience had the reforms not been implemented.

The difficulty with this method is that the comparison group may be affected by a systemwide reform or it may have experienced changes in outcomes that are not the same as those that would have occurred for single mothers (and other people eligible for welfare). To the extent that structural and systemwide reform of welfare for single mothers affects marriage rates and the economic support received by men, for example, the outcomes for men will be affected. Likewise, the pool of married women with children may change as single mothers marry and thereby affect the outcomes of married women who are supposed to comprise the control group. These threats to the credibility of the method can be minimized by comparing low-income single mothers with high-income men and married women. However, this then increases the risk that the two groups are experiencing other different economic and social changes. Thus, there is a tradeoff in using this method between picking comparison groups that are close in socioeconomic characteristics and geographic location to the group of policy interest (in this case, single mothers) and picking comparison groups that are significantly different in socioeconomic characteristics and geographic location. If the estimates of program effects differ depending on the comparison group chosen, there is little guidance on which estimate is best. Finally, this method must also confront changes in the economic and policy environment that occur at the same time as welfare reform, although in this case only for those that differentially affect single mothers and those in the chosen comparison group. For example, differential effects are likely to occur if overall changes in the policy environment (such as the enactment of a new program that affects everyone in the population) interact with the tax, transfer, and other programs facing the comparison group, because those programs are generally different than the programs being assessed and for which the group is serving as the control.

Nevertheless, as with time-series modeling, the results of this method contribute information to the effects of welfare reform if they are treated as generating approximate estimates and if they are considered as capable only of detecting large effects. Their value also depends on the credibility of the comparison group, as well as whether there is a sufficiently long time series to provide a reasonably reliable indication that the outcomes of the comparison groups were not trending at different rates than those of single mothers.

Aside from these two methods, there are other nonexperimental methods that could occasionally be used to evaluate overall effects, although all have disadvantages. For example, some econometric studies have used variation in the date at which states implemented PRWORA to estimate the effects of reform (Council of Economic Advisers [CEA], 1999). Unfortunately, most states adopted PRWORA within a fairly narrow time interval, and the few states that did not are likely to be different in other ways.[11] Other studies estimate the effects of PRWORA-like policies from waivers that were adopted pre-PRWORA, because in that period there was considerable variation in the time at which states adopted waiver policies and because a few states never adopted waivers (prior to 1996). This method, of course, requires that the PRWORA legislation and waivers be sufficiently similar. Unfortunately, there were quite a few important differences between them, which threaten the credibility of this method.

Implementation, process, and qualitative analyses are very important when considering overall effects. Because the available quantitative methods provide, at best, only approximate estimates that almost certainly contain some degree of bias, data obtained from the individuals involved in or affected by the welfare system are important as confirmatory evidence for the more formally estimated quantitative estimates. To be credible, large estimated effects obtained from the nonexperimental methods would require that the evidence from welfare administrators, front-line workers, and from welfare recipients (and welfare leavers) is

---

[11]For example, California implemented its TANF program in January 1998 (Council of Economic Advisors, 1999), but differences between California and the rest of the country make it hazardous to rely on this variation to identify TANF effects.

consistent with such large effects. Small estimated effects from a formal model should likewise find support in the evidence from those same groups. While the qualitative data cannot by their nature provide formal evidence on what would have happened in the absence of reform, information from the people involved on what has changed and, from their perspective, why it has changed, provide at least some evidence for the issue. The combination of the quantitative results with qualitative data when both point in the same direction is considerably more powerful than either taken separately.

Although many of the threats to valid conclusions of studies that use time-series and differences-in-differences methods are inherent in their designs, the problems can also be reduced with good data. Time-series modeling, for example, is heavily dependent on the availability of good historical data at the individual level on welfare histories, labor market experiences, and other demographic events and at the area level on historical data on policies and measures of the economic environment. Controlling for differences across individuals in their welfare and labor market experience, for example, is important to predicting postreform outcomes and hence to separating what would have occurred from what did occur because of reform. Policy measures and economic measures over time are needed in order to estimate the effects of those forces and project them to a postreform period. These same data requirements manifest themselves in the difference-in-difference group method as well, for which comparisons at the individual level are also important and for which individual, programmatic, and environmental histories on the individuals in the program and comparison groups are needed to control for differences in their histories. In both methods, a fairly detailed geographic disaggregation is needed in order to compare individuals, either cross-sectionally or over time, who live in the same areas and hence are experiencing the same environmental influences.

Unfortunately, as we discuss in more detail in Chapter 5, it is not possible to meet these data requirements with the data infrastructure for welfare evaluation currently in place in the United States. Some of the main national level survey data sets used for evaluation, such as the CPS and the Urban Institute's National Survey of America's Families (NSAF), are not longitudinal and hence, do not track individuals over time. Other data sets have little or no information pre-PRWORA. Those longitudinal data sets that do have pre-PRWORA information have relatively small sample sizes (discussed more below), difficulties with high rates of nonresponse, or slow rates of public release. Administrative data bases at the state level are often not available in usable individual form and sometimes do not go back far enough because some welfare agencies have not archived old records.[12] Measures of the policy environment are particularly difficult to gather

---

[12]The need to track benefit receipt to enforce the limits will presumably force states to keep records longer. See UC-Data, 1999 for a summary of states' practices with regard to archiving data bases for welfare and related programs. We discuss this further in the next chapter.

historically and at a disaggregated geographical level. Thus, time-series modeling and difference-in-difference methods of comparison groups of ineligibles are handicapped by the availability of rather crude data to estimate program effects.

Studies that use pre-PRWORA cross-area variation in waiver policies face data difficulties of another type, which is overly small sample sizes in the major data sets available. We consider this problem further below in the context of estimating the effects of broad individual components with cross-area variation.

Estimating the Effects of Individual Broad Reform Components

The possibilities for evaluating the effects of individual broad reform components are greater than for evaluating overall effects. There are both traditional experimental and nonexperimental methods that can be used for this type of evaluation, albeit not without difficulties.

Experiments for example, are usually suited for the evaluation of the effects of adding or subtracting, or otherwise changing, the individual components of welfare reform. Experimental and control groups that differ only in the availability of single components, or combinations of components, are more feasible and credible because it is unlikely that macro and systemwide effects would contaminate the outcomes in the control group, which is the main problem in using these methods to assess the overall effects of a reform. It should be immediately noted, however, that experiments that changed only one feature of the old AFDC program, and not any others (such experiments were not conducted) would not have had the systemwide effects intended by welfare reform advocates and, hence, would have had more limited interest, however feasible. Now that systemwide change has occurred, testing individual component reforms is both feasible and interesting to a wide range of policy makers. Incremental reforms in the current welfare reform structure are eminently testable with experimental methods.

As noted above, however, experiments also have certain inherent drawbacks that are still present in the case of estimations of the effects of individual component changes. The difficulty of incorporating entry effects into the analysis is one example, for entry effects are likely to be important if any major component of a welfare program is eliminated or added. The problem of generalizing the results of an experiment to populations and environments different from the ones in which the experiment is conducted is also a major issue; hence, the inability for cost reasons to test reforms nationwide or separately in most states and areas is a significant drawback. Therefore, for future changes in broad components, experimental methods will still need to be supplemented by nonexperimental methods to obtain a complete and generalizable picture of effects.

Nonexperimental evaluations of the effects of individual program components can also rely on traditional methods, such as the cross-area method discussed above, at least to the extent that there is cross-state variation in those components. Family caps, for example, are not present in all states. This difference affords an opportunity to estimate their effects by a comparison of outcomes for individuals in states with and without those caps. In comparison with experiments that test the effects of family caps, the nonexperimental strategy is likely to yield a broader range of environments and policies to estimate and hence increase the ability to generalize. The price is that all other differences across areas must be adequately controlled for (a requirement that is necessarily met by a well-run experiment). Nonexperimental evaluations of effects of family caps can, in addition, capture entry effects in a way that experiments cannot. In principle, they can also capture macro and feedback effects. Thus, nonexperimental evaluations are necessary to fill in some of the holes that experimental evaluations leave. However, like experiments, nonexperimental estimates of the effect of the addition or subtraction of individual broad components obtained from cross-area variation in policies can only produce estimates of the incremental effects of such provisions given an overall program structure. For example, family caps added on top of the old AFDC program would likely have had quite a different effect than family caps added post-PRWORA.

The cross-area nonexperimental method cannot be used if there is no cross-sectional policy variation in a individual component. For example, it is not suitable to evaluate broad components like work requirements and time limits, which are necessarily present in some form in all states because they were mandated by PRWORA.[13] Time-series and cohort comparison methods are likewise not appropriate to estimate the effects of broad components if those components are introduced in all states at the same time. Even difference-in-difference methods can rarely be used because they require comparison groups of people ineligible for welfare who are unaffected by the component in question. Finding such comparison groups is typically very difficult because ineligibles—say, those exempted from time limits or work requirements—differ from eligibles in some other important characteristic (e.g., the presence of a young child). Separating the effects of the other characteristics from the effect of the component is difficult and requires various assumptions. Within-area matching usually cannot be used for the same reason, for rarely are those who do not have the component in question imposed on them likely to be similar in unobserved ways to those who do have it imposed on them. Although cases may be found where these circumstances are met, it is not a general solution to the estimation of individual reform components.

As with the discussion of methods in the previous section, good data are important to strengthening the conclusions that can be drawn from the evaluation of the effects of individual broad components of welfare reforms. Data issues are typically more important for nonexperimental evaluation than for experimental

---

[13]Variations in the type of work requirements, and the type of time limit, are more common; we classify these as detailed strategies which are discussed below. Here we are referring to the total elimination or addition of work requirements or time limits.

evaluations. To be able to test differences in policies across areas, a good nonexperimental evaluation requires good data on the individual components of policies; on the characteristics of different areas; and on the individuals in those areas. For many data sets, such as those drawn from administrative records, cross-state comparability is a major data problem that limits the application of these methods (see Chapter 5 for more discussion). Data over time is particularly useful for tracking the effects of changes in policy combining the cross-section and time-series methods, in contrast to using just a pure cross-section method. Nonexperimental evaluations usually rely at least in part, on data collected for purposes other than the study of interest, while data collection for experimental studies is usually designed specifically for the study, and may not be ideally suited for use in some cases. Finally, sample sizes are critically important in making reliable inferences on the subpopulations affected by the particular individual component in question.

Estimating the Effects of Detailed Reform Strategies

The effects of detailed strategies, such as different types of work and employment strategies, different time limit structures, different sanctions rules, and other such variations are important parts of the welfare reform evaluation effort for certain audiences, as discussed in Chapter 3.

For the evaluation of alternative detailed strategies, randomized experiments are generally the strongest evaluation methodology.[14] Macro and other feedback effects, for example, are unlikely to be large when only a detailed strategy is altered within a particular broad component and within a given overall welfare structure. Entry effects are likely to be smaller than those that follow the introduction or deletion of a broad reform component, although reforms that markedly affect the welfare experience may have entry effects.[15]

Generalizability to different environments and different populations is likely to remain a problem when conducting experiments to learn the effects of particular detailed strategies. Typically, experiments about strategies are quite localized, conducted at the local office level or in one or only a few sites, and usually only on particular populations (e.g., only on the recipients on the rolls at a particular time in the business cycle or only on applicants). This problem could be reduced significantly if sufficient numbers of experiments in different areas, at different points in the business cycle, and on different populations (recipients,

---

[14]See U.S. General Accounting Office (1999b) for a review of experimental results on a comparison of rapid employment and education approaches to work mandates in welfare.

[15]The magnitude of entry effects largely depends on whether the reform in question would markedly change the desirability or undesirability of being on welfare in the first place. A shift from a education strategy to a work-first strategy, for example, has the potential to significantly reduce the desirability of welfare to many recipients.

applicants, nonwelfare participants, etc.) were conducted. However, this is rarely feasible for cost reasons and hence the generalizability of experiments on detailed strategies is still likely to be in question. Again, complementary nonexperimental evaluations are one route to fill in the need for generalizability, by either aiding in the extrapolation of experimental results to different populations, environments, and programs, or to directly estimate the effects of alternative detailed strategies across those same variations. Process and implementation studies at each experiment site might also help in assessing the generalizability of experiments. For example, process studies across sites that reveal that experiments were implemented in the same way in each site may support the generalizability of results or cast doubt on the generalizability if the process studies reveal that the experiments were not implemented in the same way. (We discuss the issue of generalizability in more detail in the next section.)

It is possible to use nonexperimental evaluations for the evaluation of detailed strategies, but there are difficulties in doing so. Cross-area comparison methods that examine different detailed strategies on a particular welfare component (e.g., different strategies for increasing employment) in different areas require, for accurate estimation, that all other components of the programs in the different areas be controlled. This is likely to be a problem because the detailed strategies are typically only one component of a larger welfare structure that varies in multiple and complex ways and are difficult to measure and control for. When the need to control for differences in the economic and social environments across areas is also considered, as well as the need to control for other differences in program policies, the difficulties of cross-area program comparisons can quickly become insurmountable. These difficulties are made worse because most nonexperimental data sets have insufficient numbers of areas, each with insufficient sample sizes, to adequately estimate the effects of large numbers of other factors affecting outcomes. The difficulty lies partly in the expectation that the effects being estimated may be relatively small compared with the effects of the other cross-area variations that are not controlled. Thus, nonexperimental estimation is not a promising evaluation method for gauging the effects of alternative detailed strategies.

One alternative nonexperimental methodology that may be more promising for this question is the within-area matching method. Time-series and cohort comparison methods are unlikely to be useful for evaluating detailed strategies for the same reasons they were unlikely to be useful for evaluating broad components. They require areas where the detailed strategy is changed over time, leaving all other components of the welfare program unchanged. Although this is possible in principle, it is unlikely in practice. Difference-in-difference methods are difficult as well because they require the construction of comparison groups of ineligibles for multiple detailed strategies, which is generally unlikely. As mentioned above, the main challenge to this method is finding a group of individuals in the same area as those who were subjected to the reform who have, for reasons related only to their observable characteristics (age, education, labor force, and welfare history) and not to any unobservable trait, not been subjected to the reform. Usually this group is drawn from the population of people who are eligible for, but not participating in the program. Although this requirement is particularly problematic because it is unlikely that all the factors affecting their participation status are observable, the method is now under active research and there is some evidence in its support (Dehejia and Wahba, 1999). Because it is the only nonexperimental method that is likely to be possible for the evaluation of detailed strategies, it needs more investigation (see below).

Conclusions

Conclusion 4.2 Experimental methods could not have been used for evaluating the overall effects of PRWORA and are, in general, not appropriate for evaluating the overall effects of large-scale, system-wide changes in social programs.

Conclusion 4.3 Experimental methods are a powerful tool for evaluating the effects of broad components and detailed strategies within a fixed overall reform environment and for evaluating incremental changes in welfare programs. However, experimental methods have limitations and should be complemented with nonexperimental analyses to obtain a complete picture of the effects of reform.

Conclusion 4.4 Nonexperimental methods, primarily time-series, and comparison group methods, are best suited for gauging the overall effect of welfare reform and least suited for gauging the effects of detailed reform strategies, and as important as experiments for the evaluation of broad individual components. However, nonexperimental methods require good cross-area data on programs, area characteristics, and individual characteristics and outcomes.

ISSUES IN EVALUATION METHODOLOGY

The panel devoted special attention to several specific issues in evaluation methodology that are often more technical than the general principles just adduced. This section contains the panel's findings on these specific issues: (1) ways to assess the reliability of nonexperimental evaluation methods; (2) the power of cross-sectional comparison methods to detect welfare reform effects with available data sets; (3) generalizability, which comes up repeatedly in discussing the usefulness of experiments and the combination of nonexperimental and experimental methods; (4) details regarding the use of process and qualitative analysis in evaluation; and (5) the importance of an understanding of welfare dynamics for evaluation of welfare reform. Readers not interested in these special issues may wish to move to the assessment of current evaluation efforts.

Assessing the Reliability of Nonexperimental Evaluation Methods

Given the importance of nonexperimental methods for many of the evaluation questions surrounding welfare reform, it is desirable to have methods of assessing the reliability of nonexperimental methods for their accuracy. The most important threat to the validity of nonexperimental methods is that the comparison group used is dissimilar in some respect to the group affected by the reform (i.e., that internal validity is weak) and therefore that the outcomes for the comparison group do not properly represent what would have happened to the group affected by the reform if it had not occurred. Methods that focus on this key issue and assess the validity of the comparison group are needed. The same issue arises when multiple types of nonexperimental methods are used and yield different estimates of program effects. In this section we discuss three strategies for assessing the reliability of nonexperimental methods: specification tests, sensitivity testing, and benchmarking to experiments.

Specification Tests

Specification tests are used whenever some of the assumptions made to ensure that one is estimating the true effect can be relaxed and an alternative estimator that does not require those assumptions can be used (see Greene, 2000, pp. 441-444, and 827-831 for a textbook discussion of specification testing). A common example of this type of test arises in program estimates using the cross-area method, where the assumption needed for internal validity is that the different areas would have the same values of the outcome variable in the absence of any variation in policy. This assumption would be incorrect if those areas differ in unobserved and hence unmeasured ways that happen to be related to the policy variation. For example, states differ in their income levels, poverty rates, and other factors, and the differences in policies across states usually account for only a fraction of these differences. The assumption can be tested if data on the areas are available from some prior time, before any policies were adopted in any area, for if the areas differ for reasons unrelated to policy, those differences are likely to have appeared earlier as well. A formal specification test can be developed for assessing whether the pre-policy differences are related to policy variation across areas and hence create problems for the cross-area estimate.[16] Similar tests can

---

[16]The same idea was used by Heckman and Hotz (1989) to test a within-area estimator comparing program participants to nonparticipants (the comparison group) first at a single point in time, and then at a point prior to the policy implementation.

be performed for other nonexperimental methods—cohort comparison, time series, and others.

This example illustrates the need for data to conduct specification tests, in this case, data from before the policy was implemented. Although specification tests can occasionally be developed with the same data used for the initial estimate, supplemental data are usually needed to be able to test the key assumptions in the model.

Specification tests are not without limitations. The need for additional data may often be unmet, and there may be no alternative ways to test the specification. More fundamentally, there can be no guarantee when obtaining two separate estimates from alternative models that one is correct and that one is not, for both could be incorrect or the more general estimator may be incorrectly specified. For example, the outcomes at a prior time may be a misleading indicator of what current outcomes would be in the absence of the policy. This means the conclusions from the tests are somewhat uncertain and highlights the fact that all such tests are based, themselves, on additional assumptions that may or may not be correct. Nevertheless, specification tests are a valuable tool and can be informative for many nonexperimental methods and estimators. They are underused in welfare program evaluation, and they need to be refined and developed further for best use.

Sensitivity Testing

A second method of assessing reliability is sensitivity testing, in which the critical assumptions underlying the nonexperimental estimates are relaxed to some degree, or a range of plausible assumptions is examined to determine how much the estimate of the policy effect is sensitive to those assumptions. The extent to which the assumptions are relaxed is based on intuition and general credibility, not on any formal evidence or statistical procedure. For example, in the cross-state example discussed above, one could assume that 10 percent of the difference in outcomes across states existed prior and was unrelated to the effect of policy variation, and then subtract that from the estimated effect. This is the type of implicit sensitivity testing done when an analysis yields a large estimate of a program's effect. It is implicitly understood that even if some bias exists in that estimate, the true effect is still likely to be large. Sensitivity testing in less obvious circumstances, where an auxiliary assumption that only indirectly contributes to the estimation of the program effect is tested, is more common and constitutes the typical contribution of the method.[17]

---

[17]The literature on sensitivity testing lies mostly in the statistics literature rather than the econometrics literature; See Rosenbaum and Rubin (1983) and Rosenbaum (1995); see also Robins et al. (1999) for a recent contribution.

Sensitivity testing also has limitations, mostly concerning the necessity for some arbitrariness in deciding which assumptions should be subject to sensitivity testing and how much they can credibly be varied. The bounds of sensitivity testing must be set by the individual analyst or group on the basis of intuition and outside information, not on the basis of formal tests.[18] Nevertheless, sensitivity testing is, like specification testing, all too rarely undertaken in welfare reform studies and should be used more often.

Applying Nonexperimental Methods to Experimental Data

A third method for assessing the reliability of nonexperimental methods is to apply them to data from an experiment where the "true" answer is known. The typical approach is to obtain data on both the experimental and control groups from an experimental evaluation, and then to construct a comparison group using one or more of the available nonexperimental methods. The effect of a program is then estimated by comparing the outcomes of the experimental group to those of the comparison group instead of the control group to determine if the "right" answer is obtained. The indirect method of simply comparing the true control group to the chosen comparison group is an equivalent way of ascertaining the accuracy of the nonexperimental method chosen. Studies of this type include Fraker and Maynard (1987), Friedlander and Robins (1995), Heckman et al. (1997, 1998), Heckman and Hotz (1989), and Lalonde (1986).

The advantages of this approach are that the experiment allows the analyst to know the "truth" to which the effect using nonexperimental methods can be compared. However, the approach has a number of limitations as well. Aside from the issue of whether the experiment itself has internal validity—that is, that it is well executed and does not suffer from problems of attrition or contamination—a general limitation is that the approach is necessarily restricted to those nonexperimental methods that estimate the types of effects as those estimated with experimental methods. As we noted earlier, it is not feasible to estimate some types of effects with experiments. Thus, for example, time series, difference-in-difference, and cross-area methods cannot be tested against experiments because they often capture entry and macrocultural effects, which cannot be feasibly captured with experiments. Likewise, if no experiments have been conducted to estimate the effects of broad components of welfare reform, as we noted previously is the case, nonexperimental methods that aim to estimate those

---

[18]Manski (1995) has proposed that the arbitrariness inherent in sensitivity testing be replaced by construction of logical bounds within which the true effect must lie. This is an alternative approach that is also rarely used in welfare reform research.

effects cannot be tested with this approach. The generalizability, or external validity problem of experiments also limits the benefits of this approach. Even if a particular nonexperimental method that replicates the effect of an experiment tested on one particular subpopulation and in one or only a few locations can be found, it may not have many implications for whether that or any other non-experimental method would be useful for other populations or areas.

A less obvious problem with the approach is that the services received by the control group in an experiment are often not formally characterized and described, for an experiment is generally designed only to estimate the effect of a new policy relative to the entire existing environment of policies. However, if the policy options available to the control group differ from those available to a nonexperimentally constructed comparison group, it may appear that the non-experimental method has failed when in reality it has simply yielded an alternative, equally valid estimate—but an estimate of the effect of the new policy relative to a different counterfactual policy environment.

Despite these limitations, the inherent advantage of the method is revealed by the studies that have used it to date (see previously cited studies). The most recent studies in this area have compared experimental estimates with non-experimental estimates using the method of matching. While the results of these studies are interesting, much more needs to be done. Rules for determining when a nonexperimental method is or is not likely to be valid need to be developed to go beyond single examples and illustrations of cases in which particular non-experimental methods do or do not work in particular cases. The problem of characterizing the policy environment needs to be faced more squarely. The method also needs to be applied to the difference-in-difference method by constructing comparison groups from ineligibles rather than eligibles—an approach that has not yet been attempted.

The research using results from experimental studies to assess the reliability of estimates from nonexperimental studies has been primarily applied to training programs not welfare reform. ACF has recently funded one project in this general area, however, which is a good start. ASPE has also shown interest in the general issue of choice of nonexperimental method, and has worked with an external group of experts to develop an approach. Much more needs to be done in this direction and more progress needs to be made given the importance of nonexperimental methods to welfare program evaluation.

Recommendation 4.1   The panel recommends that ASPE sponsor methodological research on nonexperimental evaluation methods to explore the reliability of such methods for the evaluation of welfare programs. Specification testing, sensitivity testing, and validation studies that compare experimental estimates to nonexperimental ones are examples of the types of methodological studies needed.

Analysis of Statistical Power of Cross-State Comparison Methods

The cross-area method has been used heavily in the analysis of pre-PRWORA waiver effects to examine both the effects of an entire bundle of reforms and the effects of broad components (Council of Economic Advisers, 1997; Figlio and Ziliak, 1999; Moffitt, 1999; Wallace and Blank, 1999; Ziliak et al., 1997). It has been used to a lesser extent in the analysis of post-PRWORA outcomes to study the effects of broad components, generally examining variations in discretionary components or aspects of components across states (Council of Economic Advisers, 1999). The method can be used either with pure cross-section data, comparing states at a single time, or with either panel data or repeated cross-section data over time to control for state fixed effects (that is, to compare changes over time across states, as policies change). The cross-state methodology has a long history in evaluations of the effects of public programs and fits very much in the spirit of a federal system that uses states as laboratories for learning about which programs and policies work.

An issue in the application of this method to welfare reform evaluation that has received little attention concerns the sample sizes needed in order to have sufficient statistical power to detect reasonably sized effects of welfare reform, either overall or of broad components. The power of a statistical hypothesis test (e.g., a test of whether the policy had an effect or not) is the probability that the test will conclude that there is a relationship (or effect) when a true relationship or effect actually exists. The best applications of the cross-area method use individual microdata to compare individuals across states who are similar in characteristics (age, education, etc.) and who are members of the target population for the policies in question. Thus, adequate sample sizes are needed not so much on the general population in each state, but on the specific strata of the population in which one is interested.[19]

An important statistical and policy question arises in analyses of this kind in defining a proper target population to compare across states. A tradeoff exists between defining the target population narrowly or broadly. Defining the target population narrowly—for example, including only single mothers with young children who have income below the poverty line—is attractive because that is for whom the effects of the policy, if any, are presumed to be the greatest. But defining the population narrowly reduces the sample size in the analysis, risks

---

[19]Statistical power for detecting effects of welfare policies is a consideration for all evaluation methods, including experimental methods, not just the cross-area method discussed here. However, experimental methods are typically designed to consider sample size and statistical power issues up front in the design phase of the study. Nonexperimental methods for assessing the effects of PRWORA and broad components of reform must rely on existing national level surveys that are designed for more general purposes and not for the specific evaluation questions or for specific strata of the population identified here.

bias from endogeneity—particularly if income if used as a stratifier—and adds uncertainty about generalizing to broader groups.[20] Defining the population more broadly reduces problems of sample size and endogeneity but diffuses any effects of the program over a larger group of people and reduces power for hypothesis testing. We shall focus here not on the bias question but only on the statistical power question, although generally bias is an issue highly relevant for the issue of power.

In most of the cross-state analyses conducted on pre-PRWORA and post-PRWORA outcomes, the Current Population Survey (CPS) has been used—often only the March survey because it contains income and welfare recipiency information for the prior calendar year. The CPS is the largest of the nationally representative, general-purpose social science data sets available. It is also available over a longer time period than other surveys, which is an advantage for nonexperimental analysis as we discussed above. A disadvantage of the March CPS is that it provides only annual data and also is subject to underreporting of welfare participation. (We discuss these data sets in more detail in Chapter 5.)

In Appendix C, Adams and Hotz report the results of a power analysis for two of the cross-state analyses in the literature, the analysis of the CEA (1997) and of Moffitt (1999). The former used aggregate data to estimate the effect of pre-PRWORA waivers on AFDC caseloads and the latter used the CPS to estimate those effects for both AFDC participation and other outcomes. Moffitt estimated only the overall effect of welfare reform; the CEA also estimated the effect of individual broad components as well. The sample size in the CEA analysis was 969 and the sample size in the Moffitt analysis was 15,504.

Figure 4-1, taken from the Adams-Hotz analysis, shows the power of the CEA aggregate analysis for different effect sizes (see Appendix C for details). The upper line denotes the power of detecting the overall effect of pre-PRWORA waivers, measured as the regression coefficient on a dummy variable for whether the state had a statewide waiver of any type, "Any Waiver." The effect size is a little over 5 percent, for which there is 60 percent power (i.e., 60 percent of the time an estimated effect would be found to be statistically significant). This is a moderately high level of power but not nearly as high as one would want. The lower lines in the figure show the power curves of detecting the effect of indi-

---

[20]In this context, endogeneity means that the criterion used to narrow the sample is correlated with the outcome of interest, which could, therefore, make the estimates of the true effect of the policies biased. For example, an endogeneity bias could arise if income is used as a sample selection criterion (e.g., selecting all those with incomes below 200 percent of poverty) because it would necessarily result in excluding from the sample any women whose income gains were favorable enough to exclude them from the study. An even stronger example is welfare participation; although one could compare welfare recipients in different states and correlate their outcomes with welfare policies. This comparison would likely end in an endogeneity bias because only the "unsuccessful" families would remain on welfare.

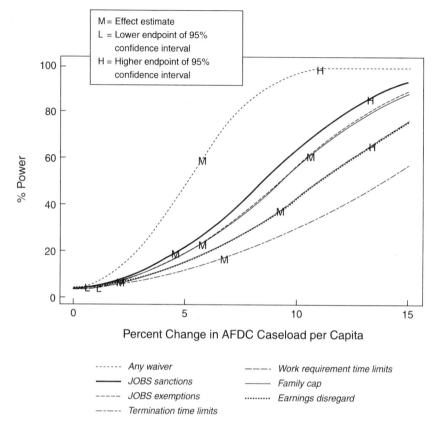

FIGURE 4-1 Power for Council of Economic Advisers analysis.

vidual components (sanctions, time limits, etc.) and demonstrate unacceptably low levels of power.

Figure 4-2 shows the power of detecting waiver effects on the probability of AFDC participation, using the larger CPS data set employed by Moffitt (see Appendix C for details). The power to detect a true effect equal to 1 percent is almost 80 percent, much superior to that of the aggregated CEA model.[21] The lower curve shows the power of the effects for education subgroups, each of which had the same sample size and hence the same power. Because each subgroup has a lower sample size than that for the total sample, power is neces-

---

[21]The 1 percent estimated effect is not comparable to the 5 percent estimated by the CEA because the latter is taken as a percent of the entire population and the former is taken as a percent of women aged 16-54.

sarily lower than 80 percent. However, the estimated effect size for the least educated group (those with fewer than 12 years of education) is quite high, even higher than the effect for the entire population.

Contrary to these rather favorable results for detecting overall welfare reform effects on the probability of welfare participation using the CPS, the Adams-Hotz analysis showed that the power of detecting effects on other outcomes in the CPS—employment, earnings, family income–is much less, almost always less than 50 percent, an unacceptably low figure (see Appendix C). This lower power is a result of a much higher variability of these outcomes in the population.

Finally, Adams and Hotz consider the effect on power of doubling the CPS sample size. The power of detecting the overall effects of welfare waivers on AFDC participation rises, at Moffitt's estimated effect size, from 80 percent to more than 95 percent. Considerably smaller effects could be detected at the initial 80 percent level as well, but "small" effects could still not be detected.

These results are quite discouraging for the use of existing household surveys to detect the effects of welfare reform using cross-state comparison methods—the dominant method in the econometric research on welfare reform in the 1990s. The sample sizes in the CPS are adequate only to detect the overall effect of welfare reform on low-variance outcomes, such as the AFDC participation rate. They are inadequate to detect the effect on individual economic outcomes at acceptable levels. In addition, the analysis of the CEA model strongly suggests

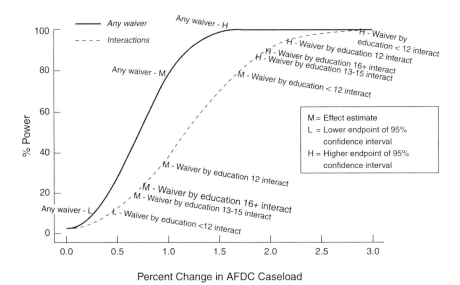

FIGURE 4-2 Power for Current Population Survey data set.

that detecting the effects of broad welfare reform components (time limits, work requirements, etc.) is also unacceptably low at CPS sample sizes.

Estimating the effects of individual welfare components, which Adams-Hotz showed to have unacceptably low power for the aggregate CEA analysis, may be problematic for the CPS as well. Some increase in power would result if the true effects of individual reform components were larger than the overall effect that Adams-Hotz examined with the CPS. But power would also be reduced by the presence of correlation between different state policies and because the implicit amount of variation of policies is less (arising only from those states, among all, who had a particular type of policy). If the individual policies were assumed to affect only a subset of the population, that would further reduce sample size and power. The problem is likely made worse by the crude characterizations of very complex state policies. Thus, it is quite likely that power will continue to be an issue when estimating the effects of reform components.

The CPS is one of the largest national survey data sets currently available. Therefore, the problem of power is likely to be even worse for other data sets. The only data set significantly larger than the CPS is the still-developing American Community Survey (ACS). It, therefore, holds the greatest promise for conducting similar nonexperimental analyses of future welfare reforms.

There are several avenues that can be explored to address these important issues. First, a more detailed analysis of the ACS is needed to assess its reliability for the estimation of welfare reform effects in the future. Although, it holds promise for relieving these sample size constraints, it would be very useful to know exactly what power it has to detect differently sized effects. Second, expansions or supplements to the CPS should be considered to increase its power. Adams and Hotz note that a simple doubling of the CPS would not be the most efficient way to increase sample size if detecting welfare reform were the only goal of the increase, for it would be more efficient to increase sample disproportionately in different states and demographic subgroups. Supplementing the CPS with state-level data sets, somewhat along the lines of the Iowa project (Nusser, Fletcher, and Anderson, 2000), is also worth exploring. Third, the power of state-level administrative data sets for estimating cross-state nonexperimental welfare effects models should be investigated. Administrative data sets are larger than the CPS when pooled across states and therefore hold promise in this regard (see Chapter 5).

Conclusions 4.5   Existing household surveys are of inadequate sample size to estimate all but the largest overall effects of welfare reform on individual outcomes using cross-state comparison methods. Research is needed to address this problem by considering the American Community Survey, state level administrative data sets, and supplements and additions to the CPS or other surveys to increase their capacity to detect welfare reform impacts in the future.

Generalizability of Evaluation Results

The issue of generalizability has emerged as an important one for many of the evaluation methods discussed thus far. There are two separate and distinct problems of generalizability. One is the problem of generalizing the results of a policy evaluation to areas, groups, and populations that were not included in the evaluation. The second is generalizing the results to policies that were not directly evaluated. With regard to the first, experimental methods, for example, are typically applied to only a few localities and on specific populations. The generalizability of their results to a national or even state population is consequently in question. Experiments also, as we previously noted, typically cannot capture entry effects or macrocultural effects and, therefore, may also not be generalizable because the total effect of the program is not measured. In this case, generalizing the experiment to a larger area and population–the nation as a whole, for example—has effects that are not captured in the small-scale study. Nonexperimental methods are typically estimated on more comprehensive groups of the population and in more areas, and sometimes capture entry and macrocultural effects. However, they too are sometimes not fully representative or complete. But nonexperimental methods more often suffer from the second problem of generalizability—to new policies—because those methods are necessarily applied only to policies that have actually been implemented. Nonexperimental methods, therefore, can yield no direct evidence on the effects of new policies. This is particularly important in the case of PRWORA, where, for example, a cross-state analysis on data after 1996 cannot estimate the total effects of PRWORA—it can only estimate the effects of differences across states because all have PRWORA in place in one form or another. Experimental methods often have the policy generalizability problem as well, but at least have the potential to estimate the effects of any policy that can be experimentally operationalized, even if it has never been implemented on a larger scale.

The most common method of addressing these problems of generalizability is through the method of microsimulation.[22] Microsimulation models are con-

---

[22]Our definition of microsimulation models includes any extrapolation or interpolation from an estimated model or policy evaluation to other populations or programs, even if the extrapolation is not formalized. While our discussion in this section focuses primarily on formal microsimulation models, we also include informal methods of generalization as well. However, there is a critical difference between microsimulation that is based on a single empirical study, using the same data and same model and variables, and microsimulation that uses different data and combines estimates from multiple underlying studies. In the latter case, all covariances across mutually exclusive data sets and parameter estimates must be set to zero (or some other arbitrary value), although sensitivity testing to the sign and magnitude of such covariances can be conducted as part of the analysis. In the former case, this is not necessary, but then extrapolation is necessarily limited to the populations, policies, and models estimated in the single study—which defeats the main purpose of microsimulation as defined here.

structed by selecting a database containing records on individuals and families and simulating the effects of different policies on the population. In the simplest accounting microsimulation models, the eligibility and benefit rules of each program are applied separately to each individual (or family) and the individual's participation in the program as well as the amount of benefit received is simulated. In more behavioral simulations, responses of recipients to participation in the program are estimated, using results from existing research on the behavioral responsiveness to program parameters. Microsimulation is a complex and often expensive tool and requires experience and sophistication in its use, particularly for calibration and validation (National Research Council, 1991). It can also lead to erroneous predictions, particularly when the model structure and equations depart too far from what empirical evidence supports. However, it is also a powerful tool because it can incorporate multiple relationships that interact in situations in which interactions among programs and markets are complex, and because it can generalize evaluation results to virtually any population or alternative program.

The most transparent advantage of microsimulation is in the generalization of any research results to populations and areas other than those upon which the original evaluations were conducted. Because there is no direct evidence for whether policy effects would be the same or different in areas in which they have not been tested or estimated, this type of exercise necessarily involves extrapolation of evaluation results beyond the range of their data. This, in turn, implies that the degree of certainty associated with simulated outcomes is necessarily lower than that for the actual outcomes in the evaluations. This difficulty can be reduced if evaluations are available for even a small number of different areas and populations from which some of the determinants of variability can be studied and ascertained. Many microsimulation models in other contexts also take information on variation in program effects across individuals and families of different socioeconomic characteristics and use that to generalize policy impacts to individuals in other areas and populations who have similar characteristics. In the end, of course, sensitivity testing is required, as it is in all microsimulation, to determine the range of uncertainty involved in the extrapolation.

Likewise, microsimulation models have the capability to generalize results to new policies not previously tested. However, this explicitly requires that policies be parameterized or characterized by its features and that the effects of individual features alone be estimated. This is required if, for example, a new policy with a different combination of components is of interest.

Extrapolation to both new populations and policies is made easier if the underlying evaluation studies whose results are the basis for calibrating a microsimulation model are conducted in a way that aids generalizability. For example, evaluations that estimate the impact of a unique program on a unique population and that do not attempt to estimate the way in which outcomes vary by program characteristics—e.g., by the estimation of outcomes as a smooth function of those characteristics—are difficult to use directly in microsimulation without assumptions on whether the same results would apply if the program and population characteristics were different. Often microsimulation developers must obtain the underlying data and estimate new models in order to make extrapolation possible.

A less obvious advantage of microsimulation is in the combination of experimental and nonexperimental results, each with its own advantages, to achieve a result that is superior to either individually. For example, entry effects, which are typically not estimated in experiments, can be estimated from nonexperimental data and applied to a dynamic microsimulation model containing entry and exit from the TANF rolls. Effects of the policy on those who are on the rolls, once they are on, could be drawn from experimental evaluation estimates. The model could be calibrated to both types of evaluation estimates.

Microsimulation can be large scale or small scale, for it can attempt to capture all behavioral relationships and policies affecting the population or it can focus only on a few. Given the complexity of welfare reform evaluation, it is not clear which approach would be best for this purpose. It is quite likely that a small scale model focusing on the delineation of key aspects of the welfare system but representing other programs in the policy environment less precisely, would be the most appropriate way to proceed.

While microsimulation has a long history in social science research and in government agencies (National Research Council, 1991), it has not been used on any significant scale for simulating the effects of PRWORA. However, the diversity of the types of evidence that welfare reform research is generating—ranging from econometric studies to experiments to monitoring studies of leavers, each generating estimates for different groups and different aspects of welfare reform—gives microsimulation more potential than it would have otherwise. When no single type of study can, or is intended to, provide evidence on more than one piece of the response to welfare reform, microsimulation is one means by which to incorporate all the pieces together into a coherent and internally consistent whole. Microsimulation thus could play a role in the synthesis of results, when those results come from very different types of studies.[23]

Conclusions 4.6 The problem of generalizability of the evidence from welfare reform evaluations on specific populations, areas, and relationships to more general populations, to a national level, and to

---

[23]We should emphasize that this role of microsimulation—as a tool to synthesize results from diverse studies and to generalize them—is distinct from other roles, that we do not assess and that microsimulation may be less well suited for. Pure time-series predictions of how outcomes will evolve over the future, for example, is a different role, and may not be the best for current problems. Nor is microsimulation an evaluation tool itself—experimental and nonexperimental methods are suitable for that function. On the other hand, a valuable role of microsimulation is in the estimation of the distributional consequences of policy and programmatic changes, i.e., who is helped and who is hurt and by how much. These issues are discussed in National Research Council (1991).

new policies, has not been sufficiently addressed. More use of micro-simulation models as a tool to address generalizability is needed. Microsimulation is also needed to assist in the synthesis of diverse types of results.

Process and Qualitative Analysis

The complexity of the current welfare program system has led the panel to conclude that multiple research methods need to be used in order to answer key evaluation questions of interest. Research should include process and implementation methods and qualitative and ethnographic research methods, which have become increasingly important in welfare program evaluations. Features of PRWORA and the subsequent changes that have been implemented on a state and local level have fueled the growing importance of process evaluations. The initial period after PRWORA has been characterized by a wide variety of evolving programs and practices as states adjusted their programs to meet their own goals and to fit the needs of their populations. It is during this period of an evolving programmatic environment in which process studies can be especially useful to help inform administrative decisions and to fine-tune implemented programs. Process analyses are an important tool for going beyond descriptions of legislated programs because they provide a more realistic picture of how programs are actually implemented and how services are actually delivered to participants.

Similarly, ethnographic and qualitative studies are becoming increasingly important tools to aid evaluations. Policy makers and administrators are recognizing the value of these methods to learn about early reaction to new policies and for understanding how a policy actually affects clients' lives. Evaluators are recognizing that qualitative and ethnographic methods can be used to help interpret study results or to generate hypotheses for further exploration and to guide further data collection or research. These potential payoffs to process and qualitative studies lead the panel to conclude that both methods have important roles to play in evaluating welfare reform.

Chapter 2 described several process studies that are under way in welfare policy research. The U.S. Department of Health and Human Services has sponsored process evaluations targeted to programs serving specific subpopulations of low-income families (families with infants and toddlers) and specific program features (welfare-to-work screening and assessment practices and mental health and employment program practices). These studies will provide useful descriptions of the specific program implementations. They do not, however, comprehensively cover TANF programs and are being conducted in only a limited number of states and sites or cover only special services for specific subpopulations. The Rockefeller Institute's State Capacity Study and its extension, the Front-line Management and Practice Study (which has funding from ACF), are probably the largest efforts to document state policy implementations. The State Capacity Study covers program implementation in 20 states and the Front-line Management study will cover, among other things, program implementation in 12 local areas of four states. In addition, implementation studies are being conducted in conjunction with monitoring and outcome studies in each of the four metropolitan areas of Urban Change Project, and in the 13 states of the Assessing the New Federalism Project.

However, there is no a systematic effort to conduct process evaluations of how states and local areas have implemented TANF policies, and process studies are not routinely used in conjunction with outcome evaluations. Although it would be impossible to conduct process studies for every local area, a more comprehensive effort is needed. Studies of implementations at both the state and local levels should be sponsored in as many areas as possible and across areas with a wide range of characteristics: for example, across regions of the country; urban and rural areas; areas with different approaches to TANF policies; areas with different special subpopulations such as immigrants; areas with different macroeconomic conditions; or perhaps on a random sample of sites. The panel believes that such an effort will be valuable for understanding how states and local areas have used their block grant funds and leverage for program design to implement programs, information that is now only being provided on a limited basis.

> **Recommendation 4.2 The panel recommends that U.S. Department of Health and Human Services sponsor process research in a number of service delivery areas to better understand how service delivery administrations have implemented new welfare programs and the benefits and services families and children are receiving under these new programs.**

Despite the growing potential for process studies to provide needed information about what is happening in program implementation, methodological improvements in how process studies are conducted are needed for them to be maximally effective. Currently, there are no standard protocols for methods to conduct process studies and, as a result, they are often of uneven quality. Part of this lack of protocols stems from the nature of process studies in that they typically rely on qualitative and subjective data sources (e.g., caseworker interviews concerning problems that arise in delivering services). But too often process studies are conducted on an informal basis, do not carefully design their studies, visit only a few convenient sites or talk to only a few key administrators and as a result, are not reproducible. Carefully designed and credible process studies that use such techniques as formal fieldwork protocols for observation and data collection, repeat visitation or data collection at one site, and data collection across multiple sites are needed.

Integration of process evaluations with impact evaluations at the level where results of process evaluations are used to describe or are part of the planned variation of the policy treatment are, thus far, limited. This lack of integration is due in part to the difficulty of measuring program processes in a quantifiable way. Furthermore, because the processes may vary considerably across sites, common terms for different processes are needed, but, they are not easily agreed to.

Recommendation 4.3 Process and implementation studies have grown in number and importance in the evaluation of welfare reform but often have design defects and are insufficiently integrated with outcome evaluations. As a consequence, their potential use in evaluation has not been fully reached. The panel recommends that the U.S. Department of Health and Human Services sponsor methodological research on process and implementation studies to improve methods for systematizing the documentation of program policies and practices, to develop protocols and best practices, and to further integrate them with impact evaluations.

Ethnographic and other qualitative studies can complement quantitative evaluations. They have become increasingly popular as an aid to program evaluation and have augmented both nonexperimental and experimental welfare reform studies. They are also an important component of several of the current major studies to monitor and evaluate welfare reform (Urban Change, Three-City Study).

In the period following major changes in policy, such as PRWORA, qualitative studies may be particularly useful. For example, the new program rules and implementations may not be well understood by potential or current program participants. Qualitative studies can be used to determine what information and attitudes administering offices are sending to potential program participants (e.g., program outreach or diversion). Focus groups could be used by local or state benefit administering agencies to understand, for example, how well policies of the agency are understood by relevant populations or what barriers some groups face to self-sufficiency.

Information gained from qualitative studies is often complemented with results from statistical evaluations of policies to help interpret results by providing more textured information about the experiences of a sample of cases that are part of the larger evaluation study or a sample of similar cases that are not part of the study. Such efforts might be particularly useful in conjunction with smaller scale or single-site studies, perhaps in conjunction with experimental studies or matching studies, because it will be easier to specifically target a small population for in-depth interviews. In analyses of the effects of treatment bundles, researchers may have difficulty identifying which treatment had the most profound effect on the outcome of interest. Qualitative studies focused on individual clients can provide information as to which of the treatments may have had the greatest effect. This information could also be valuable for guiding future evaluations and data collection efforts or about future designs of experimental or nonexperimental evaluations. Finally, qualitative and ethnographic studies can also provide more elaborate outcome measures. For example, surveys may include open-ended questions that can provide detailed information from respondents to complement quantitative data. This type of information might be used in monitoring or evaluation studies, as well as to frame hypotheses for quantitative studies.

> **Recommendation 4.4 Qualitative and ethnographic studies of the low-income population and its relevant subpopulations and of social service agencies that provide services to these populations are an important part of the overall welfare program evaluation framework. The panel recommends the further use of well-designed qualitative and ethnographic studies in evaluations of welfare programs to complement other evaluation methods.**

The Importance of Welfare Dynamics to Evaluation

As we emphasized in our interim report (National Research Council, 1999: Ch. 2, pp.22-26), a caseload dynamics perspective is important to welfare reform research. It has long been recognized that an understanding of welfare dynamics—entry and exit from the rolls and the length of spells on welfare—is necessary for an understanding of the welfare population. It has also long been recognized that different welfare recipients exhibit different patterns of participation, and that this reflects their general abilities to exit welfare. As we noted in our interim report, the most common classification of patterns is that which divides recipients into long-termers, short-termers, and cyclers (Ellwood and Bane, 1994). Long-termers have a few long uninterrupted spells on welfare; short-termers have short spells and spend only a brief period of their lives on welfare; and cyclers have short spells but tend to return to welfare frequently after leaving and hence may end up spending a substantial proportion of time on welfare.

These distinctions are essentially just a simple way to classify what is really a continuum of welfare program use. Which of these three groups a welfare recipient falls into is generally presumed to be an indirect indicator of a host of other characteristics of the recipient and so serves as a convenient proxy for those characteristics. Generally, long-termers are presumed to have the lowest job market skills, the most difficult life circumstances, and therefore, the lowest probability of leaving welfare. Short-termers have the best job market skills, the least difficult life circumstances, and therefore the highest probability of leaving welfare. Cyclers are somewhere in between, having job market skills and life circumstances that permit them to leave welfare but not sufficiently favorable to prevent them from returning. Knowing the composition of the welfare population with respect to these welfare "experience" measures provides an indirect indication of the heterogeneity of the welfare population and how many recipients are the hardest to serve. Other indicators—levels of education, work experience, poverty status, health, transportation and day care problems, and other variables—are additional indicators of need and may become more useful indicators of disadvantage as time limits take effect and people can no longer continue to receive cash assistance. However, we focus on welfare experience because it is a useful overall classification that is an indirect indicator of many other features of a recipient's degree of disadvantage and because of its particular relevance to studies of specific welfare populations—welfare leaver and diversion studies.

The level of welfare experience is important to the study of welfare reform because some groups are more likely to be affected by reform than others. Leavers are presumably more likely to be short-termers or cyclers, for example, meaning those who stay on welfare may be disproportionately long-termers. Some long-termers leave the rolls, however, and it should be expected that their outcomes after leaving may be worse than those of other leavers. For those who stay on the rolls, the effects of new work requirements and other provisions of PRWORA are also important issues, particularly whether work-first policies are successful. This information is valuable to welfare administrators who must decide how to target their resources across these different groups. Indeed, one of the goals of PRWORA legislation was to reduce the problem of welfare "dependency," which could be interpreted as a goal primarily aimed at long-termers and cyclers.

In this section we report the results of three explorations of these issues. Two are included in our companion volume (Moffitt, 2001; Ver Ploeg, 2001) and one consists of an unpublished paper prepared for the panel (Stevens, 2000). The analysis by Moffitt uses a nationally representative data set of young women (the National Longitudinal Survey of Youth 1979 [NLSY]) to document the proportions of long-termers, short-termers, and cyclers on AFDC and how their labor market and other characteristics differ. The analysis by Stevens uses an administrative data set from one state (Maryland) that contains merged data on AFDC recipiency and unemployment insurance (UI) wage data to present the same sort of analysis conducted by Moffitt—documenting the proportions of long-termers, short-termers, and cyclers—but for multiple cohorts over time, thereby demonstrating how the composition of the caseload has been changing. The analysis by Ver Ploeg focuses on leaver studies by analyzing data on welfare leavers from Wisconsin to explore how leaver outcomes differ for long-termers, short-termers, and cyclers and how other aspects of a leaver analysis are affected by incorporating the caseload dynamics perspective.

The analysis by Moffitt tests alternative definitions of long-termer, short-termer, and cycler in the NLSY data. He finds that approximately one-third of the caseload in the 1980s and early 1990s (of those who had at least one spell of receipt) was composed of each of these three types and that these compositions were fairly consistent across most definitions of long-termers, short-termers, and cyclers. A somewhat unexpected finding is that the degree of total welfare dependence—measured as the total time a woman spends on welfare in a long nineteen-year period, 1979-1997, was greater for cyclers than for long-termers. This is contrary to expectations for the ordering of recipients. The greater number of spells experienced by cyclers led them to a longer total time on welfare than long-termers. Some long-termers had one or two long spells but then left welfare for the rest of the period. This finding raises the issue of defining long-termers, cyclers, and short-termers; it is discussed more thoroughly by Moffitt (2001).[24] In examining the characteristics of the three groups, Moffitt found, as expected, that short-termers had the highest earnings when off welfare and the highest levels of education. However, again rather surprisingly, he found that cyclers had about the same levels of education as long-termers but lower levels of earnings off welfare. Thus, cyclers in his analysis seem to be the most disadvantaged of the three experience groups.

Stevens used Maryland administrative data and decomposed the AFDC-TANF caseload from 1985 to 1998 into the three experience groups (using all AFDC cases opened and closed sometime during this period). He disaggregated the data into four separate birth cohorts, each observed for a 10-year period, within this time interval. Using similar definitions to those of Moffitt, Stevens found that almost 50 percent of the Maryland caseload were short-termers (a higher fraction than Moffitt found), about a third were long-termers, and the smallest group (about 20 percent) were cyclers. Moreover, he found that the fraction of short-termers had fallen slightly over time and the fraction of cyclers had risen, perhaps the result of welfare reform or changes in the economy. When he examined earnings off welfare for the three experience groups, he found the expected ordering—highest earnings for short-termers, lowest for long-termers, and in between for cyclers, at least for the majority black population. However, for the white population, he found a changing ordering over time, beginning with the expected ordering (as for blacks), but, by the last cohort, cyclers had lower off-welfare earnings than long-termers. This interesting result, combined with the increase in the number of cyclers, suggests that many of the more disadvantaged women on welfare have become cyclers, again possibly as a result of welfare reform or changes in the economy.

---

[24]For example, one could define both long-termers and short-termers not by the number of spells and their lengths, but simply by the level of total time on, defining long-termers as those with long total time on and short-termers as those with little time on. How cyclers would then be defined is unclear. If they are defined as those with a lot of time on and with a large number of spells, long-termers would have to be restricted to those with a small number of spells. Moffitt argued that the common sense idea of a cycler is not based on total time on but is based simply on the number of spells, and that the degree of total time on should be an outcome measure from the definition rather than part of the definition.

Ver Ploeg analyzed the welfare leaver data used in one of the well-known Wisconsin leaver studies (Cancian et al., 2000). The sample included all those who received AFDC July 1995, some of whom subsequently left welfare and some of whom stayed on welfare. AFDC and earnings records for the years 1989-1995 were used to classify leavers and stayers by their pre-1995 welfare experience, using similar definitions to those of Moffitt and Stevens. Ver Ploeg found that about 50 percent were long-termers, about 35 percent were short-termers, and the residual (about 15 percent) were cyclers. These percentages are different than those of either Moffitt and Stevens and suggest that there is considerable diversity across states in the composition of the welfare caseload. Ver Ploeg also found that long-termers were much less likely to be leavers than were stayers, short-termers were much more likely to be leavers, and cyclers were somewhat more likely to be leavers than stayers. When looking at other characteristics, Ver Ploeg found that those who were more welfare-dependent—longer spells and those with less work experience—were considerably less likely to leave the rolls subsequent to 1995 than those with less welfare dependency—shorter spells and more work experience.

When looking at the differential wage and employment outcomes of leavers, she found, perhaps surprisingly, differences by the three welfare experience groups that were quite modest: virtually all three groups had employment rates of 55-65 percent and all had approximately the same level of earnings. However, there were much stronger and more marked differences in leaver outcomes by the level of past work experience. Ver Ploeg also defined a "high barrier" group of initial recipients who had low levels of education, weak employment histories, and high levels of welfare dependency, and she found that they had much lower leaving rates and much worse outcomes after leaving than others. Overall, although Ver Ploeg failed to find as strong a correlation of earnings off welfare with welfare-experience groups as found by Moffitt and Stevens, she found high levels of heterogeneity between welfare stayers and leavers and between different types of leavers. This substantiates many of the points made in our interim report (National Research Council, 1999) about the need to differentiate leavers into different subgroups and to make comparisons within such groups across states, rather than comparing of overall averages.

The lessons of these three studies for the importance of welfare dynamics for welfare reform are many. First and foremost, these studies show that the welfare caseload is extremely heterogeneous with respect to welfare experience, employment history, and other key variables. They further suggest that this heterogeneity is quite different across different states, which could lead to differences in outcomes as a result of that heterogeneity.[25] Second, two of the studies show that heterogeneity in welfare experience is strongly correlated with employment and

---

[25]As individual states continue to modify their programs to meet the needs of their populations, the heterogeneity of the caseload across states is likely to increase.

earnings off welfare and that heterogeneity in general is highly correlated with those variables. Third, the Ver Ploeg study demonstrated specifically for a leavers study the importance of disaggregating the caseload by heterogeneity measures, and how variable leaver outcomes are for different groups. These studies are the first in the welfare reform literature to focus on these issues and show the value of disaggregation along these dimensions. The panel recommends that this perspective be incorporated into more welfare reform studies, both within and across states, in future research and evaluation.

> **Recommendation 4.5 A welfare dynamics perspective should be incorporated into more welfare reform studies, including leaver studies. In general, more disaggregation by levels of heterogeneity among leavers and stayers is needed given the importance of disaggregation for outcomes on and off welfare.**

ASSESSMENT OF CURRENT EVALUATION EFFORTS

The scope, volume, and diversity of existing studies on welfare reform described in Chapter 2 is impressive. However, a large fraction of those studies, if not the majority, are not concerned with formal outcome evaluation. Many are concerned with monitoring the well-being of the low-income population or segments of it and are not aimed at estimating any of the effects or outcomes discussed in this chapter. The National Survey of America's Families, the Devolution and Urban Change Study, the Three-City Study, and many of the studies using census and other data sets to track the progress of the low-income population are not intended to formally evaluate the effects of welfare reform but, instead, have as their primary purpose the monitoring of different welfare-affected groups.[26] Although some have evaluation, neither these studies nor the many excellent implementation studies of welfare reform mentioned in Chapter 2 are reviewed here, for their goal is not formal evaluation.

There are only three major types of existing projects whose primary goal is formal evaluation. These are studies of welfare leavers; randomized experiments; and caseload and other econometric studies. Even the first of these—leaver studies—is included only for discussion purposes, for most analysts agree that they are not intended as formal evaluations, at least as presently conducted.

Leaver Studies

The most common type of welfare reform study is the welfare leaver study, which examines the outcomes of a group of welfare recipients who have left the

---

[26]Some of these studies, like the Urban Change Study and Three City Study, and in certain uses, the National Survey of America's Families, have evaluation components. However, the major contribution of these studies to date is in their monitoring function.

welfare rolls in the postreform era. Taken as an evaluation methodology rather than a monitoring method, the question such studies aim to answer is that of the overall effects of structural welfare reform, rather than the effect of any individual component or detailed strategy. For this purpose, these studies are weak and do not deserve the emphasis that they have received in the discussion of the effects of welfare reform. Aside from problems of the underlying data, (see Chapter 5 and also National Research Council [1999]), leaver studies suffer from a narrowness of focus, lack of cross-state comparability, and, most obviously, lack of a comparison group. The narrowness of focus results from examining only a subset of the population affected by reform, generally ignoring stayers as well as divertees, rejected applicants, and discouraged nonapplicants. ASPE has begun to address the latter problem by funding projects to study applicants and diversion, but these efforts have yet to produce results and need to be strengthened and reinforced. The lack of cross-state comparability in the way leavers are defined, (who is classified as a leaver and who is not) and how outcomes are measured is a major barrier to being able to compare effects across areas and to correlate those with policy differences. The grantees whom ASPE funded to conduct new leaver studies have made some decisions on uniformity of definition. While ASPE deserves credit for this, it falls short of what is needed, for there remain many differences in composition across states.

Finally, the lack of a comparison group makes the results of leaver studies difficult to interpret because it is not known whether their outcomes are any different from these for welfare leavers prior to welfare reform. This problem has also begun to be addressed by ASPE as part of its encouragement of multiple cohort designs. However, few states have embraced this method and thus few results are available.

Constructing a comparison group for current leavers from past cohorts of leavers is more difficult than it may appear. Most of the multiple cohort studies discussed in Chapter 2 compare early post-PRWORA leavers to later post-PRWORA leavers, but what is needed is a comparison of post-PRWORA leavers to pre-PRWORA leavers. In addition, using pre-PRWORA leavers is problematic if a statewide welfare waiver was in place prior to 1996, for in that case even cohorts leaving AFDC just prior to PRWORA may have been affected by welfare reform. Another problem in the existing multiple cohort studies is that the question to be answered with such cohorts is not clearly defined. Most multiple cohort studies take any evidence of changing outcomes for leavers over time— such as, lower employment rates—as an indication that more women with low skills are leaving the rolls over time. However, this interpretation ignores the original purpose of multiple cohort designs, which is to estimate the effect of a policy change on the outcomes that a given recipient or type of recipient would have. Differences in leaver outcomes could reflect either changes in the characteristics of those who leave welfare or the true effects of a change in policy. None of the cohort studies conducted thus far attempt to separate these alternatives, nor do many even acknowledge that it is an issue. Finally, even with a correct cohort definition, more than one pre-PRWORA cohort is needed. Estimating the effects of the unemployment rate and other policy developments requires several cohorts over time.

Conclusion 4.7 Studies of the outcomes of welfare leavers contribute only one part of the story of welfare reform and, as an evaluation method, have been disproportionately emphasized relative to other methods. Studies that compare current leavers to those who left welfare prior to welfare reform and studies of divertees, applicants, and nonapplicant eligibles need more emphasis.

Recommendation 4.6 More methodological research is needed to assess and improve the credibility of the multiple cohort method of evaluating the overall effects of welfare reform. This research needs to study the best method to control for the time-series effects of other policies and the economic environment and how many cohorts are enough to do this.

Randomized Experiments

The number of randomized experiments about welfare has declined in number since the passage of PRWORA. Most of the experiments in the early 1990s were the result of requirements by DHHS that any state granted a waiver from federal AFDC regulations was obligated to conduct an evaluation of that waiver, usually a randomized experiment. Since PRWORA, the federal government has lost its authority to mandate experiments; as the task of evaluation has moved to the states, there have been fewer experiments.

To a considerable degree, this decline has been a natural result of the recognition that experimentation is not particularly appropriate, for assessing the overall impact of a state's new welfare program. Another reason for the decline of experiments has been a lack of interest among many state policy makers in using the old AFDC program as a counterfactual, for their general belief is that a return to the AFDC program is unlikely. Still another reason for the decline in experimentation is that most states have been doing considerable work in developing new programs in the post-PRWORA environment and have not faced a sufficiently settled and stable policy environment to consider experimentation.

There are a number of experiments ongoing from the pre-PRWORA waiver phase of experimentation and even one experiment that was initiated after the 1988 Family Support Act to evaluate the JOBS program. These experiments are of mixed usefulness for a number of reasons. In many cases the policy environment has changed. In addition, the many systemwide changes that have occurred over the 5 years since PRWORA was passed have unquestionably had spillover effects into the control groups, whose members are now unlikely to have outcomes that are the same as would have occurred if welfare reform had not taken place. This problem is particularly acute when a reform in question is implemented statewide, and the control group on the old AFDC program is only a small group of recipients in the context of a statewide altered programmatic environment.

The experiments that have been undertaken over the past decade have generally been aimed at estimating the overall effects of a bundle of separate welfare reforms, including work requirements, sanctions, time limits, and other provisions, all enacted and tested simultaneously. With rare exceptions, there have been no experiments that have isolated individual broad components or detailed strategies, varying each while holding all the other features of welfare reform fixed.[27] Although experiments of similar policy bundles have often been tested in more than one site, there has been no attempt to coordinate those bundles in a way that would permit isolation of broad components or detailed strategies (i.e., with two sites differing only in one respect). Thus, although it would be advantageous to examine the effect of broad components, experiments have not been designed to do so.

Although the recent experiments on welfare reform therefore have many problems of usefulness and validity, there is considerable scope for new experimentation on alternative detailed strategies and, to some extent, broad components. As noted above, experiments have their greatest advantage in doing so because incremental change is of most interest and the overall welfare environment would be more settled. As states continue to study the issues of what works and for whom, experiments should play an increasingly prominent role in evaluation efforts. ACF is planning experiments on alternative employment retention strategies, which is a good example of tests of detailed strategies. Such experiments need to be supplemented by nonexperimental data collection in order to reach a complete picture of reform effects and to provide adequate generalizability. Experiments are also, in principle, still one of the better methods to test the effects of individual broad components—time limits, work requirements, sanctions, and other provisions—while holding other components fixed. Whether they should be used to do so depends on the degree of policy interest in those components. When they are appropriate, well designed and conducted, and with an adequate sample size, experiments offer uniquely strong evidence.

Recommendation 4.7 Experimental methods are underused in current designs of new welfare policy evaluations and should be employed in future studies evaluating different detailed reform strategies and different individual broad components.

---

[27]Some of the waivers did include evaluations of broad components of reform, for example, randomizing clients into a labor force attachment group or a human capital development group.

One of the obstacles to using experimental methods is that evaluation is predominantly now in the hands of state welfare administrators, who do not have a great deal of experience in designing experiments or know the operational implications of conducting experiments. Historically, state welfare agencies have not conducted much evaluation of their programs (although there are notable exceptions, many times including partnerships of state administrators with universities). Most evaluation has been initiated at the federal level and conducted by national research organizations. The devolution of legal authority for program design embodied in PRWORA was accompanied by a devolution of program evaluation, for the most part. Consequently, the lack of experienced evaluation personnel at the state level is a significant barrier to the use of experimentation, and to evaluation in general, on welfare reform.

Much welfare evaluation expertise still remains in academia or with federal agencies, particularly in ASPE and ACF. It is therefore natural for those federal agencies to continue to play an active role in sponsoring experiments at the state level and to promote such activities. In the absence of a strong federal presence, the lack of experienced personnel at the state level will result in many lost opportunities for fruitful experimentation. The federal government has a role in assisting in the design of an overall coherent strategy of controlled variation across different states. A study within one state can be a substantial benefit to that state and can contribute to the overall pool of knowledge about programs and their effects; a cross-state experimental evaluation program with comparable studies can go further in yielding generalizability of findings and can subsequently benefit all states.

Recommendation 4.8 The federal government should take a proactive role in sponsoring experiments at the state and local levels and should encourage planned variation and cross-state comparability to yield the maximum general knowledge.

Caseload and Other Econometric Models

A number of caseload and other econometric models have been used in evaluating welfare reform, as described in Chapter 2. All of them aim to estimate the overall effects of welfare reform, and a few attempt to estimate the effects of individual broad components as well. Perhaps the most distinguishing feature of these studies is that they are the only welfare reform studies that have attempted to control for economic conditions and to isolate the effect of welfare reform from those conditions.

While ambitious and deserving of investigation, these modeling efforts have thus far yielded a mixed record of success. They have produced some interesting findings and, in fact, the only findings on the overall effect of PRWORA controlling for the business cycle. However, there are significant problems with the studies that cast doubt on their validity. One problem is that the majority of the studies have used cross-state and over-time variation in pre-PRWORA programs to estimate the effects of welfare reform. Although the pre-PRWORA waiver programs are of significant interest in and of themselves, in most cases they cannot yield reliable information about PRWORA. PRWORA accelerated and greatly strengthened most of the provisions that were in waiver plans and also created overall structural changes in the welfare system. In addition, the sample sizes available in the major data sets are only barely capable of capturing welfare reform effects of the size to be expected. Thus, data limitations significantly reduce the value of these studies.

A handful of studies have been conducted using comparison-group designs with ineligibles and differences-in-differences methods (see Chapter 2). These studies have yielded significant and interesting results of overall effects. However, the validity of these comparison groups (see discussion of this method above) has not received sufficient examination, leaving the results from these studies in a state of considerable uncertainty.

Despite the problems with the existing caseload and other econometric models to estimate overall effects, they have yielded reasonably credible estimates because they have found significant effects on the outcomes that would be expected and because the magnitude of the expected effect is large. Thus, there is a reasonable chance that the biases that may exist are outweighed by the size of the effects.

The record of the econometric studies in estimating the effects of individual broad components is considerably worse. These studies have used pre-PRWORA cross-area variation in those components, in some cases, and post-PRWORA variation in a smaller set of policies (namely, those that vary cross-sectionally post-PRWORA). The results in these studies for the effects of components is highly variable in magnitude, sign, and significance, and are generally not robust to specification changes. The results often do not accord with sensible expectations, an indication of a underlying misspecification. It is quite probable that the combination of poorly measured policies at the broad component level, combined with sample size problems, have produced this result.

Conclusion 4.8   Caseload and other econometric models have produced a mixed set of results, partly because of data limitations and partly because of an inherent lack of policy variability. They have done somewhat better at producing ballpark estimates of the overall effects of welfare reform than at producing estimates of the effects of individual broad components.

Summary

Despite the large number of studies that have been and are being conducted on welfare reform, the record on evaluation of the three major questions we have put forth is not impressive. For the overall effect of PRWORA, a number of econometric models provide approximate estimates on individual outcomes and state caseloads, but these studies are weakened by data limitations and lack of policy variability. Experimental tests of the overall effects of PRWORA have also been conducted, have many limitations. There have also been econometric estimates of the effect of individual broad components of welfare reform, but these have more serious problems than those estimating the overall effects. Thus far, the results are not very reliable and lack credibility. There have been no experimental tests of the effects of adding or subtracting broad components. For detailed strategies, there have been almost no formal evaluations that isolate one strategy from all others (holding the others fixed) to determine the effect of the isolated strategy alone. There have been a few experiments of detailed strategies (e.g., the NEWWS demonstration), but these have the problem of control group contamination.

NEXT STEPS

For a mature society like the United States, with over 40 years of experience in evaluating social welfare programs, the record of accomplishment for a major piece of social legislation to date is not sufficient.

There are several evaluation studies in process that can help address some of these gaps (see Chapter 2). The multiple cohort leaver studies already funded by ASPE and their other studies of stayers and divertees, rejected applicants, and discouraged nonapplicants will be valuable additions. The experiments planned by ACF will begin the process of testing alternative detailed strategies.

Nevertheless, major new evaluation efforts are needed at the federal and state levels if the questions of interest for welfare reform research identified in Chapter 3 are to be addressed. The current set of evaluation efforts is an uncoordinated collection of disparate efforts without any overall coherence. Consequently, there are major gaps in the evaluation structure. Some private foundations have attempted to coordinate evaluation studies, but this is a role that should be played by DHHS because it is the agency with responsibility for program operations, access to details about the program and related programs, and the entity that is the most likely to have a long-term commitment to evaluation of the program. Setting forth a clear and carefully considered agenda for the questions to be asked and the evaluation methods that should be brought to bear on each of the questions would go a long way toward ensuring that the necessary analysis is conducted. A leadership role in this area is needed.

Recommendation 4.8 The federal government, taking all agencies as a whole, has produced and funded a great deal of valuable monitoring research and a much smaller volume of evaluation research. A greater effort to produce a comprehensive evaluation framework

for social welfare programs that considers the major questions of interest and the evaluation methods appropriate for each is needed. A comprehensive framework for evaluation should be developed and used to guide the evaluation efforts under way by private and other public evaluation organizations. This should be an on-going effort as new issues emerge and is a responsibility that should be taken on by ASPE in the U.S. Department of Health and Human Services.

In addition, the annual report to Congress recommended in Chapter 3 should include both a discussion of the important questions of welfare reform we outlined and a presentation of the alternative evaluation methods that are currently being used to study these questions, including those studies funded by ASPE as well as by others. The report should discuss the relative mix of experimental and nonexperimental methods being used and should present the agency's views on whether the appropriate balance and mix is being achieved, in light of the relative strengths and weaknesses of each evaluation method. It should discuss which nonexperimental methods are being used and whether there is an appropriate balance for them. It should also relate ASPE's own research agenda on evaluation methods to the overall landscape of evaluation and should present what it sees as its own role in support of good evaluation methods.

Recommendation 4.9 In its annual report to Congress, ASPE should review the existing landscape of evaluation methods, whether the appropriate balance of experimental and different nonexperimental methods is being achieved, and how evaluation methodology fits into its own research agenda.

At the state level, the capacity to conduct evaluations is very weak, both experimental and nonexperimental evaluations. This situation must be addressed if better and more appropriately focused and directed evaluations are to take place. Here we recommend again that the federal government exert a leadership role in assisting states. In fact, both ASPE and ACF already expend some portion of their personnel and resources toward such assistance, for example, through the welfare reform research and welfare outcomes conferences they have hosted for the past 3 years. But much more capacity-building effort is needed.

Conclusion 4.9 The panel finds that state capacity and resources to conduct evaluations of their own welfare reform programs is often below the level needed for such an important change in policy.

Recommendation 4.10 The panel recommends that the U.S. Department of Health and Human Services continue and expand its efforts to build capacity for conducting high-quality program evaluations at the state level through the provision of technical assistance,

convening of research conferences, promoting the exchange of technical assistance among the states, and other capacity building mechanisms.

Finally, given the decentralized nature of the evaluation of PRWORA, and given the disparate methods that have been and will be used and the diversity of different approaches to evaluation that have been conducted, a major attempt to synthesize findings will be needed. Reconciling conflicting findings, combining experimental and nonexperimental results when appropriate, weighing the results of different studies considering their strengths and weaknesses, combining quantitative and qualitative data, drawing lessons from monitoring studies as well as evaluation studies, and identifying and filling gaps in knowledge in order to arrive at a comprehensive, best-guess judgment on the different effects of welfare reform will be a challenging task. But it is a necessary one. Once again, we recommend that the federal government, whose interests are those of the nation as a whole as charged by the electorate, take a leadership role in this regard and fulfill the synthesizing function. ASPE, as the policy evaluation and development arm of DHHS, is the most appropriate agency to fill this role.

Recommendation 4.11 The panel recommends that ASPE be the primary agency responsible for synthesizing findings from studies of the consequences of changes in welfare programs.

5

Data Needs and Issues

Successful monitoring and evaluation of welfare reform are not possible without good data, regardless of how clearly the questions of interest are delineated and how strong the available evaluation methodologies are. Good data are therefore critical to studying welfare reform.

In Chapters 3 and 4 we showed that there are a wide variety of questions of interest and that answering those questions requires a number of different methods. It should not be surprising that addressing the questions of interest for monitoring and evaluating welfare reform will therefore require use of multiple types of data from multiple sources. We categorize data sources into four generic types for our discussion. First are household surveys, both national and state level, which have been the data sources that have informed much of what is known about the low-income population. Second are administrative records from social welfare and other programs, which are a somewhat newer and emerging data source for studying welfare reform. Much of the new administrative data is available at the state level, but there are also a few federal-level data sets. Third are data describing policies and programs at the state and local levels. Fourth are qualitative data, another source of data that are increasingly being used in policy evaluation. Together, these four types of data constitute the data infrastructure for monitoring and evaluating welfare reform.

Good data have many characteristics. They have reasonably good coverage of the population in question. They contain measures of the key variables of interest for welfare reform study, either characteristics of policies or of individuals and families. They are reasonably accurate and contain few response errors, understatements, or missing values. Good data are also available for a reasonably long time frame and are comparable across time. The sample sizes in good data sets are large enough for reliable statistical estimation, in many cases at the state and local level. Finally, for the purposes of many welfare reform studies, though not all, good data are comparable across states and use the same concepts and definitions, so that valid cross-area comparisons can be made.

What constitutes good data for addressing one question of interest may not suffice for another question of interest. Correspondingly, different evaluation methods require different types of data with different strengths and weaknesses.

This chapter describes the various sources of data available for welfare program research. In doing so, we discuss their potential use for addressing the research questions of interest using the available evaluation methods, their use in current studies under way, and we compare them with the characteristics of good data. We also include a section on data confidentiality that has implications for almost all data collection.

We note that most of these recommendations for improvements are specific to the current data infrastructure for social welfare program monitoring and evaluation. The panel concludes that this infrastructure has limitations and that the devolved nature of social welfare programs has exacerbated the limitations. The main limitation is that no agency within DHHS has the specific responsibility to collect data to monitor the well-being of the low-income population nor for evaluating the effectiveness of social welfare programs. The panel believes that this responsibility needs to be allocated to some administrative entity within DHHS to coordinate data collection activities at the federal level and to work with states to coordinate data collection activities at the state and local level. The final chapter of this report discusses this need in more detail. However, many of the specific recommendations for data improvements made in this chapter could be addressed more easily if this administrative authority is assigned. Therefore, in discussing these specific recommendations, we highlight areas where the existence of such an authority will help spur data improvements.

Devolution has had important consequences on data needs for the study of welfare reform. It has resulted in a proliferation of different programs in different states and localities around the country, each mixing a different bundle of reform components and strategies and each targeting somewhat different populations. Adding these differences to existing cross-state variation in Medicaid and other welfare programs and to ever-present differences in labor markets, demographic profiles, and general socioeconomic environments, the demands for state-level and local-area data have grown tremendously.

Devolution lies behind many of the recent developments in data collection for welfare reform studies and behind much of our discussion here. It affects the value of national-level surveys which have less to contribute in the current wave of reform than they had in past reforms. The number of state-level and local-area surveys, which historically have been quite rare, is growing. The value of state-level administrative data, which have the potential to capture state and local-area details in a way that has not been important in past reforms, is also growing. At the same time, the comparability of these state and local data sets is of greater concern if generalizations about the consequences of reform are to be understood on a broader basis. Finally, it affects the need to collect state and local area program and policy information itself, a need which is now much greater.

SURVEY DATA

Data from question-and-answer surveys have been heavily used for social welfare program monitoring and evaluation in the past and will continue to be useful for future studies. This section of the chapter discusses the strengths and limitations of existing surveys for monitoring and evaluating social welfare programs and gives the panel's recommendations for improving survey databases. It covers national-level surveys, which are designed to be representative of the U.S. population, and state- and local-level surveys, which are designed to be representative of state or local populations or subpopulations (like welfare leavers). The merits of particular surveys for particular purposes are discussed in terms of population coverage, sample size, content, nonresponse, response error, and periodicity.

National-Level Survey Data

There are several national-level surveys that are relevant to welfare program monitoring and evaluation. They cover such content areas as income, earnings, employment, program participation and benefit receipt, adult and child well-being measures, family structure, and demographic and other background information. The surveys discussed here (and summarized in Appendix D) include the long form of the decennial census, the March Supplement of the Current Population Survey (CPS), the American Community Survey (ACS), currently in the development stage, the Survey of Income and Program Participation (SIPP), the Survey of Program Dynamics (SPD), the National Survey of America's Families (NSAF), the National Longitudinal Survey of Youth (NLSY), and the Panel Study of Income Dynamics (PSID). The CPS, ACS, SIPP, SPD and the census long form are all surveys funded by the federal government and conducted by the U.S. Census Bureau. NLSY is privately conducted but funded by the U.S. Department of Labor and the National Institute for Child Health and Human Development of the U.S. Department of Health and Human Services. PSID is conducted by the University of Michigan and supported by grants from the federal government and private foundations. NSAF is conducted by the Urban Institute with private funding. The NLSY, PSID, SPD and SIPP are longitudinal data and so have the added feature of tracking the changes in the well-being and outcomes of sample members over time. Table 5-1 contains basic summary information about these surveys.

Although these surveys all include content relevant to welfare reform evaluations, most are conducted for purposes other than welfare population monitoring and evaluation. Only the Survey of Program Dynamics has as its primary purpose the evaluation of welfare reform, although the SIPP, which was established before PRWORA, also has a special role as it was created to measure government and welfare program participation.

Population Coverage

National-level surveys are designed to produce analyses that are representative of the national population and, hence, are useful for producing estimates of the well-being of the nation as a whole.[1] Most of these surveys are not, however, representative of smaller geographic areas, which is a significant disadvantage for studying welfare reform in an era of devolution. Data from the census long form are representative of state and local areas, but they are only produced once every 10 years, and so are not appropriate for timely monitoring or evaluation purposes. The ACS will be representative of smaller areas on an annual basis, and, hence, will be a major improvement in providing state and local level data on a far more timely basis. The ACS will be representative of states, large counties and governmental units with populations over 65,000. Eventually, multiyear averaged data representative of smaller areas will also be produced. Other national-level data sets (SIPP, SPD, NLSY, PSID) are of limited use for state-level monitoring because the state sample sizes are too small for precise estimates of state-level measures. The March CPS is large enough to produce annual state-level estimates, but the precision of estimates in most states is low.[2] Other national surveys are representative of some states. For example, the Urban Institute's NSAF is designed to be representative in 13 states (Alabama, California, Colorado, Florida, Massachusetts, Michigan, Minnesota, Mississippi, New Jersey, New York, Texas, Washington, and Wisconsin), though sample sizes for the low-income welfare participant population per se are quite modest. The SIPP and SPD are not representative of all states, but sample sizes are large enough in some states that state level estimates of outcomes can be produced with reasonable precision.

---

[1]Except for the census long form, these surveys exclude institutionalized persons, much of the military, and the homeless populations, although the NLSY and PSID studies do follow sample members in and out of institutions. The NLSY79 is representative only of those aged 14-22 in 1979; the NLSY97 is nationally representative of youths aged 12-16 in 1997. The NSAF is representative of the nonelderly population.

[2]The Census Bureau has funding to improve the precision of state-level estimates of the number of children with health insurance coverage by family income, age, race and ethnicity. Initial plans call for a significant increase in the sample size of the March Supplement, which should enhance the use of the CPS for state-level monitoring and evaluation.

TABLE 5-1 Key Features of National-Level Surveys Relevant for Monitoring Low-Income Populations and Evaluating Welfare Reform

Feature	2000 Census Long Form	American Community Survey (ACS)	March Current Population Survey (CPS)	National Longitudinal Surveys of Youth (NLSY79)
Populations Represented	U.S. households and individuals	U.S. households and individuals	U.S. civilian noninstitutionalized population age 15 and over	Youth aged 14-21 in 1979
Levels of Geography	National, state, local	National, state, local	National	National
Social Welfare Program Content	Limited benefits information, specifically public assistance benefit amount and SSI benefit amount; income	Limited benefits information—includes SSI, food stamps, cash assistance, and housing; income	Moderate benefits information—includes AFDC, SSI, food stamps, cash assistance, school lunch, and public housing; income	Extensive benefits information—includes AFDC, food stamps, cash and other public assistance; child outcomes; income
Sample Size and Design	Cross-section of approximately 18 million housing units in 2000	"Rolling" cross-section of three million households per year	Rotating panel design of 50,000	Panel of approximately 13,000 initially; roughly 12,000 in 1985 when discontinued interviewing the military sample
Oversampling	Small governmental units	Small governmental units	Hispanics	Hispanics, blacks, economically disadvantaged non-blacks and non-Hispanics (until 1990), enlisted military youth (until 1984)

Periodicity	Once a decade	Monthly	Annual (income supplement)	Annual until 1994 and biennial since
Data Collection Mode	Mail survey, personal follow-up for nonresponse	Mail survey, phone follow-up, then personal follow-up for one-third of mail and phone non-respondents	First and fifth interviews in person; other six interviews by phone	Personal interviews, except in 1987 when phone interviews were conducted due to budgetary constraints
Response Rates	1990 mailback response rate=60%; 2000 mailback response rate=54%	Weighted response rate of more than 95%	Until recently, response rates have been quite high. In recent years, they have been in the 80-82 percent range.	Round by round response rates are high. Cumulative retention rate through 1998 is 84% of original sample (not adjusting for mortality)
Data Release Dates	Long-form data planned to be released in 2002 for 2000 census	Goal is to publish six months after data collection	Income and poverty data published for nation and population groups 6 months after data collection; limited data published for states on the basis of 3-year averages	Most recent data available in 2000 was from 1998 survey; publish update biennially
New Features	Long form may not be included in 2010 or later censuses	May replace census long form	Recently received funding to expand sample size for state estimates of low-income children not covered by health insurance	NLSY97 began in 1997 with nationally representative sample (oversample of blacks and Hispanics) of roughly 9,000 youths aged 12-16 years old

continues

TABLE 5-1 Continued

Feature	National Survey of America's Families (NSAF)	Panel Study of Income Dynamics (PSID)	Survey of Income and Program Participation (SIPP)	Survey of Program Dynamics (SPD)
Populations Represented	U.S. civilian noninstitutionalized population under age 65	U.S. civilian noninstitutionalized population of households and of low income families	U.S. civilian noninstitutionalized population	U.S. civilian noninstitutionalized population in 1992-1993
Levels of Geography	National and 13 states	National	National	National
Social Welfare Program Content	Extensive benefits information, including AFDC, SSI, food stamps, WIC, and child outcomes; income	Extensive benefits information, including AFDC, SSI, food stamps, low income health services, and housing subsidies; child outcomes; income	Extensive benefits information, including public assistance, food stamps, school lunch, health insurance, and WIC; income	Extensive benefits information, including AFDC, SSI, food stamps, WIC, and health insurance; child and adolescent outcomes; income
Sample Size and Design	Repeated cross-section of 48,000 households	Panel, originally 4,800 families and 6,434 as of 1999	Panel, size has varied from 11,000 to 37,000 households	Panel of 18,500 households for 1998
Oversampling	Children and low income	Blacks; Hispanics in 1990-1995	Low income starting in 1996	Children and low income
Periodicity	1997 and 1999; planned for 2002	Annual until 1997 and biennial since	Every four months	Annual
Data Collection Mode	Telephone for those with access to a phone; in person and by cell phone for people in the area sample without a telephone	In 1999, 97.5% by telephone; all interviews used computer-based instruments	First, second, and one interview in each subsequent year of a panel in person; other interviews by phone	In-person and two self-administered surveys, one for adolescents; will conduct reinterview

Response Rates	Overall response rate for adults was 62% in 1997 and 65% for children.	97-98.5% annually (mortality-adjusted) PSID does not attempt to interview attriters. Cumulative response rate was 39% in 1994	91-95% households to first wave (cumulative response rate was 69% by wave 8 of 1996 panel)	82% in 1997, 85% in 1998, 1999, 2000. Cumulative non-response was near 50% by 1998. Since then, attempts to interview noninterviews from previous years were made and the cumulative response rate has been not risen.
Data Release Dates	First data from 1997 released in January 1999	1999 data were added to the Wealth Files in February 2000; most recent data in all other files is 1997	Historically, one to two year (or more) lag from data collection to publication	1997 and 1998 data available. Longitudinal file for the years 1992-1998 will be released in the summer of 2001.
New Features	1999 survey incorporated ways of measuring changes in child well-being	Child Development Supplement (CDS) began in 1997 with in-home interviews of 3,500 children aged 0-12 years with over-sample for blacks; these children will be followed into adulthood	Requested funding to expand sample size and number of panels and to implement state-representative design	Will be conducted through 2001 to collect data that enable evaluation of the 1996 federal welfare reform legislation and its impact on the American people

SOURCES: Information from Brick (2000) and National Research Council (2000b).

National-level surveys have experienced some problems with undercoverage. The CPS has some population coverage problems, especially for specific subgroups that might be of interest for welfare program research. The average monthly coverage ratio (the ratio of the CPS population estimate compared with the census-based population estimate) for the CPS in early 1996 was 0.93. But for specific subgroups of black women between 16 and 39, the coverage ratio ranged from 0.82 to 0.87 (U.S. Census Bureau and Bureau of Labor Statistics, 2000). Continuing SIPP panels do not represent new entrants into the population such as immigrants and people returning from institutions (e.g., jail or longer term substance abuse facilities) which are relevant to welfare policy studies.

Population Subgroups

The national-level surveys are aimed to be representative of the population as a whole, but this implies that sample sizes for the population subgroups relevant to welfare reform, namely, single mother families who have lower incomes or welfare recipients specifically, may be problematic. For broader subgroups, such as single mother households, many national-level surveys are, in general, large enough to produce reliable estimates of well-being for the nation as a whole but rarely can they provide state-level reliable estimates.[3] Moreover, studying specific subgroups who may be of interest for welfare reform, such as immigrants, disabled adults, or families with disabled children is more difficult, for the sample sizes in national-level surveys are almost always quite small for these groups, even for the nation as a whole.

Subgroup analysis is necessary not only for description and monitoring but also for nonexperimental evaluations of the overall effect of welfare reform and of the broad components of reform. Of the currently available data sets, only the CPS has the sample size and statistical power for needed subgroup analyses, and even its usefulness is limited to estimating the overall effect of PRWORA and only for low variance outcomes, like the program participation rate (see the discussion of power in Chapter 4). The ACS, as it is currently being developed, has considerable potential for use in such cross-area subgroup analyses of broad components of reform, but it is untested.

Nonresponse

A major threat to the representativeness of all surveys is nonresponse. Nonresponse may bias estimates of outcomes if those who do not respond are systematically different from those who do respond. In a longitudinal setting, the inability to reinterview families for multiple waves of surveys may also cause bias problems. For surveys of low income populations, there may be particular

---

[3]Table 5-1 shows which subpopulations are oversampled in national level surveys.

reasons to suspect there is bias due to nonresponse and attrition: it is likely that factors making it difficult to interview and reinterview respondents (in a longitudinal setting) may be correlated with their outcomes. For example, a lack of stable residence may indicate financial trouble for a family and may make it more difficult to locate a survey sample member. Homeless persons are rarely included in survey sample frames, as we noted earlier, and longitudinal survey respondents who become homeless are generally lost for future reinterview attempts.

Weighting and imputation procedures can potentially reduce nonresponse biases although they can rarely eliminate them (see Kalton and Kasprzyk, 1986 and Little and Rubin, 1987). With specific attention to surveys of low-income populations, Groves and Couper (2001) discuss survey design considerations for reducing nonresponse and nonresponse adjustments and Mohadjer and Choudhry (2001) provide more detail on weighting adjustment procedures. Incentive payments to encourage sample members to respond to surveys have also been effective in increasing response rates in surveys. Initial evidence from a small number of experiments further suggests that incentive payments may be particularly effective with low-income populations (Singer and Kulka, 2001). There has been some movement towards using incentives payments for the SIPP and SPD.

Response rates in the key national-level surveys vary considerably. CPS response rates are around 94-95 percent each month, although the response rates for the March CPS Supplement are a little lower.[4] The ACS is still undergoing field tests and response rates are not available. However, in a 1996 test in four sites, the weighted response rates for the ACS were about 95 percent. The NSAF, which oversamples low-income households, had an overall response rate of 70 percent for the 1997 round and about 64 percent for the 1999 round (Safir, Scheuren, and Wang, 2001).

For the longitudinal surveys, nonresponse and attrition over multiple waves is a significant threat to data quality. For the SIPP and SPD, response rates in the initial waves were high (between 91 and 95 percent for first panels of SIPP from 1984-1996 and 91 percent for the first wave of the SPD—which corresponded to the 1992 and 1993 panels of SIPP), but many first-wave respondents in both surveys have not been reinterviewed. By the eighth wave, the cumulative nonresponse rates for the 1984-1991 panels were between 21-22 percent, 25 percent for the 1992 and 1993 panels and 31 percent for the 1996 panel. This attrition seems to be the result of refusals, rather than the inability to track sample members (U.S. Census Bureau, 1998). The SPD sample is comprised of the 1992 and 1993 SIPP panels. The first SPD survey, the "bridge survey" in 1997, attempted

---

[4]For example, in the 2000 CPS March Supplement, the response rate for the basic monthly labor survey was just over 93 percent, but 8 percent of the basic sample did not respond to the supplement and so the total response rate was 86 percent (U.S. Census Bureau and Bureau of Labor Statistics, 2000).

to interview all 1992 and 1993 SIPP panel members who had responded to each intervening SIPP wave, which was only 73 percent of the original 1992 and 1993 SIPP sample members. The bridge survey interviewed 82 percent of those households. For the next SPD interview in 1998, budget constraints resulted in a decrease in the sample size. Of the eligible households for the 1998 collection, 89 percent were interviewed. Accumulated over these waves, the response rate through the 1998 survey was only 50 percent. The Census Bureau has explored the degree to which attrition has affected the representativeness of the sample; it concluded that in comparing estimates of population well-being measures and characteristics, the SPD produces estimates similar to those of the CPS (Weinberg and Shipp, 2000). (We discuss this further in the section on longitudinal data.) Cumulative nonresponse has also been a problem for the PSID. The NLSY 1979 cohort has had good cumulative response rates, which can probably be attributed in part to keeping sample members in the sample even if they are nonrespondents for one or more waves of the survey.

Timeliness

In order to be useful for continual monitoring of the well-being of welfare prone populations, the data used in monitoring studies should be produced on a regular basis. The March CPS and SPD collect data on an annual basis. The decennial long-form collects data every 10 years. The NSAF collected data in 1997 and 1999. A fully implemented ACS will collect data every month. The SIPP collects data every 4 months.

The timeliness of the release of the data is just as important, and is a severe limitation for some surveys. While the March CPS data are produced on a very timely basis (the data are usually available in the fall after collection), other data sets are not and are thus less useful for monitoring the well-being of the low-income population than they could be. This has been an especially significant problem for the SIPP, for which data release has often taken much longer than a year. For example, while the core data from all 12 waves of the 1996 panel have now been released, only the first few topical modules have been released as of yet, and no longitudinal file has been produced. Data release for the SPD is only slightly better; 1998 data were available in early 2001 and the first longitudinal file of the data set, covering 1992-1998, is scheduled to be released mid-2001. Thus, for two of the key surveys for monitoring welfare program participation, only very limited post-welfare reform data are available in early 2001, nearly 5 years after the reforms were enacted.

Survey Content

Another important aspect of the data for studying welfare reform is content. All of the national-level surveys discussed collect basic information relevant to welfare and low-income populations (employment, income, and public assistance benefits). Some are more inclusive in their coverage of income (CPS, NSAF, NLSY, NSAF, PSID, and SIPP) and include questions about many resources that might be available to the sampled individual or household, while other surveys do not collect as much detail on resources (the long form and the ACS). Some also include more detailed measures of employment than others (again, the long form and ACS are short surveys that do not include many questions detailing employment). Obtaining more detailed information on these two types of measures is important in many monitoring and evaluation settings in order to get a fuller picture of well-being.

Receipt of public assistance benefits is also an important part of these surveys. The census long form covers very limited program benefit receipt information (cash assistance and supplemental security income [SSI]). The ACS collects a bit more program benefit information (receipt of and amount of cash assistance, SSI, food stamps, public housing, and energy assistance). The March CPS collects more detailed information about receipt of public assistance benefits, but it does not collect much information about noncash benefits, such as job search assistance, wage subsidies, or transportation benefits. The major surveys that provide the most detail on program participation and benefit receipt are the SIPP, SPD, and NSAF.

The devolved and ever-changing nature of welfare programs has made it more difficult for all of the national-level surveys to capture the welfare program benefits received by survey respondents. Under AFDC, there was a common program name for benefits across states, so that a common question naming the common benefit (AFDC) could be asked of all respondents, nationwide. However, there is now no common name for cash assistance benefits across all areas, which makes it more difficult to design a survey question that is relevant for respondents in different states. A further complication is that cash assistance is only one of the entire range of services that states now offer low-income families. This wide range creates a major barrier for surveys trying to measure benefit and service receipt and has so far limited the use of national-level surveys to address both monitoring and program evaluation questions. Efforts to incorporate survey questions to probe sample members in different states about the benefits and services received have been hindered by the slow development of good data on programs and policies enacted in each state. Furthermore, recognizing the need for new questions and then developing, testing, and incorporating the questions into the major national surveys takes time and adds to the problem these surveys have in keeping up to date with the changes to state programs. As a result, these surveys are not well suited to fully capture benefit receipt and program participation.

Some of the national surveys collect considerable data on other topics that are relevant for monitoring the well-being of low-income and welfare populations. Most of the longitudinal national surveys collect information on moving and on the state of residence. Therefore, it is possible to measure migration across the country with the longitudinal data sets. The 1999 SPD included a topical module on child well-being that will be repeated in 2001. The 1998 SPD included a module that interviewed adolescents that will be repeated in 2001, although the 1998 module had sizable nonresponse (Bass and Downs, 1999; Downs and Bass, 1999). The NSAF also collects extensive measures of child and adolescent well-being and a great deal of information on health and health care. These surveys are unique in their national coverage of child outcomes, and so will be valuable for monitoring child well-being on a national level. The NLSY and PSID both collect extensive child well-being measures, but these surveys are quite small for some purposes.

Measurement Error

Measurement error for key concepts of interest for welfare program monitoring and evaluation, such as income, benefit receipt, employment and earnings, is also a concern for the quality of data from national-level surveys. For income and earnings measurement in SIPP and CPS, there is some evidence that these are measured well (see Hotz and Scholz, 2001 for a review). Reporting of program participation and benefit levels in national surveys is more problematic. Marquis and Moore (1990) found small differences in overall participation rates in transfer programs when comparing SIPP data with administrative records. However, reports of participation in the SIPP were underreported when comparing the individual survey responses of those who (according to administrative records) actually participated in the program. Underreporting of food stamp participation in SIPP has also been found (Bollinger and David, 2001). For the CPS, underreporting of welfare program participation has been documented for some time, although the extent of underreporting varies from year to year (Bavier, 1999). There is some evidence that the amount of benefits reported (for both AFDC and food stamps) is getting worse (Primus et al., 1999). Moore et al. (1997) review the literature in general on reporting of income from programs and include a discussion of early assessments of reporting for the CPS and other surveys. Mathiowetz et al. (2001) and Hotz and Scholz (2001) both review the literature on survey reports of program participation and benefit levels in more detail. Accurately measuring program participation and benefit levels is likely to continue to be problematic for national surveys as the services offered and program names become more diverse across the country.

Longitudinal Data

For some of the questions of interest for welfare reform monitoring and evaluations identified in Chapter 3, there is a need for longitudinal survey data to track the same individuals and families over time. Longitudinal survey data can be used to help understand the dynamics of welfare program participation as families move on and off public assistance as their life situations change. More broadly, longitudinal survey data can also help understand the dynamics of the income and economic status and the marital, fertility, family composition, and migration across localities or states.

The SIPP, SPD, PSID, 1979 NLSY and 1997 NLSY are all longitudinal data sets. The SIPP interviews sample households every 4 months so that data on marriage, fertility, and family composition are collected over time frames that are short in relation to the frequency and duration of change. Income and economic data are collected every 4 months as well, but respondents report these on a monthly basis. Most of the other longitudinal studies collect information annually, obtaining most characteristics as of the interview date and a few variables for the past year (e.g., income). Thus, the SIPP is unique in providing short-term information on the dynamics of poverty, income, and family situations. Further, understanding the interplay between the family composition and economic situations of sample members (e.g., a decrease in household income after one household member moves or enrollment in a welfare program after the birth of a child) is more feasible with SIPP because these changes are measured over short time frames. Both of these features make the SIPP particularly useful for some monitoring and evaluation questions that require longitudinal data.

Of the other longitudinal data sets, the SPD was specifically designed to study outcomes of families before and after the 1996 reforms (1992-2001). It has a large sample size compared with NLSY and PSID, but nonresponse, attrition, and sample size reductions after budget cuts have hurt the overall size of the sample. Although the Census Bureau has concluded that attrition has not severely hurt the representativeness of the sample in comparison with other national-level surveys, attrition rates are higher for sample members with lower incomes (Weinberg and Shipp, 2000). Cumulative attrition through the 1997 SPD for those with incomes of less than half of the poverty level was 53 percent, compared with 43 percent for those with incomes at the poverty level, and 35 percent for those with incomes twice the poverty level (Weinberg and Shipp, 2000). This analysis also found that the 1997 and 1998 SPD overall interviewed samples have significantly fewer high school dropouts (which is another subpopulation particularly relevant to welfare policy studies) than the 1997 and 1998 March CPS surveys. Thus, there is reason to doubt that this attrition is random and that the population of interest for studies of welfare reform are adequately represented in the SPD.

The NLSY and PSID surveys are both long-term longitudinal studies and have much information on behavioral outcomes that require a longer time frame to study (e.g., some child outcomes, life time family and fertility decisions, or intergenerational welfare dependency). They both collect extensive information on family formation and dissolution and on child-bearing—information that is important for monitoring these outcomes over time. However, both have small sample sizes and the NSLY surveys do not contain data on people outside of the age cohorts sampled.

Use for Monitoring and Evaluation

The national-level data sets currently available are of considerable value for monitoring welfare reform, but still fall short on some criteria. The data sets are of less value for addressing formal program evaluation questions.

The CPS is probably the best all-around national data set for monitoring the well-being of the adult population at the national level because it contains sufficient measures of most income and employment outcomes for individuals and families, is reasonably representative of the overall population and major subgroups of interest, is produced on a timely basis, and is available prior to PRWORA. However, it has many weaknesses as well. Its survey content relevant to welfare participation is quite limited, measuring only cash receipt and only over annual periods. Welfare receipt is also not measured at the same time as most other individual characteristics and, as a consequence, it is not possible, for example, to determine basic questions like whether families are working while on welfare. Further, welfare receipt is significantly underreported in the CPS. Finally, it is too small for state-level monitoring of welfare programs because there are too few observations of low-income, single-mother groups to produce estimates with acceptable levels of error.

The other national-level data sets are weaker for the monitoring function. Although the sample sizes are still adequate for estimating trends in well-being of the nation as a whole, they are inadequate for conducting extensive subgroup analysis and for state-level analysis. The SIPP has the advantage of more frequent periodicity of data collection and more extensive program participation coverage, but it has the significant disadvantage of being extremely slow in release, which greatly diminishes its usefulness for monitoring welfare reform. Another issue for monitoring is that the 1996 SIPP panel does not include some new entrants into the sample frame, (primarily immigrants and those who move from the institutional to the noninstitutional population). The 1996 SIPP also has differential attrition of higher and lower income sample members, which is a problem for monitoring income and poverty. The SPD has significant problems of nonresponse which may be correctable, but nevertheless reduce sample size, may introduce bias, and limit its ability to monitor outcomes. Panel data sets, such as the PSID and NLSY, are too small even for adequate monitoring. The NSAF is large and is representative of 13 states but have only been collected post-PRWORA (in 1997 and 1999 and next in 2002) and are not longitudinal in nature.

The usefulness of these surveys for formal evaluation is more limited. Their primary use is for nonexperimental evaluation of the overall effect of welfare reform at the national level (using pure time-series analysis or comparison-group designs of the type discussed in Chapter 4). For these purposes, many of the data sets provide adequate sample sizes and at least the minimally necessary outcome and program participation information needed. However, for any analysis that is based on cross-state comparisons, the sample sizes in these data sets are either on the borderline of the minimum necessary or below it. The CPS is minimally adequate for estimating the overall effect of pre-PRWORA waiver evaluations, but neither the CPS nor the other data sets have sufficient sample sizes to reliably conduct evaluations of the incremental effect of broad components or evaluations of detailed strategies (see Chapter 4 and Appendix C).

In the absence of sufficient state-level household data sets, the ACS, if it is fully implemented and sustained, has the potential to be used in future program participation modeling at the state level that could assess the effects of future changes in broad components of reform. The survey will produce yearly state-level estimates of the number of individuals participating in broadly defined social welfare programs. It is not yet clear how well the questions included in the ACS will capture program participation, given the potential problems in measuring the wide array of services and benefits offered to poor families, which is a difficult problem for all the surveys. However, if measures of participation are sufficiently accurate, the ACS will be quite valuable for understanding changes in broad components of welfare policy and how larger macroeconomic and social conditions affect program participation outcomes. It is, however, not available for evaluation of the overall effect of welfare reform.

Using nonexperimental methods and national-level data sets to assess the overall effect of PRWORA and the effects of both broad and specific program strategies is also limited by confidentiality issues. Most national-level data sets do not allow researchers access to information that can identify where a sample member resides below the state level (although these data can be accessed with proper permission through the Census Bureau data research centers). Non-experimental methods used to address evaluation questions about the overall effects of reform, along with the broad and specific effects of reform, must control for the larger program and economic environment faced by each sample member to separate out effects of these conditions from the effects of the policy in question. If the data cannot identify in sufficient detail where a sample member resides (localities, counties, or states), it is not possible to match data from other sources on local conditions to control for these conditions in the analysis. (We discuss these confidentiality restrictions on data below.)

Nationally representative longitudinal survey data are needed to address some monitoring and evaluation questions. For example, studies that evaluate the effect of policies on family formation use longitudinal data on individuals and families, tracking their behavior over time. Some specific nonexperimental evaluation methods require historical data on an individual level to control for individual characteristics that might be correlated with outcomes of interest (e.g., current labor force or program outcomes may be correlated with past employment or program participation histories). As Chapter 4 described, both time-series modeling and comparison group methods that use microdata require such longitudinal data to separate the effects of policies from differences due to individual characteristics.

Currently available longitudinal data sets meet some of these needs but fall short on others. The SIPP provides valuable information about the short-term dynamics of poverty, income, and family formation and composition that has a particular use for some policy questions. Some outcomes require a longer time frame with which behavior can be observed. All of the currently available national-level data sets have limitations in this respect. The SPD covers a longer time frame than SIPP, but it does not cover a long enough time frame to examine long-term outcomes, and has serious data quality issues as discussed above. The NLSY and PSID are long term, but are not large enough for precise estimates of outcomes for some populations of interest. Thus, another gap in the data infrastructure for welfare program monitoring and evaluation is the lack of a large, nationally representative longitudinal survey with welfare program-relevant content covering a long-run time frame.

Use in Current Welfare Projects

As we note in Chapter 2, several projects are using national surveys for monitoring purposes and are producing interesting results. The CPS has been used most often for these analyses. The SIPP and PSID have been used extensively for monitoring efforts, such as the ongoing series of reports on well-being and dependency issued by DHHS. However, the SIPP has been used mostly for pre-PRWORA monitoring because so little post-PRWORA data have yet been released. The NSAF has been used for a large number of descriptive studies of the welfare population as well. The SPD and ACS, as relatively new sources, have been used less. As for evaluation studies, the CPS has also been used for much of the caseload and econometric modeling we discussed in Chapter 2. Other surveys have been used less frequently for specific evaluation questions.

Conclusions and Recommendations

National-level data sets are particularly valuable for monitoring the well-being of the nation as a whole and for many relevant subpopulations of the nation. They are less valuable for the evaluation of welfare reform and welfare programs as they evolve. Overall, the current set of national-level surveys is inadequate for fully addressing the research needs for monitoring and evaluating welfare reform, and improvements will be needed to make them effective. Nonresponse is a significant threat to how well many of these surveys cover the populations of interest and, hence, limits their use for monitoring well-being. Furthermore, all the national-level surveys must deal with the new realities of welfare programs, where there is no common set of definitions and terms for assistance and there is wide variation in states' social welfare programs. The abilities of national-level surveys to fully capture all benefit receipt and program participation across the nation is hampered because of this. The lack of timely release of the key national surveys is also a threat to adequate monitoring of the population of interest. Evaluations of the overall effect of reform and the effects of different program components and detailed program strategies across states are also limited by sample size.

Conclusion 5.1 The panel finds that each of the major national household survey data sets most suitable for monitoring and evaluation has significant limitations in terms of sample size, nonresponse levels, periodicity, response error, population coverage, or survey content.

Although the national-level data sets have these limitations, there is a role for them to play in monitoring and evaluation of welfare programs. National-level surveys provide some of the best data for monitoring the well-being of the low-income population of the nation as the whole and for some broad subgroups of interest. They also often contain rich measures of child and adult well-being not found in other data sources. Some national-level data sources will be valuable for assessing the overall effects of welfare reform and the effects of broad components of reform. There are areas where improvement is needed, however, so that the key questions of interest for welfare reform research identified in Chapter 4 can be addressed.

Because a key purpose of monitoring studies is the early detection of changes in the population of interest and its well-being, it is essential that the data are produced on a timely basis. The SIPP is unique in that it is an on-going survey that provides detailed coverage of program participation and income for low-income populations and collects needed information on the short-term dynamics of program participation. Thus, it could be a very useful data set for monitoring the well-being and program participation status of the low-income population. However, the lack of a timely release of these data is problematic. The SPD also provides detailed information on program participation. It has a smaller sample, but follows respondents for a longer time frame than the SIPP and covers the years before and after PRWORA. Although it may be limited by nonresponse and attrition, it could be used for current and future monitoring purposes through the period over which the survey extends. However, the data release for this survey has been delayed. Because these data are not released in a timely manner, their value for monitoring purposes is significantly weakened.

Conclusion 5.2 Key national-level survey data sets used to monitor low-income and welfare populations are currently not being produced on a timely basis. The value of these data for monitoring low-

income and welfare populations would be enhanced if they are produced on a more timely basis.

Assessing the overall effect of welfare reform necessarily relies on data that were available at the time of the reform. National-level survey data, specifically the March CPS, is the best hope to address this evaluation question. As the analysis by Adams and Hotz shows (see Appendix C), the March CPS has reasonable sample size and power for detecting overall effects of reform on program participation. However, its power for detecting overall reform effects on outcomes with greater variance, such as employment and earnings, is limited. All other available national-level survey data sets are not large enough for assessing the overall effects of reform.

Nonexperimental methods of evaluating the effects of changes in the broad components of welfare programs, particularly those relying on cross-area variation, rely on national-level survey data. These data are important because they contain comparable measures of outcomes and other variables across states and because some collect longitudinal data on individuals before and after policy changes. However, sample sizes for conducting cross-state analyses is a serious limitation for these data. The CPS is the only currently available national-level data set that is a viable candidate, and its power for detecting the effects of broad components of reform is suspect. The ACS is a hopeful future alternative for cross-state analyses of broad policy components, but its power for detecting the effects of broad components and detailed components of reform is untested. Moreover, as it currently stands, the ACS does not collect much detailed information on program participation and benefit receipt that can be used to assess the effects of some specific program components or detailed strategies on outcomes.

Sufficient sample size in at least one of the data sets that measures program participation and benefit receipt is necessary so that reliable cross-state analysis of the effects of broad policy components can be conducted. This may mean that sample sizes in either the CPS or the SIPP will need to be increased substantially or that state-level supplements to these surveys are given more serious consideration. A promising development along these lines is recent funding for the Census Bureau to increase the March CPS, to the extent of almost doubling its size, to produce statistically reliable state-level estimates of the number of low-income children who do not have health insurance. The implications of this for evaluations of welfare reform need to be explored.

Recommendation 5.1 To improve the abilities of national-level survey data sets to measure the effects of changes in broad welfare program components across states, the panel recommends expansions or supplements to the CPS or other surveys.

The prototype American Community Survey has much to offer for welfare program evaluation and monitoring. Its key benefit is that it will be representative of states and larger cities every year. It is likely to be large enough to use in conjunction with time-series and comparison group models for assessing the effects of future changes in broad policy components. It also includes broad measures of well-being and measures of welfare program benefit receipt and so it will be very useful for monitoring efforts, at the national, state, and city levels.

The ACS is currently in development stages and is being field tested throughout the country. Full funding has not yet been secured. The ACS has great potential for use in social welfare program monitoring and evaluation the survey and therefore deserves full funding and support.

Recommendation 5.2 A fully implemented and continuous American Community Survey has significant potential for use in future welfare policy research. The panel recommends that sufficient funds be devoted to fully implement the survey and that support for the survey at its currently proposed sample sizes is sustained over time.

The ACS does not and was not designed to collect detailed data on social welfare program participation. It was designed to provide general economic, social and demographic data to communities every year instead of the census long form. It includes several questions about public assistance benefits received by sample households, but it does not collect the more detailed program participation data that the SIPP and SPD, and to a lesser extent, the March CPS do. It does not, for example, ask about low-income child care benefits, transportation benefits, diversion payments, job search or job training benefits, all of which might be provided along with or instead of cash assistance. Furthermore, the reference period for program benefit receipt is the past 12 months, which is long enough to raise issues of the accuracy of respondent recall. Unlike the CPS, the ACS does not contain follow-up questions in the survey to serve as checks on the quality of reported benefits. A potential solution to the lack of detailed program participation data in the ACS is to use the population-based data from the ACS and link it to program-based data from state- or local-level administrative data sets that contain better program participation data. However, the ACS is a mandatory survey and is protected under Title 13, which means that individual-level data (which would be necessary for linking) cannot be released to anyone outside of the Census Bureau. One possible enhancement to the ACS is state-added supplemental questions.

The lack of sufficiently detailed questions on welfare program benefit receipt may mean that the ACS, as it is currently planned, will not reach its full potential for welfare program monitoring and evaluation. If sample size in the CPS is increased, the need for more detailed questions on program participation in a larger survey like the ACS is reduced. However, if the ACS is the only sufficiently large and reliable data source to use for nonexperimental, cross-state evaluations of welfare program components, this lack of detail in the ACS will be a serious limitation for national-level welfare policy analysis.

The ACS will have many competing demands for additional questions, and the number of questions that can be added to the survey is likely to be limited. However, because welfare program devolution has increased the need for state and local data, the panel believes that, with more detailed questions on program participation, the ACS could serve as a very useful data set for welfare program monitoring and evaluation.

Recommendation 5.3 The potential of the American Community Survey for evaluating welfare policies would grow considerably if the survey included more extensive questions about public assistance benefit and service receipt. The panel recommends adding more detailed questions on public assistance receipt to the survey questionnaire.

Even with more detailed questions on program participation, it is unlikely that the ACS, will be able to fully capture the wide array of benefits states and localities are offering welfare recipients. Indeed, capturing welfare benefit and service receipt is a problem for all national-level surveys. With state and local control over welfare programs, an increasingly wide array of benefits and services are now being offered. As noted above, there are no common names of, nor terms for, cash and noncash assistance programs and benefits across states. The Census Bureau, which conducts all of the federally funded national-level surveys relevant to welfare policy (March CPS, ACS, SIPP, and SPD), is aware of this problem in measuring welfare program participation and has taken steps to test new questions and incorporate them in surveys. The Census Bureau should be commended for beginning to address this issue, but it does not have the resources or expertise to do it alone. As a statistical agency, the Census Bureau has expertise in collecting survey data, but lacks it substantive knowledge of welfare programs and how states have implemented them. This expertise lies in DHHS and state welfare program agencies. This mismatch of expertise and responsibility has impeded data collection for program participation and is an area for which the proposed new organizational entity for collecting data relevant to social welfare programs outlined in Chapter 6 could be particularly beneficial in the long run. Short-term efforts will, however, need to rely on extensive coordination among the Census Bureau, DHHS, and state welfare agencies. Staff from the Census Bureau and from DHHS and other federal agencies offering assistance to low-income populations (e.g., U.S. Department of Agriculture, U.S. Department of Housing and Urban Development) should meet regularly with each other and with state welfare program agencies to stay on top of what states and localities are offering as part of their welfare programs so that survey questionnaires can better capture the program services and benefits received by survey respondents. Continued efforts by the Census Bureau to test and develop new questions for capturing program participation should be supported. In addition, the process by which questionnaires are changed to reflect new program realities needs to be accelerated.

Recommendation 5.4 The wider array of services provided in social welfare programs and the variation in these programs across states both make measuring program participation and benefit receipt more difficult, especially on a national level. For national household surveys that measure participation in and benefits received from programs serving the low-income population, it is critically important to regularly and frequently review survey questions to keep in step with program and population changes. The panel recommends to the Census Bureau that more resources be devoted towards improving questions on program participation and benefit receipt to better capture program participation. The panel also recommends that DHHS work with the Census Bureau to develop mechanisms for regular communication with states to stay abreast of programmatic and implementation changes in the states.

State and Local Surveys

As states and localities have implemented their own TANF programs and have more control over designs of their programs, they now also have more of a vested interest in understanding the effects of programs and for monitoring population well-being. Thus, demand for state and local-level surveys has grown considerably.[5]

Most of the welfare-program-related state and local surveys that have been conducted thus far are not representative samples of the entire state's population in the same way national surveys are of the national population. (An exception is NSAF, which is partly national and partly state specific and is representative of the states it samples.) Surveys of welfare leavers, for example, are one of the types of useful surveys being conducted, although, as we stressed in previous chapters, it is also important to survey stayers and other groups. Indepth surveys of the welfare participants or of the general low-income population in particular cities or neighborhoods can be useful because they provide depth in exchange for geographic breadth. Surveys of other special populations, such as immigrants, individuals with substance abuse problems, and others would also be valuable.[6]

State and local surveys confront issues of population coverage, coverage of subgroups, nonresponse, timeliness, survey content, and measurement error, just

---

[5]Appendix Table B-1 contains many examples of welfare program studies that use state and local level survey data.

[6]Matching these types of surveys to administrative data is an important issue as well (see below).

as national surveys do, although the relative importance and nature of the issues is not always the same. For population coverage, for example, generating a sample frame from the traditional counting and listing process of households at the block level is an expensive enterprise even for very local surveys. Also, to be effective for monitoring and evaluating programs serving low-income populations, surveys would need to oversample low-income households. Screening for low-income households can be an expensive task because initially contacted households may be reluctant to provide sensitive information about their income or because income is often measured with more error than other background variables otherwise used for screening (Cantor and Cunningham, 2001). Using random digit dialing telephone surveys instead of in-person surveys is an alternative that can cut expenses, but they raise issues of population coverage because a sizable proportion of the low-income population may be without telephones.[7] Further problems are posed by caller identification screening and the use of multiple phones, although it is not clear how much of a problem these factors are for the low-income population.

State-level surveys of welfare populations (stayers and leavers) thus far have predominantly generated survey samples from lists of program participants—for example, persons receiving cash assistance or food stamps during a certain time period or persons in the control and treatment groups of a state-level experimental program. There are benefits to using such administrative lists for a sample frame (additional information from the administrative records on the universe of sample members is the key one). However, such a sample frame limits the population of interest to only those that participated in the program during that time. Therefore, results cannot be extended to the overall low-income population, which includes people who were not participating in the program at the time the sample was drawn.

Nonresponse is a serious issue for many state-level surveys of welfare recipients and other low-income families. Many of the early welfare leaver studies had low response rates (Acs and Loprest, 2001; U.S. General Accounting Office, 1999a). These populations are often hard to locate because they move more frequently than the full population (Groves and Couper, 2001; Cantor and Cunningham, 2001) and, as mentioned above, are more likely not to have telephone service. Conducting an interview may also be problematic for those with language barriers and those with literacy barriers. Contacting sample members can be problematic because contact information from administrative records (e.g., addresses and phone numbers) is frequently inaccurate. This lack of accurate initial contact information contributes to nonresponse in many of these studies (Cantor and Cunningham, 2001).

---

[7]Thornberry and Massey (1988) report that 30 percent of those in poverty do not have phones. Weiss and Bailar (2001) cite similar findings.

Like national surveys of low-income populations, error in measuring outcomes relevant for welfare program research, such as income, earnings, employment, and program participation is also an issue for state level surveys. State-level surveys must still address the problem of response error in collecting information on program participation, income, and other related concepts in general, although measuring program participation is likely to be less troublesome at the state level. Unlike the national-level surveys that must design questions about program participation for many states with many different programs, state-level surveys need only cover the programs in their own state. However, with the many different programs offered, survey respondents may have difficulty recalling each of the programs they have participated in and so may misreport such information on a survey. Data from state-level surveys can be linked to state-level administrative data to supplement survey data measures of program participation or to serve as a quality check of survey reports more easily than national-level data can be linked.

The lack of cross-state comparability of data limits the use of state-level surveys for cross-state monitoring and evaluation. In the current round of welfare reform, state-level surveys have been primarily developed for evaluations only in the state in which the survey is being conducted. Exceptions to this are the ASPE-sponsored studies of specific welfare populations (welfare leavers and divertees), for which a variety of states were given grants to follow these populations so that a national picture of the circumstances of these groups across the country could be developed. There was some coordination across these state- and county-level studies in terms of common definitions of populations and sharing of questionnaires. However, each state was inherently interested in different topics and so questionnaires were not coordinated. Furthermore, sample frames, designs, reference periods, and the timing and frequency of interviews varied across the surveys. Thus, while these surveys are more comparable than surveys of other welfare leavers, there are still issues of comparability that will make it difficult to compare data across states.

Use for Monitoring and Evaluation

An advantage of state and local surveys for monitoring and evaluation purposes, in comparison with national-level data sets, is that they are able to collect more detailed information relevant to the particular populations and programs of the state (e.g., information of particular interest for rural states or information on a particular state program). Most administrative data sets used in welfare program evaluation are state based. Therefore, matching state-level survey data to state-level administrative data is another advantage (see below). It is also more feasible to follow a local group of welfare recipients, leavers, or divertees or simply a sample of families in the low-income population in particular cities, counties, or other service areas at state or local levels.

A significant handicap at the state and local level thus far is the relative lack of experience of state governments in conducting and using survey information, as well as a lack of resources to conduct surveys. The expense and expertise required in traditional sampling frame methods makes most government agencies hesitate to use them, and they more often rely on telephone surveys or do not use survey data at all (relying on administrative data alone). More surveys have been conducted locally by private research organizations who are funded by foundations or federal-level research agencies. More needs to be done in this area, given the importance of state and local surveys for monitoring purposes.[8] The quality of many of the telephone surveys that have been conducted is also rather low; these surveys need to be of higher quality if they are to be useful for monitoring and evaluation purposes.

State and local surveys used for evaluation purposes are thus far quite rare. For nonexperimental evaluations, cross-area comparisons within states require comparing different counties or different agency offices within states. Attempts to conduct surveys for such studies are rare. Within-area nonexperimental methods are also rare, although they are more feasible. This method of finding comparison groups for ineligibles or nonparticipating eligibles in a particular area has been used in the evaluation of other social programs and could be explored for welfare reform. Finally, there is an issue of whether surveys in multiple states could be used together to conduct cross-state nonexperimental comparisons, which would require sufficient comparability in the survey designs as to permit valid conclusions. This approach has not been attempted to date.

Surveys conducted in conjunction with experimental evaluations are more common, for those evaluations are almost always local in geographic coverage (many experiments use only administrative data, however). These surveys face the same nonresponse and measurement issues discussed above for surveys in general. However, with adequate resources and the use of experienced survey organizations, high-quality survey data in conjunction with experimental evaluations can be collected.

Use in Current Welfare Reform Studies

State and local surveys are only now beginning to be developed for welfare program and evaluation. Many of the welfare leaver studies described earlier in this report include state-level surveys of former welfare participants (see Acs and

---

[8]There are examples of federal support for state-based surveys for monitoring purposes in other fields. An example of particular relevance here is the Center for Disease Control's Behavior Risk Factor Surveillance System, in which state health departments conduct or contract out monthly telephone surveys to track health trends and potential health problems. We discuss other examples in Chapter 6.

Loprest, 2001, for a review of leaver study surveys). There has been very little exploration into the quality of data from these studies: for example, whether the surveys are representative of their universe and how different measures of key variables, such as employment and wages, compare with measures from administrative data sources. For studies of formally and informally diverted populations (see Chapter 2), data issues for both survey data and administrative data are in some ways likely to be more severe. Sometimes very little information is gathered for cases that have been diverted, so there is very little information with which to track individuals in order to survey them. Some areas are using past participants in other social welfare programs who are not or have not participated in TANF to identify informally diverted cases. For these studies, there is the additional burden of finding these cases with what may be out-of-date information.

Surveys at the city, county, or local level are also being conducted as part of the Three-City Study, The Project on Devolution and Urban Change, and the Los Angeles Families and Neighborhood Survey. In a unique example of a national survey conducted at a state level, Iowa State University, in conjunction with the Census Bureau, conducted a modified SPD survey in Iowa (with modifications to questions that were of particular relevance to state policy makers) to explore the feasibility of conducting state-level surveys that could be integrated with the national-level surveys (Nusser et al., 2000). The state of California has also recently launched a large telephone survey to collect information about health and health care access. This survey will also collect information relevant to studying welfare policy.

Conclusions and Recommendations

Devolution has contributed to the growing demand for more localized data on low-income populations. States do not have a great deal of experience in sponsoring or conducting surveys, and thus far, data quality for some state-level surveys has been less than adequate. DHHS-ASPE has recognized the lack of experience for such surveys and has taken steps to help develop state-level capacity to conduct surveys or to manage surveys conducted through contractors. So far these efforts have been geared mostly towards those states and local areas that have grants to study those who leave or are diverted from cash assistance. For this group of states, ASPE has held conferences that provide technical assistance for conducting surveys and has hired a contractor with survey research expertise to provide technical assistance for these states. ASPE staff have also compiled information relevant to developing better surveys, such as survey instruments that include welfare-relevant questions and references to key survey methodology literature. Funding for further enhancements to surveys of welfare leavers and divertees for three states and two county groups with previous grants to track leaver and divertee outcomes has also been allocated. The ACF annual welfare evaluation conferences have also included sessions on state-level surveys.

These capacity-building efforts for states and localities to conduct or contract for their own surveys should be greatly increased. Future activities should be expanded to states other than those conducting leaver or diversion studies. One such activity would be regular conferences that primarily focus on topics in surveying low-income populations with state-level research staff and with experts in survey methodology. DHHS could also consider funding short courses on survey methodology topics for state-level staff. Further interaction with federal-level survey practitioners (e.g., at the Census Bureau and other statistical agencies) could also be beneficial. Some states have more experience in conducting surveys than others and can share valuable hands-on experience and lessons learned. Mechanisms for fostering communication between these groups should be developed and is another area in which DHHS can take a leadership role.

Recommendation 5.5 State-level capacity to conduct household surveys of low-income and welfare populations is limited. DHHS has begun an important effort to build state capacity for conducting surveys. These efforts need to be continued and expanded.

ADMINISTRATIVE DATA

Administrative records that contain information collected as part of administration of programs or services are crucial sources of data for current and future welfare program monitoring and evaluation. Most data relevant for social welfare programs are collected at the local level but linked and maintained at the state level. Some programs further require states to provide administrative data to the federal government. States are required to provide microdata (data on individuals) to DHHS on persons receiving assistance from the TANF program and from separate state programs funded with TANF block grant funds under maintenance of effort requirements. The Child Support Enforcement Program also requires states to provide data to the federal government. This system, the Federal Parent Locator Service (FPLS), consolidates state data (earnings and employment status, employer information, employee social security numbers and names, and unemployment insurance benefit information) on mothers and fathers of children with child support awards and consolidates them in a national database that will be available for some research purposes. The Urban Institute program also maintains records of wage and employment information for individuals that have been used for social welfare program monitoring and evaluation. Administrative data on households, business firms and government entities are being linked to employer and household surveys from the Census Bureau in the Longitudinal Employer-Household Dynamics Pilot Project and the related

Dynamic Employer-Household Data and the Social Data Infrastructure Project. Child protective services, foster care, Women, Infants, and Children Program (WIC), Medicaid, and Food Stamp Program data are other sources of administrative data for social welfare program evaluation.

Administrative data in general have become increasingly important for monitoring and evaluation purposes in the devolved social welfare program environment. These data sets are available on the state and local level, which makes them particularly attractive for use in state- or local-level analysis (Hotz et al., 1998). Aggregate data on program caseloads have been used to estimate the effects of welfare waivers on outcomes. Such data could also be used on an aggregate level to assess the overall effect of PRWORA on cash assistance caseloads and benefits (as described in Chapter 4), with time-series modeling. Using administrative data for cross-state nonexperimental evaluations of changes in broad policy components and changes in specific detailed strategies is also possible since these data sets are typically larger state samples than national-level surveys. Cross-state comparability is a potential limitation for using administrative data for these purposes. Their use is further limited because they are not representative of all persons potentially eligible for programs. However, if information from population-based surveys can be linked with administrative records, these data could be used for evaluations of program participation. Administrative data also have an advantage over survey data in that administrative records contain more detailed and reliable data on program participation.

There are many examples of state- and local-level monitoring and evaluation efforts using administrative data. Administrative data are usually integral parts of experimental program evaluations. Often the outcome measures of program participants—both control and treatment group members–are tracked with administrative data. A number of states are linking administrative data from social welfare programs and from UI wage records to track the status of families that leave welfare. The administrative data used in welfare leaver studies are also used as sample frames for surveys conducted as part of these studies. Administrative data are also being used for other types of welfare program evaluations. For example, the Urban Change Project used administrative records from food stamps, Medicaid, and AFDC/TANF to identify their populations of interest for the four-county sites of the study and will use the data to track some outcomes. A Department of Labor study of six cities (Atlanta, Baltimore, Chicago, Ft. Lauderdale, Houston, and Kansas City—managed by the University of Baltimore) is using administrative records on program participation, employment, and earnings to understand the dynamics of welfare-to-work patterns of low-income individuals. Administrative data are also being used to assess the quality of and improve survey data collections related to welfare program surveys. For example, the California subsample of the SIPP will be merged with data from California UI wage records and AFDC/TANF administrative data to assess the accuracy of self-reported program participation data (Hotz et al., 2000). The Iowa SPD

Feasibility Study examined the use of samples of welfare program participants from administrative records to reach households targeted for surveys (Nusser et al., 2000).

General Issues

As is the case with survey data, population coverage, sample size, data quality, content, and periodicity are important aspects of the value of administrative data for the monitoring and evaluation of social welfare programs. When the question of interest requires data on both participants and nonparticipants, administrative data alone will not be of great use. For such needs, however, administrative data can be used in conjunction with survey data to provide needed information. If the population of interest is programmatically defined, such as those who once received welfare, then administrative data are a relatively inexpensive source of data for monitoring or evaluation questions concerning these populations. There may still be issues of coverage for administrative data sets.

A major weakness of administrative data is their limited content, for they typically include only the information on an individual or family necessary to establish eligibility and benefits. Thus more general household demographic characteristics or indications of health problems, transportation difficulties, or child care obstacles, to name only a few, are missing. Administrative data do not include information on household members who are not part of the benefit unit or whose characteristics are not considered for eligibility determination. This lack of data on other household members limits the use of administrative data for studying family-level outcomes. The problem can be reduced if other sources of administrative data containing information on other household members, such as UI wage records or tax records, can be linked. However, both UI and tax records have coverage problems (see Hotz and Scholz, 2001). It is also difficult to measure child-bearing, family composition changes, and family structure with administrative data.

Administrative data sets generally have much larger sample sizes than surveys, which is a major advantage for monitoring and evaluation. Administrative data sets are usually quite large since records for each person that participates in a program are kept. Similarly, administrative data sets do not have the problems that national surveys have in accurately collecting benefit information because good records on what benefits and services were received are crucial to operating the program. The diversity of programs and services does have implications for administrative data systems, however. In some states, TANF-funded services are being targeted to children and their noncustodial fathers in addition to their mothers, who have traditionally been the primary component of the TANF case unit through which services have been funneled. Thus, for some purposes, it may be important to track benefits received by families rather than by individuals. Doing so may require a greater degree of linking of data from different family members.

If historical information about program participants is needed for an evaluation, administrative data can be very valuable. Historical information about benefit receipt is particularly useful in some evaluation settings, such as the nonexperimental methods of time-series modeling and comparison group modeling, that require good information on the past program or employment status of individuals in the study. Longitudinal survey data can capture such information, but if questions are asked retrospectively, then measurement error can be a serious problem for surveys trying to collect this information. Administrative data would presumably provide very reliable data on benefit receipt, and if they can be linked with population-based survey data, they may be useful for measuring the effects of changes in program components on program entry or on measuring macroeconomic and other feedback effects. A challenge to doing so is that in the past, administrative data have not been maintained or retained for long periods of time, so that historical information is sometimes not available. How long these records are kept varies from data set to data set and from state to state (UC Data, 1999). Because states must now track time limits for cash assistance recipients, records must be kept for longer periods.

Data that are not crucial to administering benefits (e.g., the educational level of a woman applying for TANF) may not go through as rigorous quality checks as data crucial to administering the program (e.g., benefit levels) and so are more likely to be of suspect quality (Hotz et al., 1998). Other items may be collected only when a case is opened and so may not be accurate after the initial period (Goerge and Lee, 2001). For some items collected as part of eligibility determination, applicants may provide inaccurate or incomplete information, such as total earnings. Such issues for collecting administrative data can be key for understanding the quality of administrative data (Goerge and Lee, 2001; Hotz and Scholz, 2001).

There is generally a short lag in the availability of administrative data so they are potentially available on a very timely basis. However, they are collected for administrative purposes and thus are not always readily available for research purposes. To be used for research purposes, the data typically need to be cleaned—that is, the quality of the data needs to be assessed and where possible, improved.[9] Preparation for research purposes also typically includes linkages to other administrative data sets or to survey data sets to improve coverage and content. Linking data often requires obtaining data from other agencies, which may have different definitions and data formats so that formats, definitions, and units of reporting between two data sets need to be reconciled before the data can be linked. Thus, comparability of definitions and data across programs is an

---

[9]This work includes making sure that items recorded the same way over time, that similar definitions are used throughout, that reported items are within a valid range, and, when possible, that comparisons of similar information are reported in other data sets.

issue. For national-level monitoring purposes, administrative data need to be comparable across areas.

Linked administrative data sets and linked survey and administrative data sets have great potential as sources for welfare program evaluations (for details, see Goerge and Lee, 2001; Hotz et al., 1998; National Research Council, 1992). Such linkages can improve coverage of populations. For example, linked data from many programs serving low-income populations (TANF, Medicaid, food stamps, and many others) can improve coverage of program participation. Linking administrative data sets can also improve coverage of needed content areas. For example, unemployment insurance data can provide some employment and earnings data. Child outcome measures, such as test scores from schools or child abuse and neglect information, can improve content coverage if they can be linked to other data sources (see Barth et al., 2001).

Administrative data may also be used to assess the quality of data from different sources. For example, the degree of nonresponse bias in surveys can be assessed by matching administrative records that are available for both respondents and nonrespondents to survey questionnaires to determine how different nonrespondents are from respondents on important variables of interest.[10] Administrative data from food banks or homeless shelters may be a source of information on those who cannot be contacted or who do not respond to surveys.

There are, however, challenges to linking data sets. One challenge is in gaining access to data sources. Within a state, this can be a problem, as data sets often come from separate administering agencies, each with their own protocols for sharing data and for protecting confidentiality of the data. Data sharing across states is even more difficult, as agreements across multiple agencies in multiple states must be obtained. The federal government may be able to collect administrative data across states if it has legislative authority to do so, as in the case of the FPLS and the TANF reporting requirements. Without such authority, data sharing among states is voluntary.[11]

Another challenge to data linking is the availability of high-quality information on which data sets can be matched to one another. If data items that are used to actually link data sets (names, common identifiers such as SSNs, addresses) are of suspect quality or are incomplete, then matching across data sets becomes problematic. Reconciling differences in definitions, units, and protocols for collecting and storing data across different programs is another problem for data linking. This problem is even more severe when linking data across states be-

---

[10]Some welfare leaver studies are planning to compare earnings of survey respondents and nonrespondents. The Census Bureau is planning to match Social Security Administration records to the SPD to assess the effects of attrition in the SPD.

[11]Linkage of the FPLS data with TANF data would be a valuable research product in particular.

cause programs (especially TANF programs) are different across states and, therefore, data may not be easily converted to common standards.

The availability of administrative data at the state level and its relatively accurate measures of program participation measures make them a vital component of the data needed for evaluating welfare reforms. Its familiarity and accessibility to state-level program officials is also important as states now have more interest in monitoring and evaluating their own programs. The development of administrative data sources for research and evaluation purposes should, therefore, be a priority.

Because most administrative data for welfare program evaluations are collected at the state level, development efforts should be focused there. Many state- and local-level administrative data sets are only now beginning to be used for research purposes. Such efforts are uneven across states, although some states have been linking and using administrative data for such purposes for some time now (Cyphers and Kinsella, 2000). In general, states have varying degrees of expertise and resources for preparing and using administrative data sets for research. Technical assistance and funding to develop and link administrative data systems should be provided to help all states develop, clean, and improve the quality of administrative data. Some states also need guidance in negotiating data-sharing agreements across agencies in their states. For many of these capacity-building items, states that already have expertise in developing administrative data can help those with less experience. Federal statistical agencies also have expertise in matching administrative data that can be exploited.

Recommendation 5.6 Administrative data, primarily at the state level, are an important emerging source of information for both monitoring and evaluation. However, there are many significant challenges that prevent them from fulfilling their potential, including the conversion to research use from management use, preservation of data over time, improvements in the quality of individual data items, comparability of data across states, confidentiality and access, and barriers to matching across different administrative and survey data sets. Much more investment in this data resource is needed.

DHHS has sponsored some projects to develop administrative data for research purposes, such as assistance in the development of data for welfare leaver studies, a recent effort to develop public-use files for these studies, and the development of federal level administrative data sets (FPLS, the National New Hires Directory, and the TANF reporting requirement data) for research purposes. These efforts are important beginnings for the development of administrative data. The resource and expertise requirements for a more long-term and comprehensive effort to develop administrative data for social welfare program evaluation are great, however. Such an effort would require a great deal of coordination with states, both in developing the data and in making them more comparable across states. Neither of the relevant agencies within DHHS (ACF and ASPE) can devote the kind of resources needed and still fulfill their own missions. The need for a more comprehensive, long-term effort to develop administrative data sources is another factor that leads the panel to propose the establishment of an authority within DHHS that is responsible for social welfare program data collection (discussed in Chapter 6).

Cross-State Comparability

Any multistate monitoring or evaluation study must confront the issue of comparability of administrative reporting. This is a special issue for TANF program administrative data since the programs and administrative structures for operating the programs now vary widely across states. Some state TANF administrative data sets contain certain types of recipients while other states contain other types of recipients. For example, Wisconsin has moved administration of child-only TANF cases to its child welfare system so these cases would not be part of the TANF data sets, unlike other states. Definitions of a case and family unit also vary across states. For example, some states classify cases in which the adult has been sanctioned as child-only cases, while other states consider children receiving TANF benefits that do not live with a parent as child-only cases. States are providing a wide variety of services to beneficiaries and, as the population being served changes, these services are evolving. As a result, there are few standard definitions of services or even types of services. The services provided under job search assistance in one state may not be classified the same way in another state. All these differences need to be well understood and reconciled if data from multiple states are to be used for research purposes.

Conclusion 5.3 The lack of cross-state comparability is a major barrier to the use of state-level administrative data sets for cross-state monitoring and evaluation.

The panel concludes that more can and should be done to improve the cross-state comparability of administrative data sets if these data are to reach their full potential. These improvements should move toward a common set of definitions of services and service units, which will not be an easy task. However, as the programs become more stable, it should be easier to identify broad types of services that can be defined and to implement common types of service units. Child-only cases are a good example of those for which a standard definition and service unit could be created.

Improvements in common data formats must also be made, including updated systems for storing and managing administrative data. Systems vary significantly across states and agencies. For example, some records are still kept on paper and so are far from being ready for research use, while others are readily available on an electronic basis for research requests. Some data are organized around families or case units while others are organized on the basis of individuals. Not all administrative data systems can easily switch between organization units and so are difficult to match and use with other data. Documentation of formats and definitions is also not standardized in any way.

Improvements in comparability will require cooperation between state and federal agencies.[12] The administrative databases must meet the requirements for use in each state individually. Therefore, complete comparability across all states is probably not feasible. However, the federal government should take the lead for stimulating and supporting improvements in comparability. DHHS can fund and support states to develop their administrative data sets for welfare program research and help develop standard definitions for services and service units and standard protocols for documenting data. DHHS has some experience in this area and can build upon it for future activities. For example, in ASPE-sponsored welfare leaver studies ASPE staff worked with state grantees to develop common definitions for the studies as much as possible across states. ASPE is also working with states conducting welfare leaver studies to produce restricted-access data files from the administrative and survey data collected that are as comparable across states as possible.

> **Recommendation 5.7 The panel recommends that DHHS, in conjunction with state social service agencies, take steps to further improve the comparability of administrative data across states. These steps should move toward comparable definitions of services and service units and data formats. Building comparability across states will have to be a cooperative effort between the federal government and states and will likely require federal funding of state activities.**

Research Uses of TANF-Required Data

States are required to collect and report microdata to the federal government on TANF cases and on cases receiving benefits provided under other programs under maintenance-of-effort grants. States are also required to provide similar data on cases that stopped receiving benefits in the given time period. These data were required as part of state accountability measures in PRWORA and are used to assess whether these requirements are met and to award high performance bonuses. The final rule about what data need to be reported was established in 1999 and is effective for fiscal year 2000. Broadly, states must report informa-

---

[12]Again, this is an area where the sustained and coordinated efforts of an organizational entity responsible for social welfare program data collection that involves cooperative efforts with state data centers, as proposed in Chapter 6, could most effectively make needed improvements to the data infrastructure.

tion about how much and what assistance each case received, information collected for determining eligibility (earnings, work participation activities) and basic demographic data about adults and children in the case (age, race, ethnicity, gender). Monthly data are reported on a quarterly basis to the federal government.

Although these data are collected for federal administrative functions, they are a potential source of data for welfare program monitoring and evaluation. They are potentially useful for monitoring caseload characteristics, benefit levels, and participation in work activities, for example, on a national level. Social security numbers of cases are also reported so there is a potential to link these data with other administrative and survey data sets. For example, data on cases that stop receiving benefits could potentially be matched with other data sources (such as UI employment and earnings records) to provide a national picture of earnings of welfare leavers to compare with results now being reported from state-level studies. These data might also be used in conjunction with national-level surveys to supplement information available from them and to assess data quality (like the SIPP and California administrative data match noted above).

Time-series and cross-state, cross-time caseload modeling of the overall effect of PRWORA could be conducted with aggregated data on welfare caseloads from administrative records (see Chapter 4). To do so, the aggregate data on TANF participation that is being reported to ACF will be crucial. A critical factor for the use of these data for time-series modeling is whether the data are comparable over time. The AFDC program had its own data reporting definitions and protocols. The reporting requirements established in 1999 use new definitions and protocols. In between the passage of PRWORA and when the final reporting requirements went into effect, states reported data under emergency reporting requirements. It is not clear how comparable data reported under these three systems are. If these data are to be used for such purposes, the comparability between these needs to be explored.

Another limitation of these data is that their coverage of program benefits is not comprehensive. DHHS specified a definition of assistance for the reporting requirements—that is, states must report data on cases receiving benefits, where "benefits" are defined only as cash or vouchers for basic ongoing needs such as food, clothing, shelter and utilities (see *Federal Register*, April 12, 1999, for an exact definition). This definition does not include many types of benefits that are currently offered by states, such as nonrecurring short-term benefits, work subsidies, support services such as child care and transportation, employment-related services such as job retention and advancement services, counseling, or child care information and referral. The definition is thus quite limited: data for families receiving noncash types of benefits will not be reported. For example, Florida is using some of its TANF money for abstinence education programs. Other states are using TANF money for programs that specifically attempt to engage poor fathers in the lives of their newborn children. Participants in these programs will presumably not be part of data collected through these federal reporting requirements. Thus, the data do not cover all types of benefits received.

Information on those receiving noncash benefits is also important as states are increasingly using TANF funds for noncash benefits. To do so, a broader definition for whom microdata needs to be reported is needed. It may still be desirable to retain a delineation of the different types of benefits received (e.g., cash assistance separate from noncash assistance, such as child care or work support services) in the data reporting, but a broader definition will give a more comprehensive picture of the services being received.

The definition of assistance for these reporting requirements was a point of contention between the federal government and the state governments. The original federal proposal for a definition was broader than the current version. States, however, wanted a narrower definition, partly to reduce the burdens of reporting, as the broader definition would require states to report more data. In many cases, states do not have a great deal of funding to develop these data and to get their information systems geared up for the reporting. The narrower definition, however, seriously limits the use of these data for program monitoring and evaluation.

Recommendation 5.8 The current definition of assistance used to guide state data reporting requirements is very narrow and will not capture many recipients of different forms of assistance provided by states. The panel recommends that the Administration for Children and Families consider broadening this definition to include as many types of assistance and services provided as possible.

Another limitation of the administrative data reported under TANF is that some states are reporting samples of data, while others are reporting the entire universe of data (i.e., data for all persons receiving benefits in the month). DHHS has given states the option to report either a sample or the universe. For research purposes, however, there are key advantages to having the universe of data available. If the universe of data is reported, data can be linked longitudinally so that past program participation and benefit receipt for each individual can be tracked. The data could also be used to collect information on past welfare receipt histories of cases that move across states. Linkages with other data sets, including survey data, will be more feasible if the universe of data is collected. These linkages could be used to provide additional information about individuals in surveys—particularly program participation and benefit receipt. The full universe of administrative records could also be used to assess the accuracy of survey data reports of program participation.

In some respects, it will be less burdensome for states to provide data on the universe of their cases than on a sample, since a sample of their cases will not have to be drawn. The federal government would have an extra burden of storing the full universe of data, although electronic storage is becoming much less expensive. However, the assessment of data quality and preparation of these data for research use will be significant endeavors. The panel believes, however, that efforts to obtain the universe of data and to make them available for research purposes should be pursued to the greatest extent possible.

Recommendation 5.9 Administrative data reported by states as part of the TANF reporting requirements will be of limited use for research purposes unless steps are taken to improve them. The usefulness of these data will be improved if the data can be linked to other data sets and if the full universe of cases is reported. The panel recommends that ACF take steps to improve the linkability of these data and encourage states to report the full universe of cases.

DATA ACCESS AND CONFIDENTIALITY

Answering important questions about the effectiveness of welfare programs requires a greater reliance on multiple sources of data and linkages between sources—including linkages among administrative data sets, between administrative and survey data sets, and across levels of government. Although the needs for multiple sources of linked data are great, restricted access to data, instituted to prevent individuals who provide data from being harmed by the improper use of the data, limit data currently available for use in research contexts. There are restrictions to access for both survey and administrative data. Such restrictions range from completely limiting the use of the data to only those within the collecting agency to no restrictions at all on the use of individual data. For many data sets, restrictions on data access are somewhere in between. Different models for data access include: granting access to group-level data instead of individual-level data; releasing scrambled data so that any data items containing individually identifying information are either not released or are modified to prevent individual identification; granting permission for researchers to access data at a centralized data holding center (e.g., as done in the Census Bureau data centers); housing data in secure holding centers but allowing researchers to specify the analyses they want conducted with the data as long as they are within the bounds of confidentiality requirements; and releasing individual data to those who agree to abide by terms for the use of the data and are subject to penalties if they are found to be using the data in ways other than the agreed-upon terms.

The panel believes that confidentiality and access restrictions are often drawn in ways that unnecessarily limit the use of important sources of data for welfare program monitoring and evaluation. Confidentiality protocols limit the use of survey data for evaluation purposes. For example, nonexperimental methods of evaluation that compare outcomes of individuals across different areas must be able to control for the economic conditions and other characteristics of the local areas in which study participants live. This requires information about where the individuals live (for example, a county, census tract, or zip code). Often, this information is not available from surveys, and therefore, poses a barrier to use of these data for evaluation.

The state-based nature of the TANF program and limited budgets for evaluation magnify the importance of administrative data sets and linkages of administrative data sets for program evaluation. Although these data are needed now more than ever to inform policy decisions, they are often not accessible. A barrier to data access that is particularly acute with the devolved program structure for TANF is that rules and protocols governing data access vary considerably across states and even across agencies within states (Brady et al., 2001). A study examining state social service administration practices for releasing data found that some state social service agencies had well-developed policies for release, while other states did not (UC Data, 1999). Cross-agency data sharing at the federal level is also hampered by the variation in data sharing protocols among federal agencies (National Research Council, 1993a, 2000a).

Variation in policies and practices regarding release of data and confidentiality protections across both state and federal agencies is a particularly complex problem for linking administrative data from different agencies for research purposes. Gaining access to data from multiple agencies is more difficult because data-sharing agreements with each agency providing data must often be negotiated separately, a process that may take considerable time. Linking data from different sources requires some individually identifying information for each data point to be matched with similar information from another data set. Social security numbers are a typical example of such information. However, some agencies have moved away from using SSNs as identifiers and assign their own identifying numbers to cases. A problem then for linking is that identifiers in each of the data sets being linked may differ across each agency.

Different agencies also have varying degrees of experience, resources, and technical know-how for releasing data for research purposes, and, thus, policies and practices for releasing data have developed unevenly. This is especially true across state agencies, partly because data collection and evaluation efforts were not previously focused at the state level and resources for data collection and linkage were more limited. With an increased focus on state-level data and evaluations, state agencies could use advice on different models for data sharing and new technical advances that can be used to protect confidentiality of individual data. This is another area for which DHHS can convene conferences or meetings with state and federal agency representatives and with experts in data access and confidentiality. In the longer term, leadership in coordinating data linkages from the proposed data collection authority in DHHS that is responsible for data collection for social welfare programs (see Chapter 6) could speed the coordination of confidentiality protocols and take steps to lower data access barriers.

It is crucial for data collection agencies to ensure that the individuals who provide data are not harmed from misuse of the data. The reputation of the agencies charged with collecting data or administering programs may rest on whether individuals believe that these data will be used appropriately or that they will not be harmed by providing the data. The issues of data access and confidentiality are, however, much deeper and more complex than any single agency or state. The larger scientific, legal, and governmental communities will need to be involved in resolving current tensions between opening data access while protecting individual privacy.

One factor in the tension between open data access and protecting privacy is that current laws governing the use of data often do not specifically address the use of the data for research purposes.[13] Most privacy laws allow administrative data to be used for activities in accordance with the program's purposes or include clauses for "routine use" of the data. It is often through these provisions of the laws that agencies grant access to the data to policy analysts outside the agency (Brady et al., 2001). But because the laws do not directly address the use of data for research purposes, these laws can be interpreted quite differently. Policy makers and agency officials with control of the data are not always aware that researchers have no interest in the personal identities of specific individuals providing data, but rather, only have a need for information on random individuals. Because they do not understand how researchers use the data, agencies that control data too often limit access to the data for research purposes, even though the data could be valuable for monitoring and evaluation.

Rules governing the use of individual data collected from state and federal government agencies need to clarify how the data can be used for research and evaluation purposes. Provided such clarifications can be made and agreed on, an effort to implement them as consistently as possible across and within state and federal agencies is needed. The benefits of access to data for program monitoring and evaluation purposes need to be better communicated to agency officials that grant data access. Alternatives to simply eliminating access to data includes stricter enforcement of rules governing the use of restricted data to discourage improper disclosure (National Research Council, 2000a), as well as advancing the development of techniques for data disclosures that protect confidentiality, such as data masking or data perturbations (Brady et al., 2001). New technologies may help to provide external access to linked data sets while meeting confidentiality requirements. For example, the Longitudinal Employer-Household Dynamics Pilot Project at the Census Bureau and the related Dynamic Employer-Household Data and the Social Data Infrastructure projects are exploring the use of web-based and video teleconferencing tools to provide research data.

The panel has found that data access and confidentiality restrictions are

---

[13]See Brady et al. (2001) for a review of legislation specific to administrative data uses and National Research Council (1993a) for a review of legislation regarding data collected through federal agencies and for a review of agency-specific confidentiality practices.

significant barriers to the availability of data for social welfare policy evaluation. As these issues begin to be addressed on many fronts, the panel emphasizes the need for data linkages in welfare program evaluations and encourages steps to remove barriers to data access.

> **Recommendation 5.10 Confidentiality, privacy, and access concerns with administrative and survey data and the linking of multiple data sets are important issues, but are currently serving as a barrier to socially important evaluation of welfare reform programs. The importance of access to these data for monitoring and evaluation of programs should be emphasized and efforts to reduce these data access barriers while protecting privacy and maintaining confidentiality should be expanded.**

PROGRAM DESCRIPTION DATA

Another type of data that are crucial for social welfare program evaluation are program description data, or descriptions of the TANF and related programs that states have adopted and are operating. The importance of such data for evaluation seems obvious—programs cannot be compared if the rules of the programs are not known. Yet as the panel stated in its interim report, good program description data on post-PRWORA state and local programs were slow to develop. This lack of data has been a major limitation for welfare reform evaluation, especially for cross-state monitoring and evaluation. In relation to monitoring the low-income population on a national level, it is important to know what the different state programs are so that national surveys can ask respondents the right questions about the program benefits they receive. Nonexperimental methods of evaluating the overall effect of welfare reform and of broad components of reform rely on fairly detailed program description data for both TANF policies and other related non-TANF policies in states and localities so that these variables can be included in models to control for the different policies that apply to each case. Program description data need to cover programs in effect during the entire study period. For national-level evaluations, program description data are needed from every state and for every locality within states for which different rules apply. For state-level evaluations, program description data are needed for a given state only, unless different localities within the state have different policies.

The federal government's efforts to collect program description data are, thus far, limited. States are required to provide summaries of their state TANF programs every 2 years in order to receive block grants. The first collection was in 1997 and the second in 1999. States are given general guidance on what to report, but there are no specific requirements. As a result, the level of detail that the states have provided about the programs varies greatly. These state summaries are just now being organized so that they can be made accessible to the public.

Aside from the state plans required to be reported to DHHS every 2 years, there are several efforts under way to document state policies and practices (see Chapter 2). The most comprehensive effort has been conducted by the Urban Institute as part of their Assessing the New Federalism Initiative. This database is the most comprehensive in time documenting rules from 1996-2000. It includes data on eligibility rules, asset rules, benefit levels, work activity requirements, time limits, sanction policies, behavioral requirements, and child support requirements. The data have been coded to be more readily usable in quantitative analyses and are publicly available (see http://www.wrd.urban.org). The 2000 round was sponsored by ACF and current plans call for updates in 2001 and 2002.

In another effort, the Center for Law and Social Policy and the Center for Budget and Policy Priorities are jointly collecting information on state TANF and Medicaid policies. Currently, this database includes information on state policies regarding: TANF applications, cash diversion programs, emergency assistance, categorical and financial eligibility rules, family cap policies, minor living arrangement provisions, school and training requirements for minors, abstinence education programs, and Medicaid (see http://www.spdp.org). This information was collected for legislation enacted before and updated through 1998. In the future, information about time limits, work activities and requirements, sanction provisions, child care assistance, child support, and drug-related provisions will be included in the database. While this database contains some information not included in the Urban Institute database, it does not cover the full time frame since PRWORA that the Urban Institute database does.

The Congressional Research Service (CRS) has also used state TANF plans reported to DHHS-ACF to produce reports summarizing state program rules on different topics. For example, the last summarized key features of state TANF programs, such as: treatment of earnings and savings, welfare diversion, work requirements, personal responsibility plans, division of the welfare caseload, and benefit levels (Burke et al., 1999). Every 6 months states are surveyed to collect information about financial eligibility and benefit determination rules in effect. The last update includes rules in effect through January 2000 (Abbey et al., 2000), and future updates of this report are also planned. Finally, the CRS has a continuing series of reports called Cash and Noncash Benefits for Persons with Limited Income that covers over 80 federal programs that serve low-income people that is produced every other year. The latest version was produced in 1999 (Burke et al., 1999), and another version is due in late 2001.

It may seem that all these ongoing efforts to collect TANF program description data would translate into sufficient, even redundant, program description data, but this is not the case. Most of these data collection efforts are not conducted on a regular basis and do not cover the entire time frame of interest. Only the Urban Institute database comprehensively covers programs and changes in programs in operation between 1996 and the present. The state plans provided to ACF and summarized by the joint effort between ACF, Welfare Information Network, American Public Human Services Association, and National Governors Association (discussed in Chapter 2) will eventually be available every other year. The State Policy Document Project only covers programs in effect at one point in time, thus far.

Another weakness of many of these efforts is their coverage of all programs and rules. It is not at all clear that data submitted to the federal government will be detailed enough in every state and consistently reported across states to comprehensively cover all TANF and other state welfare programs, since there are few detailed requirements of what states have to report. Again, the Urban Institute's database is probably the best source of detailed data, but it does not include information about other related non-TANF program rules. Other data collection efforts provide some needed information, but these efforts do not comprehensively cover all programs. Thus, evaluations that depend on full descriptions of TANF and non-TANF program rules (such as time-series modeling, comparison group modeling, and cross-state policy and timing variation models) will have a difficult time controlling for all the policies that may affect individuals in the study, and thereby, isolating the effects of specific policies. A further limitation of these data is caused by the changes in the ways agencies have actually implemented their policies. None of these sources of program description data collect detailed information on program implementation (see below).

A key issue for the collection of program description data is whether efforts like the Urban Institute's can be sustained. There are positive signs in this direction as ACF funded the 2000 round of the rules update, and plans for future rounds are now set. However these data need to be continually updated and expanded to cover other related programs. Data collection of program rules, in a sufficiently comprehensive, detailed, and consistent manner across states, should be an institutionalized component of DHHS's duties for administering social welfare programs. This work requires the institutional commitment of a government agency to ensure that the data are collected and provided to users in a readily usable form.

Recommendation 5.11 The monitoring and documentation of the actual policies, programs, and implementations of welfare reform at the state and local levels by the federal government has been minimally adequate to date. The panel recommends that the Department of Health and Human Services take active and direct responsibility for documenting and publishing welfare program rules and policies in every state and in every substate area where needed. Continuing updates documenting changes in state and local area rules should also be produced.

In Chapter 4 the panel recommends that more process studies should be funded in order to provide more detailed descriptions of how state and local policies have actually been implemented. These detailed descriptions are needed in evaluation efforts, especially in evaluating the effects of specific detailed welfare reform strategies, to fully characterize the policies that cases are subject to and in turn, to use these characterizations to assess the effect of the policies on outcomes. We emphasize the need for more process studies that can provide this detailed data on program policies.

QUALITATIVE DATA

Qualitative data on individuals are another important source of data for welfare program monitoring and evaluation. While Chapter 4 highlights potential uses of qualitative data for evaluation purposes, the discussion in this chapter focuses on data collection. The collection of qualitative data for addressing key monitoring and evaluation questions posed in Chapter 3 is likely to be most useful when conducted as part of other data collection efforts, such as surveys or administrative data collections (see Newman, 2001). Sometimes these data collections are incorporated into larger surveys, more often they are not. Open-ended questions, or questions that do not require a respondent to choose among a fixed set of answers (yes or no, numbered choices, etc.) allow respondents to provide detailed responses or explanations in their own words. These are typically conducted within the framework of a larger survey with other closed-ended questions. In-depth interviews are question-and-answer interviews that include more open-ended questions than a survey instrument and typically do not include fixed choice questions. Such interviews may be conducted on a subsample of a larger survey sample, or on an independent sample of individuals. Qualitative longitudinal studies with in-depth interviews conducted on the same individuals or families over multiple interview sessions are also common. Focus groups are conducted with small groups of individuals to discuss topics of interest, with a facilitator prompting participants and guiding discussion. Finally, participant observation fieldwork directly observes behavior of study participants. Data are collected through notes the researcher takes while observing the behavior of study participants, usually on a day-to-day basis. Participant observation is typically combined with interviews of study participants.

Process analyses may also collect qualitative data to provide detailed information on programs or on a system that administers benefits and are another use of qualitative data. Data for process studies is gathered by visiting program offices (often across multiple service delivery areas); conducting surveys, in-depth interviews or focus groups with key stakeholders in the delivery system such as program participants, caseworkers, and administrators; directly observing client and caseworker interactions; reviewing documentation of individual cases;

and special tracking of a cohort of participants through the processes of the program.

The goals of qualitative data collection are generally to provide more detailed information and sometimes more subjective information on individuals or groups that is not easily quantified or measured with survey or administrative data. Besides providing more detailed insights into the outcomes of individuals, qualitative data can also be used to improve quantitative data collection. Open-ended questions embedded in surveys can be used to develop future survey questions (Newman, 2001). For example, an open-ended question may solicit answers that are fairly consistent across respondents. In future surveys, those responses might be incorporated as fixed-choice questions. Qualitative studies, perhaps through in-depth interviews or longitudinal in-depth interviews, might also be useful for understanding family organization, which can be used to improve the design of surveys that are designed to gather information about family members (Newman, 2001). Participant observers and in-depth interviews may be used to understand how surveys can be successfully targeted to hard-to-interview populations for surveys.

Despite their potential use for welfare program monitoring and evaluation, qualitative and ethnographic data collections have several limitations. Qualitative studies are not always designed to statistically represent a population of interest. Because qualitative and ethnographic studies are expensive to conduct, the sample sizes of these studies are generally small, so that even those studies with representative samples of the population of interest are often too small for precise statistical analyses. Thus, qualitative studies are often most effective when nested within a larger survey or administrative records study to complement the information collected from quantitative data sources. A data collection issue here that qualitative and ethnographic researchers disagree on is whether it is more desirable to draw a separate sample of individuals within the same geographic area and with similar demographic characteristics as the survey or administrative records sample (as is the case with the Urban Change Project and the Three City Study) or to draw a subset of the survey or administrative records sample (as the ethnographic component of the Fragile Families Study has done). While the subsample strategy has the advantage of providing quantitative and qualitative data for a subsample of the study participants, the in-depth nature of many qualitative studies increases respondent burden for the subsample, which may make differential attrition an issue (Newman, 2001). Yet recruiting a separate sample of study participants for the quantitative component can be costly.

Replication of results is rare for qualitative and ethnographic studies, which is a serious shortcoming. To remedy this problem, qualitative and ethnographic researchers should work closely with one another to coordinate their efforts so that there is some consistency in sampling and data collection across multiple locales; this is rarely done. The exception is for those studies that use qualitative or ethnographic studies across multiple areas. Moreover, qualitative and ethnographic studies often do not sufficiently detail the methods by which the sample was selected and the data were collected, stored, sorted, and analyzed. This deficiency contributes to the problem of trying to replicate studies. Thus, it is incumbent on qualitative researchers to better specify their data and methods when reporting their results.

While the potential uses of qualitative data in evaluation settings are becoming more apparent, these data are not routinely collected as part of evaluations of programs. The barrier is usually budget constraints, when quantitative outcome evaluations are of foremost importance for the sponsoring agencies. This priority is especially true for state program agencies sponsoring evaluations of their programs. Although many administrators see a useful role for ethnographic research (Newman, 2001), government-sponsored ethnographic studies are rare, especially at the state level.[14] In the absence of a great deal of funding for extensive large-scale qualitative studies, smaller-scale studies embedded in larger quantitative studies may be the most feasible way to obtain needed qualitative data (Newman, 2001).

SUMMARY AND ASSESSMENT OF THE
CURRENT DATA INFRASTRUCTURE

This chapter reviews the state of currently available data for welfare program evaluation and monitoring needs. Our discussion has focused on four types of data: survey data, administrative data, data describing programs and policies, and qualitative data. Addressing the key questions of interest for evaluating welfare reform requires the use of all of these kinds of data.

While in many respects the existing data are very rich and extensive and furnish a wide range of valuable information on the low-income population and welfare recipients, in many critical respects they have significant weaknesses. These weaknesses are sufficiently severe that the panel has concluded that inadequacies in the nation's data infrastructure for social welfare program study constitutes the major barrier to good monitoring and evaluation of the effects of reform.

National-level surveys have an increasingly difficult task of measuring program participation in a setting in which programs vary widely from state to state. In addition, the sample sizes of many national-level surveys, though completely adequate for nationwide totals, are inadequate for the study of most of the state-level welfare program components (such as time limits, work requirements, etc.). The surveys often have major problems of nonresponse, which is often concen-

---

[14]One exception is a study under way in South Carolina conducting in-depth interviews with a sample of welfare leavers (Medley et al., 1999).

trated in the lower income groups in the sample. Finally, timeliness of data release and availability is a major barrier to the analysis of welfare reform, a problem particularly acute for SIPP, which has released very little post-PRWORA data at the time of this writing.

State-level surveys are in much worse conditions, primarily because states are only beginning to conduct such surveys. Most such surveys are conducted by telephone and response rates are often very low. Currently, they cannot be a major resource for the study of welfare reform.

State-level administrative data hold more promise in an era of devolution because they provide fairly large samples at the state level. But their use as research tools, rather than as management information systems, is still in its infancy. Administrative data sets are usually quite complex and usable only by those who are expert in understanding the coding of the data, which makes the data difficult to use by any wide set of evaluators or researchers. The data are sometimes not available over time, because states have had no reason to save them in the past. The lack of historical information on individuals in data sets puts limits on their use for evaluation and monitoring. Evaluation efforts are also hindered by the lack of cross-state comparability in data items and variable definitions, which makes cross-area methods of evaluation problematic with these data. An inherent limitation of administrative data is, of course, that they are only available for those who receive welfare.

Data describing state policies and programs have improved in quality and quantity in the last year. However, the development of databases with this critical information will need to continue and will need significant support from DHHS. Furthermore, the databases need to be significantly widened to cover more than TANF program rules, while at the same time maintaining historical dimensions with regularly recorded rules for all the states going back several years. Collecting information about the actual implementation of the official rules continues to be a very difficult problem.

Qualitative data in the form of ethnographic information on families is an underused source of information in program evaluation on social welfare reform. Neither administrative nor survey data can fully characterize the complexity of individual families' lives and the way different types of families respond to welfare reform. However, researchers working with qualitative data need to continue to develop standardized protocols for collecting data and documenting how the data were collected, and they need to extend the data to cover a more representative set of areas and population groups. To date, these data have not played a major role in welfare reform evaluation despite their potential.

There is a critical need to address the data barriers hindering good evaluation and monitoring as these data barriers limit what is known about the effects of PRWORA and welfare reform. As we note in our previous two chapters, ASPE has an important role to play in addressing these barriers. ASPE has already committed significant money and staff resources to the improvement and maintenance of national-level survey data sets and has assisted states in developing their own databases, both administrative and survey. However, much more needs to be done.

The panel concludes that the overall weaknesses in the data infrastructure have not been fully realized by the wider community of evaluators and policy makers. In part, this is because there is no established mechanism for assessing data quality and reporting on it to the public. Consequently, the panel believes that ASPE should include, in the Annual Report to Congress, a review of the state of the data infrastructure for welfare reform research. The review should cover survey and administrative data at federal and state levels. It should identify strengths and weaknesses of existing data and should note gaps that need to be filled and give an assessment of what the highest priorities for filling the gaps are so that resources can be effectively allocated to those projects.

Recommendation 5.12 In its Annual Report to Congress, ASPE should review current availability and quality of data for welfare reform research, identify high-priority data needs, and discuss its own research agenda for data development and technical assistance.

Building a data infrastructure for welfare program monitoring and evaluation will take a concerted effort from federal and state governments, all of whom have interests in social welfare program evaluation and monitoring.

6

Administrative Issues for Maintaining the Data Infrastructure

Our investigation of data needs in Chapter 5 demonstrated that the national infrastructure for data collection on social welfare programs and populations has many severe limitations. These limitations are so important that they have seriously constrained the ability of the government and private analysts to monitor and evaluate the effects of welfare reform in the 1990s and of the PRWORA legislation. Despite the best intentions of analysts, there is unlikely to be any significant additional progress made in learning the effects of welfare reform until the nation's data infrastructure undergoes major improvements.

The inadequacies appear at all levels, federal, state, and local, and in both survey and administrative data. National-level survey data sets are of limited sample size, and have suffered serious problems of nonresponse, and their questions on welfare program participation are not adequate to capture the new devolved structure of programs. In addition, serious delays in producing key data sets have limited publicly available data for the post-PRWORA period, constraining the analysis of outcomes for that important time frame. Furthermore, national-level administrative data sets, such as those based on TANF reporting requirements from the states, which should provide information on those still on TANF, are of dubious quality for research purposes and are unlikely to be used for this purpose. Data on what program characteristics and rules states and local areas have been adopted are a necessary ingredient in knowing what welfare reform actually has constituted. But these data have only lately been developed and will need continuing and significant support to be maintained.

State-level administrative data have considerable potential to yield information on families still on TANF, as well as families who have left TANF or been discouraged from applying, but they have historically been used primarily for management purposes and need much additional work to be made useful for research. State data sets of this type also vary greatly in quality and quantity across states. States often use noncomparable definitions and categorizations, making it difficult to use them for cross-state assessments. In addition, state-level administrative data sets are not often available for many past years because states do not generally archive them; so, for example, it is often difficult to compare current TANF families to those who were on AFDC prior to PRWORA. State-level TANF administrative data sets also have significant limitations in terms of content. These limitations could be partly addressed by matching different state-level administrative data sets across different programs, but such matching has been limited by confidentiality and access rules. Finally, state-level surveys of current TANF recipients, former recipients, and other groups affected by welfare reform—which could provide important information on how families are doing and what their needs are that are not available elsewhere—are in their infancy and need support and development if they are to be a significant resource for evaluation.

Although there are many reasons for this discouraging state of affairs, the panel concludes that it is partly the result of inadequacies in the structure of federal administrative authority and responsibility for data collection in this area. No existing federal agency has general authority and responsibility for data collection on social welfare programs and populations (nor the necessary staff to implement such authority). To remedy the situation and improve the data infrastructure, there is a set of distinct, specific administrative functions that need to be carried out. We list these functions later in this chapter. None of these functions are now seen as the responsibility of any agency.

In this chapter, we first describe the current structure of federal responsibility for data collection on social welfare programs and populations and identify gaps. We then discuss what the federal role should be in an era of devolution. Finally, we lay out the functions that need to be carried out, and we discuss some alternative organizational structures that might be developed to carry out those functions.

THE CURRENT SYSTEM

Responsibilities for collection of data relevant to social welfare programs are currently spread across several different federal agencies, none of whose primary purpose is the maintenance and development of data on these programs. Within the U.S. Department of Health and Human Services, both the Administration for Children and Families (ACF) and the Office of the Assistant Secretary for Planning and Evaluation (ASPE) are responsible for components of the data collection system, but neither has general responsibility. Neither agency is a statistical agency and so all data collection activities conducted by these agencies are secondary to its main mission. Those activities tend to be short-run in nature and designed only to carry out other current responsibilities.

ACF is responsible for administering the department's social welfare programs for families and children, of which TANF is one of the major programs. As part of this charge, ACF is responsible for collecting TANF and related administrative data from states. However, ACF's primary responsibility is to use these data to check the compliance of states with various provisions of PRWORA and to assess performances of states for monetary awards under PRWORA. For example, ACF is charged with monitoring the compliance of caseload employment requirements by state TANF programs. ACF also monitors aspects of child support enforcement provisions and other provisions that can entail the administration of sanctions and bonuses to states by the federal government. Therefore, the mission of ACF is considerably narrower than what is required to support a general-purpose data infrastructure for social welfare and human service programs at the federal and state levels.

ASPE is responsible for strategic planning, policy development, research, and evaluation for the Department's programs, including TANF and related social welfare programs for families and children. As part of these duties, ASPE currently has some responsibilities to collect data, to support data collection undertaken by others, and to support data use for policy planning, development, and evaluation. In the area of state-level data sets, ASPE has taken a new leadership role in guiding the states in data development. As noted above, for example, ASPE is currently funding 17 state and local welfare leaver and diversion studies and has worked with the contractors for these studies to develop state-level databases for such welfare research, including the provision of technical assistance on data collection (both administrative and survey). ASPE also made an attempt to persuade these states and localities to use common definitions of variables in their analyses of welfare leavers. This activity is a relatively new role for ASPE, which has not traditionally been as heavily involved in state-level data collection. ASPE has been led in this direction by the devolution of responsibility for welfare programs to the states and by the need to sponsor high-quality, state-level welfare research. But the ASPE staff are not survey statisticians and methodologists; they are primarily from other disciplines and see their mission as consumers of data rather than producers of data. Furthermore, ASPE's resources are far too limited in terms of funding and staff to be able to take a major oversight role in state-level data collection. ASPE also does not have the resources or administrative responsibility for ensuring that investments are made in the long-run state data infrastructure, for ASPE is usually fully engaged in carrying out short-run policy functions needed by the administration and by Congress. Consequently, while ASPE has done very well with the resources it has had and has been a major force in achieving what gains there have been in the improvement of state data sets, it would require a major change in resource levels, staffing, and mission for ASPE to take on the larger role of carrying out the significant changes to such data that are needed, while yet simultaneously fulfilling the other parts of its mission.

ASPE has been and continues to be heavily involved in the development of federal-level administrative and survey data sets. It is the primary research and evaluation agency overseeing the Survey of Income and Program Participation (SIPP), for example, although other agencies are involved in SIPP oversight as well. (SIPP is sponsored and operated by the Census Bureau and not by ASPE.) In its role in welfare reform, ASPE has also been involved in the "new hires" data set, the matching of administrative data (e.g., social security records) to survey data for research purposes, and a number of other related important activities. ASPE has a long history of supporting data collection for national-level data sets. However, in order to fulfill its planning and evaluation role within DHHS, ASPE has traditionally been a data user rather than a data collector. Its mission, as already noted, is research and evaluation; it is not a statistical agency.

The lack of any agency within DHHS that has the distinct administrative authority and responsibility, and the requisite staff expertise, for federal and state-level data collection on social welfare programs and populations has, the panel believes, been partly responsible for the limitations in the data infrastructure.

> **Conclusion 6.1 No agency within DHHS has distinct administrative authority and responsibility for the collection and development of data relevant to social welfare and human service policies and pro-grams. This administrative gap is a major reason for many of the inadequacies in the data infrastructure for monitoring and evaluating welfare policies.**

Other agencies outside DHHS are, of course, also involved in data collection for human service and social welfare programs. Most notable is the Census Bureau, which currently has primary responsibility for SIPP, the chief on-going nationally representative survey on participation in various social programs, as well as the Survey of Program Dynamics (SPD), the offshoot of the SIPP that was mandated under PRWORA to monitor the progress of welfare reform. As part of these survey programs, the Census Bureau is responsible for developing the content of the surveys (the questions on program participation, income, and re-sources and background characteristics to be asked of survey respondents) as well as fielding the surveys and producing and maintaining public-use data sets developed from them.

It is an atypical organizational structure for the Census Bureau, which is a data collection agency, to have primary responsibility for such mission-specific data sets as SIPP and SPD. Usually, primary responsibility for such data sets rests with a sponsoring agency that uses, or represents the users of, the data being collected. More typically, the agency administering programs for which the data are collected or whose mission is most closely related to the substance of the survey has primary responsibility for survey content but works together with the Census Bureau (or other outside contractors, in some cases) in the translation of that survey content into a survey instrument form.

One example of the more typical model is the employment and wage data collection program. For this program, the Census Bureau collects the data through the Current Population Survey (CPS) and the Area Wage Survey; the Bureau of Labor Statistics (BLS) contracts with the Census Bureau for the data collection, but has primary responsibility for the content of these surveys. Similar contracting arrangements with the Census Bureau are used by the U.S. Department of Transportation, the U.S. Department of Justice, the National Center for Health Statistics, and others to collect population-level information relevant to the mandates of these agencies. These contracting-based arrangements with the Census Bureau have the advantage of ensuring that responsibility for the substantive content of the data collection resides in the agency that is closest to the relevant policy concerns and substantive issues that drive the need for these data. Such an arrangement is missing in the case of the collection of nationally representative data on social welfare programs.

This mismatch of responsibility and expertise for data collection among federal agencies has hindered the collection of data for social welfare programs. A previous National Research Council panel charged with reviewing SIPP noted the weaknesses of the organizational structure and the need for the Census Bureau to seek outside input on the content and basic design of the survey. The study recommended a different management structure within the Census Bureau to produce income and program participation statistics partly because of the lack of a social welfare program data collection agency within DHHS that would have been a logical agency to sponsor the survey (National Research Council, 1993b). Because devolution has made the collection of information on welfare program participation even more difficult for national-level surveys, such as the SIPP and SPD, the need for such substantive expertise in the responsibility for these surveys is even greater. Because there is no agency in DHHS that has direct responsibility for such survey data development, this need is not being fully met.

The lack of direct administrative authority and responsibility for social welfare program data collection within DHHS has also hindered the development of administrative data for research purposes, which has become an increasingly important source of data in the state-based programmatic environment. In a number of social program areas, including TANF, states now must provide DHHS with microdata—individual case-level records with client and service characteristics. In addition to their use for program administration and program compliance, these data are also being developed for research purposes. Because these data are not explicitly collected for research purposes, a substantial effort is required to convert the data to usable research form, and these efforts have been ongoing at the state level and in various divisions of DHHS. But because they are primarily agencies for administering programs, they do not always have the resources and expertise to develop the data for research purposes. However, they are not independent from the programmatic functions of the agency, which is a crucial condition that improves the credibility of a data collection agency as being independent from political interests of the agency (National Research Council, 2001b).

A PROPOSED SYSTEM

The federal government's need to evaluate one of its major social welfare programs, TANF, is constrained by the realities of a decentralized program environment. Devolution has transferred much of the policy-making functions for welfare programs to states. As a result, federally centralized efforts to collect data for welfare program research, such as the national-level surveys, face more challenges than ever before, especially in collecting data for cross-state analyses and for measuring participation in state-based welfare programs. State-based but federally coordinated monitoring and evaluation efforts, such as the ASPE-sponsored welfare leaver studies, face challenges of comparability in defining terms and standards for data collection. Even the efforts of DHHS to collect data describing each state's policies and administrative data from states to check program compliance and assess performance of state programs are hindered by these same comparability issues.

Even though devolution gave states authority over program design, the panel concludes that it is necessary to reaffirm the leading role of the federal government to ensure that data needed to evaluate these programs and to monitor well-being of populations that may use the programs are collected. The federal government should clearly oversee national-level data sets because the benefits of information gained from these data accrue to all the states. The federal government has a role to play in state-level data sets, as well. Only the federal government is in a position to coordinate comparability across state-level data sets, which would make the state data sets much more than the sum of their parts because cross-state evaluation and research comparisons could be made. Those types of comparisons would benefit all states. Yet no single state has the resources or the incentives to undertake steps toward comparability by itself. In addition, states do not generally have the expertise in data collection that exists at the federal level. Nor would it be efficient for them to do so, for a concentration of expertise in each of the states would be redundant and wasteful. The federal government, with its concentration of such staff, is in a position to provide technical assistance and guidance to all the states in a more efficient manner.

Recommendation 6.1 The federal government should be responsible for ensuring that high-quality and comparable data on human service and social welfare programs and populations are collected so that the well-being of the low-income population can be moni-

tored and so that high-quality evaluations of the effects of welfare reform can be conducted.

While the federal government is in the best position to take the lead, cooperation with states is necessary as well. States are more in tune with the realities of program operations and thus can help improve federal data collection activities and provide up-to-date information on ground-level developments related to social welfare programs and the populations they serve. Federal data collection agencies, therefore, have much to gain from cooperation with the states. States interested in developing their own data infrastructures can also gain from cooperation with the federal government. The federal data collection agencies have more expertise in technical matters for data collection and data use than most states do. While the panel concludes that the federal government should retain responsibility for collecting high-quality data for social welfare program monitoring and evaluation, coordination and cooperation with states is a necessary and critical part of developing a data infrastructure.

Administrative Mechanisms and Functions

The need for methodological leadership to address the complex data collection, linkage, storage, and access needs for social program data leads the panel to recommend that alternative administrative mechanisms for lodging responsibility and authority for social welfare program data collection in some entity within DHHS be considered. The panel does not offer a blueprint of such a structure, for it does not have the expertise, time, resources, and charge to do so. There are many alternatives. For example, the functions that the panel believes need to be performed could be placed within an existing statistical agency in DHHS, such as National Center for Health Statistics. Alternatively, a new statistical agency within DHHS could be created to handle social welfare program data. Another option would be to expand one of the other agencies within DHHS with increased statistical staff and to assign that agency the responsibility for working with both federal agencies and states in developing and maintaining data. Which option is chosen will require careful consideration and joint discussions between all the agencies and departments involved. Reassignment of functions from one agency to another would be required, and departments and agencies outside DHHS would have to be involved because they have authority over other welfare programs (e.g., the Departments of Labor, Agriculture, and Education, to name only three).

The programs whose responsibility and authority for data collection would be assigned should also be considered by the relevant parties. There are human service and social welfare programs other than TANF that could be considered— excluding those concerned specifically with health programs or programs for the aged. Such programs include child care, child support enforcement, child protective services (foster care and abuse and neglect reporting), child developmental disabilities programs, Low-Income Home Energy Assistance Program, and community service programs. These programs would all be candidates for inclusion in a centralization and reorganization of responsibility and authority for data collection.[1]

Whichever organizational entity is assigned these functions, the entity should be separate from other programmatic and policy agencies within DHHS. Independence is required in order to confer credibility of the data with both data suppliers and data users. As noted elsewhere (National Research Council, 2001b; Hotz et al., 1998), the integrity of data can be compromised in situations in which the same agency that collects the data is also required to use the data to administer sanctions and other administrative actions. In order to maintain the integrity of the data, the agency needs to maintain a separation from real and perceived political partisanship and ensure data providers that their data will be kept confidential.

Data needs for monitoring the well-being of populations relevant to these programs and for evaluating these programs are on-going and will continue to change as the programs change. The panel believes that the short- and long-term data needs will be best met if some organizational entity within DHHS is given responsibility and authority for data collection activities.

Recommendation 6.2 The panel recommends that an organizational entity be identified or created within DHHS and that this entity be assigned direct administrative responsibility and authority for carrying out statistical functions and data collection for social welfare programs and the populations they serve. The entity should also coordinate data collection and analysis activities between states and the federal government.

Examples of Other Agencies

Although the panel cannot be more specific on the type of entity to be assigned responsibility or its programmatic coverage, the panel can do two things. First, in this section we describe how these other statistical agencies operate to illustrate how the functions that are required for human service and social welfare programs are addressed in other areas. In the next section we list the functions that need to be performed by the organizational entity, whatever form it takes.

In the area of health, the U.S. Department of Health and Human Services has the National Center for Health Statistics (NCHS); in the area of employment and earnings, the U.S. Department of Labor has the Bureau of Labor Statistics (BLS);

---

[1]Another welfare-related set of programs within DHHS that have more of a health orientation include those that deal with mental health, developmental disabilities, and substance abuse.

and in the area of education programs, the U.S. Department of Education has the National Center for Education Statistics (NCES). The data collection functions needed to be fulfilled for human service and social welfare programs are quite similar to those performed by these agencies. Indeed, whatever organizational unit within DHHS is assigned the new functions would necessarily work with these agencies and others. One reason for establishing separate statistical structures is the need to involve other departments and agencies in data collection and development activities (National Research Council, 2001b). For social welfare programs data, there is a need to coordinate across many departments and levels of government.

NCHS was established administratively in 1960 (by law in 1974) with a broad mandate to collect, analyze, and disseminate data on a wide range of health-related topics. To meet its mission of monitoring the nation's health, NCHS fields a complementary set of data collection mechanisms to meet current and emerging health data needs. NCHS coordinates the national vital statistics system, working with states to produce the nation's official birth and death statistics. NCHS also supports the development of state and local data through the use of telephone survey methodology linked to existing household surveys in conjunction with the Healthy People process, which sets and tracks progress in reaching health objectives at the national, state, and local levels; and through research and collaborative efforts to adapt and apply national data sets and methodology to state-based applications.

The BLS is a federal statistical agency that collects or sponsors the collection of, processes, analyzes, and disseminates statistical data on labor markets and related topics to the public, Congress, other federal agencies, state and local governments, business, and labor. The BLS has long-standing relationships with cooperating state agencies in the production of statistical data, specifically to produce economic statistics on such topics as employment and worker safety and health. The BLS contracts with the Census Bureau to conduct several surveys, for example the CPS, which is used to produce the monthly unemployment statistics. Timeliness of these data is often of utmost importance, since the unemployment indicators are required for monitoring the national economy. Working together, both agencies are able to meet the timeliness demands as the unemployment figures must be released within 22 days after the reference period for which they are collected.

NCES has overall responsibility for planning, design, statistical analysis, reporting, and dissemination of elementary, secondary, and postsecondary education, and library surveys at the national, state, and local levels. Its mandate is also to ensure that statistical quality and confidentiality are maintained. NCES sets the statistical standards, administers technology support programs, and provides state-of-the-art technology and statistical support to federal and nonfederal organizations and entities involved in statistical work in support of the Department of Education. In addition, the staff develops and operates a system of licensing for individuals and organizations to acquire access to confidential data for statistical purposes.

A notable commonality in the functions of these three agencies is an explicit mandate to coordinate activities with state counterparts and, in many instances, provide funding support for state data collection.[2] NCHS operates the cooperative federal-state vital statistics program referred to above. BLS cooperatively works with state employment security agencies to collect and provide data for programs such as Current Employment Statistics and Local Area Unemployment Statistics. Under this cooperative agreement, the states collect the data and provide them to the BLS, while BLS provides most of the funding for the data collection and defines the procedures for collecting the data, the data are then useful and comparable for state-level estimates. NCES works cooperatively with states to produce comparable data on elementary and secondary school statistics. Although NCES does not provide funding to states for this data collection, it does have funding for a technical assistance program for helping states produce high quality data that are comparable and timely. NCES also sponsors an annual data conference on educational statistics in conjunction with its National Forum on Education Statistics, where representatives from all states and from federal agencies with interests in educational statistics meet to discuss data collection activities.

Most of these agencies and others contract out survey data collection efforts to the Census Bureau or to private survey organizations. Examples of surveys contracted out to private organizations include the National Survey of Family Growth, which is contracted out by the NCHS; the Child Welfare Panel which is contracted out by ACF; the Early Childhood Longitudinal Study cohorts and the National Education Longitudinal Survey, which are contracted out by NCES; and parts of the Medical Expenditures Panel Survey, which are contracted out by the Agency for Healthcare Research and Quality. Many of these surveys involve complex longitudinal designs with which private survey organizations have more experience than the Census Bureau.

State data collection and coordination functions must necessarily be a part of the administrative responsibility for human service and social welfare programs. As in all federal-state cooperative efforts, this will create a need for organizational entities at the state level to be responsible for coordination of data collection activities with the federal government and with other states. Cooperatively developing data programs is necessary, and the DHHS entity should provide both technical assistance and some funding for affiliated state statistical centers. Indeed, such a federal-state program may require the creation of new state agencies to work with the federal government and to ensure that state-level data relevant to human service and social welfare programs are made available. One possible

---

[2]See Ruddick (1996) for a summary of federal-state data collection partnerships.

approach is for the federal entity to create a "benefits reporting area" or "human services reporting area" composed of a few states with well-developed social welfare and human services data systems who would agree to jointly work towards a common framework for data collection and reporting. Over time, more states could be added to the reporting area. Federal birth and death registration data developed this way; first with a few states and with federal financial assistance, and then gradually expanding to include all states. Other possible arrangements for state-level data collection systems should be considered as well.

The Functions Needed

We provide here an itemization of the functions that would need to be performed by whatever new or existing organizational entity within DHHS is given responsibility and authority to carry out the mission.

National Surveys   The organizational entity that is assigned responsibility would be the primary sponsor of the national surveys used to monitor and evaluate human service and social welfare programs and, in general, content related to the low income population. It would contract with the Census Bureau or with private survey organizations to conduct these surveys. These include the Survey of Income and Program Participation and the Survey of Program Dynamics, and perhaps parts of other surveys, like the topical modules in the Current Population Survey that cover social welfare program topics. As the entity with lead responsibility for content and design of these surveys, it would also work with other agencies that have interests in these surveys. It would also explore the linkage of national-level administrative data to the national survey data that address social welfare program topics.

Administrative Data   The development and management of a cooperative welfare and social statistics data and information effort with the states would also be a needed function. Existing or new state statistical agencies should be full partners in this effort. Funding or financial incentives for the states to provide data to the federal agency and determining the form and content of the data submission should also be part of the responsibilities of the federal authority. Periodic reporting would be part of this program. Benefits Reporting Areas should be considered.

The development of standards for the use of administrative data for research purposes is an additional needed function. These standards should include definitions of services and benefit units, recipients and case members, data formats, and processes for documenting administrative data files.

In order to promote sharing of data resources for welfare and social statistics research and evaluation, coordination with other federal and state data collection agencies would also be required.

Leadership in advancing the use of and accessibility to all data provided by the states to DHHS for monitoring and social welfare program evaluation purposes is another important function.

Technical Assistance Another need is the provision of technical assistance to states on the use of administrative data and on the development, conduct, and analysis of surveys. The technical assistance could be used as a tool to promote the goals of comparability, improved data quality, data linkages, and data security and access.

Reports The federal entity should have responsibility for producing periodic reports on topics related to social welfare program utilization and the well-being of those who utilize these programs. One set of reports would be based on the data submitted by the states through the cooperative data collection effort mentioned above. It should also collect and publish social welfare program rules and policies, particularly for TANF and related separate state programs, for every state and every sub-state area where appropriate.

Data Archive for Continuing Research Needs A leadership role is needed in developing data archives on particular topics for use in social welfare program evaluation and research. Archives may include state surveys and administrative data, for which the agency would be responsible for preparing the surveys or administrative data for use by researchers. Maintaining an archive of welfare policies and programs description data throughout the states, and where relevant, in local areas, should also be a responsibility.

The principles and practices of statistical agencies are described more fully in National Research Council (2001b). The panel strongly believes that following these principles and practices is a necessary condition for addressing our recommendations regarding data collection.

A federal-state data collection system, as the one proposed above, will not develop overnight. It will require strong leadership and sustained support at both the federal and state level. If the trend of devolution persists, the need for and benefits from such a system will continue to grow.

References

Abbey, C.W., V. Burke, A. Butler, C. Devere, G. Falk, T. Gabe, M. Gish, S. Harper, C. Solomon-Fears, M.A Wolfe
  2000   Welfare Reform: Financial Eligibility Rules and Cash Assistance Amounts under TANF. Congressional Research Service. Washington, DC: U.S. Library of Congress.

Acs, G., and P. Loprest
  2001   Studies of welfare leavers: Methods, findings, and contributions to the policy process in *Data Collection and Research Issues for Studies of Welfare Populations*. Panel on Data and Methods for Measuring the Effects of Changes in Social Welfare Programs, C.F. Citro, R. Moffitt and M. Ver Ploeg, eds. Committee on National Statistics. Washington, DC: National Academy Press.

Ahn, J., D. Fogarty, S. Kraley, F. Lai, and L. Deppman
  2000   *A Study of Washington State TANF Departures and Welfare Reform: Welfare Reform and Findings from Administrative Data, Final Report.* Olympia, WA: Washington Department of Social and Health Services.

Barth, R., E. Locklin, S. Cuccaro-Alamin, and B. Needell
  2001   Administrative data on the well-being of children on and off welfare. In *Data Collection and Research Issues for Studies of Welfare Populations*. Panel on Data and Methods for Measuring the Effects of Changes in Social Welfare Programs, C.F. Citro, R. Moffitt, and M. Ver Ploeg, eds. Committee on National Statistics. Washington, DC: National Academy Press.

Bass, L.E., and D. Downs
  1999   What Can the SPD Adolescent SAQ Tell Us About the Well-being of Adolescents in the Aftermath of the 1996 Welfare Reform Act? Paper presented at the Population Association of America Annual Meeting in New York City. Available: http://www.sipp.census.gov/spd/workpaper/paa3799.htm

Bavier, R.
  1999   An Early Look at the Effects of Welfare Reform. Unpublished paper. Office of Management and Budget. Washington, DC.

Bloom, D.
    1999   *Welfare Time Limits: An Interim Report Card.* New York: Manpower Demonstration Research Corporation.
Bollinger, C.R., and M.H. David
    2001   Estimation with response error and non-response: Food stamp participation in the SIPP. *Journal of Business and Economic Statistics* 19(2).
Brady, H., S.A Grand, M.A. Powell, and W. Schink
    2001   Access and Confidentiality Issues with Administrative Data. In *Data Collection and Research Issues for Studies of Welfare Populations.* Panel on Data and Methods for Measuring the Effects of Changes in Social Welfare Programs, C.F. Citro, R. Moffitt, and M. Ver Ploeg, eds. Committee on National Statistics. Washington, DC: National Academy Press.
Brauner, S., and P. Loprest
    1999   *Where Are They Now? What States' Studies of People Who Left Welfare Tell Us.* Paper Series A, No. A-32. Washington, DC: Urban Institute.
Brick, P.D.
    2000   A Descriptive Review of Ten Major Surveys. Urban Institute, Washington, DC. (January 19).
Burke, V., T. Gabe, M. Gish, G. Falk, C. Solomon-Fears, and K. Spar
    1999   *Welfare Reform: State Programs Under the Block Grant for Temporary Assistance for Needy Families.* Congressional Research Service. Washington, DC.: U.S. Library of Congress.
Burtless, G.
    1995   The case for randomized field trials in economic and policy research. *Journal of Economic Perspectives* 9(Spring) 63-84.
Cancian, M., R. Haveman, T. Kaplan, D. Meyer, and B. Wolfe
    1999   Work, earnings, and well-being after welfare. In *Economic Conditions and Welfare Reform*, S. Danziger, ed. Kalamazoo, MI: Upjohn Institute.
Cancian, M., R. Haveman, D. Meyer, and B. Wolfe
    2000   *Before and After TANF: The Economic Well-Being of Women Leaving Welfare.* Special Report #77. Institute for Research on Poverty. Madison, WI: University of Wisconsin.
Cantor, D., and P. Cunningham
    2001   Methods for obtaining high response rates in telephone surveys. In *Data Collection and Research Issues for Studies of Welfare Populations.* Panel on Data and Methods for Measuring the Effects of Changes in Social Welfare Programs, C.F. Citro, R. Moffitt, and M. Ver Ploeg, eds. Committee on National Statistics. Washington, DC: National Academy Press.
Corbett, T., and M.C. Lennon
    Forth-   *Implementation Analysis: An Evaluation Approach Whose Time Has Come.* Washing-
    coming   ton, DC.: The Urban Institute.
Council of Economic Advisers
    1997   Technical Report: Explaining the Decline in Welfare Receipt: 1993-1996. U.S. Council of Economic Advisers. URL: http://clinton4.nara.gov/WH/EOP/CEA/Welfare/
    1999   The Effects of Welfare Policy and the Economic Expansion on Welfare Caseloads: An Update. Technical Report, August 3, Office of The President. Washington, DC.
Cyphers, G., and S. Kinsella
    2000   Harnessing the Power of Data: State TANF Agencies' Use of Administrative Data for Policy and Program Management. Paper presented at the National Association for Welfare Research and Statistics 40th Annual Workshop. August 1, Scottsdale, AZ.

Danziger, S., M. Corcoran, S. Danziger, C. Heflin, A. Kalil, J. Levine, D. Rosen, K, Seefeldt, K. Siefert,, and R. Tolman
  2000 Barriers to the Employment of Welfare Recipients. Chapter 8 in *Prosperity for All? The Economic Boom and African Americans*, R. Cherry and W.M. Rodgers, III, eds. NY: Russell Sage Foundation.

Dawid, A.P.
  2000 Causal inference without counterfactuals. *Journal of the American Statistical Association* 95:407-424.

Dehejia, R., and S. Wahba
  1999 Causal effects in nonexperimental studies: Reevaluating the evaluation of training programs. *Journal of the American Statistical Association* 94:1053-1062.

Downs, B.A., and L.E. Bass
  1999 The Survey of Program Dynamics: A New Source of Data to Explore the Effects of the 1996 Welfare Reform Act on Adolescents. Paper presented at the American Sociological Association Annual Meeting, Chicago, IL. Available: http://www.sipp.census.gov/spd/workpaper/asa99.htm

Ellwood, D.
  2000 The impact of the earned income tax credit and social policy reforms on work, marriage, and living arrangements. *National Tax Journal* 53(4)(part 2):1063-1106.

Ellwood, D., and M.J. Bane
  1994 Understanding welfare dynamics In *Welfare Realities: From Rhetoric to Reform*, M.J. Bane and D. Ellwood, eds. Cambridge, MA: Harvard University Press.

Federal Register
  1999 Temporary Assistance for Needy Families Program (TANF): Final Rule. Administration for Children and Families, U.S. Department of Health and Human Services. Vol. 64, No. 69. Monday, April 12.

Figlio, D., and J. Ziliak
  1999 Welfare reform, the business cycle, and the decline in AFDC caseloads In *Economic Conditions and Welfare Reform*, S. Danziger, ed. Kalamazoo, MI: Upjohn Institute.

Fogarty, D., and S. Kraley
  2000 *A Study of Washington State TANF Leavers and TANF Recipients: Findings from Administrative Data and the Telephone Survey: Summary Report*. Olympia: Washington State.

Fraker, T., and R. Maynard
  1987 The adequacy of comparison group designs for evaluation of employment-related programs. *Journal of Human Resources* 22:194-227.

Friedlander, D., and P. K. Robins
  1995 Evaluating program evaluation: New evidence on commonly used nonexperimental methods. *American Economic Review* 85:923-937.

Goerge, R.M., and B.J. Lee
  2001 Matching and cleaning administrative data. In *Data Collection and Research Issues for Studies of Welfare Populations*. Panel on Data and Methods for Measuring the Effects of Changes in Social Welfare Programs, C.F. Citro, R. Moffitt and M. Ver Ploeg, eds. Committee on National Statistics. Washington, DC: National Academy Press.

Gordon, A., J. Jacobson, and T. Fraker
  1996 *Approaches to Evaluation Welfare Reform: Lessons from Five State Demonstrations*. Washington, DC: Mathematica Policy Research.

Greene, W.H.
  2000 *Econometric Analysis*. 4th Edition. Englewood Cliffs, NJ: Prentice Hall.

Groves, R.M., and M.P. Couper
   2001   Designing surveys acknowledging nonresponse. In *Data Collection and Research Issues for Studies of Welfare Populations*. Panel on Data and Methods for Measuring the Effects of Changes in Social Welfare Programs, C.F. Citro, R. Moffitt, and M. Ver Ploeg, eds. Committee on National Statistics. Washington, DC: National Academy Press.

Hahn, J.
   1998   On the role of the propensity score in efficient semi-parametric estimation of average treatment effects. *Econometrica* 66:315-332.

Heckman, J., and V.J. Hotz
   1989   Choosing among alternative nonexperimental methods for estimating the impact of social programs: The case of manpower training (in applications and case studies). *Journal of the American Statistical Association* 84(408):862-874.

Heckman, J.J., and J.A. Smith
   1995   Assessing the case for social experiments. *Journal of Economic Perspectives* Spring (9):85-110.

Heckman, J.J., H. Ichimura, J. Smith, and P. Todd
   1998   Characterizing selection bias using experimental data. *Econometrica* 66:1017-1098.

Heckman, J.J., H. Ichimura, and P. Todd
   1997   Matching as an econometric evaluation estimator. *Review of Economic Studies* 65:261-294.

Hill, M.A., and T. Main
   1998   *Is Welfare Working? The Massachusetts Reforms Three Years Later.* Boston, MA: Pioneer Institute.

Hofferth, S., S. Stanhope, and K. Harris
   2000   *Exiting Welfare in the 1990s: Did Public Policy Influence Recipients' Behavior.* Ann Arbor, MI: Institute for Social Research, University of Michigan.

Hotz, V.J., R. Goerge, J. Balzekas, and F.Margolin, eds.
   1998   *Administrative Data for Policy-Relevant Research: Assessment of Current Utility and Recommendations for Development.* Report of the Advisory Panel on Research Uses of Administrative Data. Evanston, IL: Northwestern University/University of Chicago Joint Center for Poverty Research.

Hotz, V.J., R. Schoeni, and N. Lim
   2000   An Examination of the Reporting of Welfare Benefits and Income in the Survey of Income and Program Participation (SIPP) in California Using Matched Administrative Records. Proposal to the Assistant Secretary for Planning and Evaluation and the Administration for Children and Families of the U.S. Department of Health and Human Services.

Hotz, V.J., and J.K. Scholz
   2001   Measuring employment and income for low-income populations with administrative and survey data. In *Data Collection and Research Issues for Studies of Welfare Populations*. Panel on Data and Methods for Measuring the Effects of Changes in Social Welfare Programs, C.F. Citro, R. Moffitt, and M. Ver Ploeg, eds. Committee on National Statistics. Washington, DC: National Academy Press.

Institute for Public Affairs and School of Social Work
   2000   *Illinois Study of Former TANF Clients: Final Report Executive Summary.* Springfield and Champaign: University of Illinois, and University of Illinois.

Issacs, J., and M. Lyon
   2000   A Cross-State Examination of Families Leaving Welfare: Findings from the ASPE - Funded Leavers Studies. Paper presented at the National Association for Welfare Research and Statistics, Scottsdale, AZ.

Kalton, G., and D. Kasprzyk
   1986   The treatment of missing survey data. *Survey Methodology* 12(1):1-16.
Lalonde, R.
   1986   Evaluating the Econometric Evaluations of Training Programs with Experimental Data. *American Economic Review* 76:604-620.
Little, R.J.A., and D.B. Rubin
   1987   *Statistical Analysis with Missing Data.* New York: Wiley.
Loprest, P.
   1999   *Families Who Left Welfare: Who Are They and How Are They Doing?* ANF Discussion Paper. Washington, DC: Urban Institute.
Loprest, P., and S. Zedlewski
   1999   *Current and Former Welfare Recipients: How Do They Differ?* DP 99-17. Washington, DC: Urban Institute.
Manski, C.F.
   1995   *Identification Problems in the Social Sciences.* Cambridge, MA: Harvard University Press.
Mathiowetz, N., C. Brown, and J. Bound
   2001   Measurement error in surveys of the low-income population. In *Data Collection and Research Issues for Studies of Welfare Populations.* Panel on Data and Methods for Measuring the Effects of Changes in Social Welfare Programs, C.F. Citro, R. Moffitt, and M. Ver Ploeg, eds. Committee on National Statistics. Washington, DC: National Academy Press.
Marquis, K.H., and J.C. Moore
   1990   Measurement errors in SIPP program reports. *Proceedings of the Bureau of Census 1990 Annual Research Conference*, 721-745. Washington, DC: U.S. Department of Commerce.
Medley, B., M.J. Edelhoch, L.S. Martin, and Q. Lin
   1999   Characteristics of Upwardly Mobile Ex-Recipients. Unpublished paper. South Carolina Department of Social Services, Columbia, SC.
Meyer, B.
   1995   Natural and quasi-experiments in economics *Journal of Business and Economic Statistics* 13:151-161.
Meyer, B.D., and D.T. Rosenbaum
   1999   *Welfare, the Earned Income Tax Credit, and the Labor Supply of Single Mothers,* NBER Working Paper No. 7363, September. Boston, MA: National Bureau of Economic Research.
   2000   *Making Single Mothers Work: Recent Tax and Welfare Policy and Its Effects.* NBER Working Paper No. 7491. Boston, MA: National Bureau of Economic Research.
Meyer, D., and M. Cancian
   1998   Economic well-being following an exit from aid to families with dependent children *Journal of Marriage and the Family* 60:479-492.
Michel, R.
   1980   *Participation Rates in the Aid to Families with Dependent Children Program, Part I.* Working Paper 1387-02. Washington, DC: Urban Institute.
Moffitt, R.A.
   1992   Incentive effects in the U.S. welfare system: A review. *Journal of Economic Literature* 30(1):1-61.
   1999   The effect of pre-PRWORA waivers on AFDC caseloads and female earnings, income and labor force behavior. In *Economic Conditions and Welfare Reform*, S.H. Danziger, ed. Kalamazoo, MI: W.E. Upjohn Institute for Employment Research.

2001   Experienced-based measures of heterogeneity in the welfare caseload. In *Data Collection and Research Issues for Studies of Welfare Populations*. Panel on Data and Methods for Measuring the Effects of Changes in Social Welfare Programs, C.F. Citro, R. Moffitt, and M. Ver Ploeg, eds. Committee on National Statistics. Washington, DC: National Academy Press.

Mohadjer, L., and G.H. Choudhry
2001   Adjusting for Missing Data in Low-Income Surveys. In *Data Collection and Research Issues for Studies of Welfare Populations*. C. Citro, R. Moffitt and M. Ver Ploeg, eds. Panel on Data and Methods for Measuring the Effects of Changes in Social Welfare Programs, Committee on National Statistics. Washington, DC: National Academy Press.

Moore, J.C., Stinson, L.L., and Welniak, E.J.
1997   *Income Measurement Error in Surveys: A Review*. Statistical Research Report. Washington, DC: U.S. Census Bureau.

Mueser, P., J. Hotchkiss, C. King, P. Rokicki, and D. Stevens
2000   *The Welfare Caseload, Economic Growth and Welfare-to-Work Policies: An Analysis of Five Urban Areas*. Columbia, MO: University of Missouri.

National Research Council
1991   *Improving Information for Social Policy Decisions: The Uses of Microsimulation Modeling, Vol. 1, Review and Recommendations*. Panel to Evaluate Microsimulation Models for Social Welfare Programs, C.F. Citro and E.A. Hanushek, eds. Committee on National Statistics. Washington, DC: National Academy Press.

1992   *Combining Information: Statistical Issues and Opportunities for Research*. Panel on Statistical Issues and Opportunities for Research in the Combination of Information, D. Draper, D.P. Gaver, P.K. Goel, J.B. Greenhouse, L.V. Hedges, C.N. Morris, J.R. Tucker, and C.M. Waternaux, eds. Committee on Applied and Theoretical Statistics. Washington, DC: National Academy Press.

1993a   *Private Lives and Public Policies: Confidentiality and Accessibility of Government Statistics*. Panel on Confidentiality and Data Access, G.T. Duncan, T.B. Jabine, and V.A. de Wolf, eds. Committee on National Statistics. Washington, DC: National Academy Press.

1993b   *The Future of the Survey of Income and Program Participation*. Panel to Evaluate the Survey of Income and Program Participation, C.F. Citro and G. Kalton, eds. Washington, DC: National Academy Press

1995   *Measuring Poverty: A New Approach. Panel on Poverty and Family Assistance: Concepts, Information Needs, and Measurement Methods*. C.F. Citro and R.T. Michael, eds. Committee on National Statistics. Washington, DC: National Academy Press.

1999   *Evaluating Welfare Reform: A Framework and Review of Current Work, Interim Report*. Panel on Data and Methods for Measuring the Effects of Changes in Social Welfare Programs, R. Moffitt and M. Ver Ploeg, eds. Committee on National Statistics. Washington, DC: National Academy Press.

2000a   *Improving Access to and Confidentiality of Research Data: Report of a Workshop*. Committee on National Statistics, C. Mackie and N. Bradburn, eds. Washington, DC: National Academy Press.

2000b   *Small-Area Income and Poverty Estimates: Priorities for 2000 and Beyond*. Panel on Estimates of Poverty for Small Geographic Areas, C.F. Citro and G. Kalton, eds. Committee on National Statistics. Washington, DC: National Academy Press.

2001a   *Data Collection and Research Issues for Studies of Welfare Populations*. Panel on Data and Methods for Measuring the Effects of Changes in Social Welfare Programs, C.F. Citro, R. Moffitt, and M. Ver Ploeg, eds. Committee on National Statistics. Washington, DC: National Academy Press.

2001b *Principles and Practices for a Federal Statistical Agency. Second Edition.* Committee on National Statistics, Margaret E. Martin, Miron L. Straf, and Constance F. Citro, eds. Washington, DC: National Academy Press.

Newman, K.
2001 The right (soft) stuff: Qualitative methods and the study of welfare reform. In *Data Collection and Research Issues for Studies of Welfare Populations.* Panel on Data and Methods for Measuring the Effects of Changes in Social Welfare Programs, C.F. Citro, R. Moffitt, and M. Ver Ploeg, eds. Committee on National Statistics. Washington, DC: National Academy Press.

Nusser, S.M., C.N. Fletcher, and D.G. Anderson
2000 The Iowa Survey of Program Dynamics Feasibility Study. Unpublished paper. Iowa State University.

Parrott, S.
1998 *Welfare Recipients Who Find Jobs: What Do We Know About Their Employment and Earnings?* Washington, DC: Center on Budget and Policy Priorities.

Primus, W., L. Rawlings, K. Larin, and K. Porter
1999 The Initial Impacts of Welfare Reform on the Incomes of Single-Mother Families. Center for Budget and Policy Priorities (August).

Quint, Janet, K. Edin, M.L. Buck, B. Fink, Y.C. Padilla, O. Simmons-Hewitt, and M.E. Valmont
1999 *Big Cities and Welfare Reform: Early Implementation and Ethnographic Findings from the Project on Devolution and Urban Change.* New York: Manpower Demonstration Research Corporation.

Research Triangle Institute
1983 *Final Report: Evaluation of the 1981 AFDC Amendments.* Research Triangle Park, NC: Research Triangle Institute.

Robins, J., A. Rotnitzky, and D. Scharfstein
1999 Sensitivity analysis for selection bias and unmeasured confounding in missing data and causal models. Chapter 1 in *Statistical Models in Epidemiology: The Environment and Clinical Trials*, M.E. Halloran and D. Berry, eds. New York: Springer-Verlag.

Rosenbaum, P.
1995 *Observational Studies.* New York: Springer-Verlag.

Rosenbaum P.R., and D.B. Rubin
1983 Assessing sensitivity to an unobserved binary covariate in an observational study with a binary outcome. *Journal of the Royal Statistical Society, Series B* 11:212-218.
1983 The central role of the propensity score in observational studies for causal effects. *Biometrika* 70:41-55.

Ruddick, M.
1996 Characteristics of Federal-State Data Collection Systems: Perspectives from Federal and State Agencies. Paper prepared for the Committee on National Statistics, Washington, DC.

Safir, A., F. Scheuren, and K. Wang
2001 *National Survey of America's Families: Survey Methods and Data Reliability, 1997 and 1999.* Washington, DC: The Urban Institute. Available: http://newfederalism.urban.org/nsaf/survey-methods.html

Schoeni, R., and R. Blank
2000 *What Has Welfare Reform Accomplished? Impacts on Welfare Participation, Employment, Income, Poverty, and Family Structure.* Working Paper 7627. Boston, MA: National Bureau of Economic Research.

Singer, E., and D. Kulka
    2001   Paying Respondents for Survey Participation. In *Data Collection and Research Issues for Studies of Welfare Populations*. Panel on Data and Methods for Measuring the Effects of Changes in Social Welfare Programs, C. Citro, R. Moffitt, and M. Ver Ploeg, eds. Committee on National Statistics. Washington, DC: National Academy Press.
South Carolina Department of Social Services
    2000   Survey of Former Family Independence Program Clients: Cases Closed During April Through September 1998. Unpublished paper, Columbia.
Stevens, D.
    2000   Welfare, Employment, and Earnings. Memorandum prepared for the Panel on Data and Methods for Measuring the Effects of Changes in Social Welfare Programs, Committee on National Statistics. University of Baltimore, MD.
Thornberry, O.T., and J.T. Massey
    1988   Trends in United States telephone coverage across time and subgroups. Pp. 25-50 in Groves, R. M., Biemer, P.P., Lyberg, L.E., Massey, J.T., Nicholls, W.L. and Waksberg, J., (eds) *Telephone Survey Methodology*. New York: Wiley.
Tweedie, J., and D. Reichert
    1998   *Tracking Recipients After They Leave Welfare: Summaries of State Follow-Up Studies*. Washington, DC: National Conference of State Legislatures.
Tweedie, J., D. Reichert, and M. O'Connor
    1999   *Tracking Recipients After They Leave Welfare*. Washington, DC: National Conference of State Legislatures.
UC Data
    1999   *An Inventory of Research Uses of Administrative Data in Social Services Programs in the United States, 1998*. Berkeley: University of California.
U.S. Census Bureau
    1998   *Survey of Income and Program Participation Quality Profile 1998, 3rd Edition*. Washington, DC: U.S. Department of Commerce.
U.S. Census Bureau and Bureau of Labor Statistics
    2000   *Current Population Survey Design and Methodology*. Technical Paper 63. Washington, DC: U.S. Department of Commerce and U.S. Department of Labor.
U.S. General Accounting Office
    1984   *An Evaluation of the 1981 AFDC Changes: Initial Analyses*. Washington, DC: U.S. Government Printing Office.
    1999a   *Welfare Reform: Information on Former Recipients' Status*. GAO/HEHS-99-48. Washington, DC: U.S. Government Printing Office.
    1999b   *Welfare Reform: Assessing the Effectiveness of Various Welfare-to-Work Approaches*. Washington, DC: U.S. Government Printing Office.
Ver Ploeg, M.
    2001   Pre-exit Benefit Receipt and Employment Histories and Post-Exit Outcomes of Welfare Leavers. In *Data Collection and Research Issues for Studies of Welfare Populations*. Panel on Data and Methods for Measuring the Effects of Changes in Social Welfare Programs, C.F. Citro, R. Moffitt, and M. Ver Ploeg, eds. Committee on National Statistics. Washington, DC: National Academy Press.
W.E. Upjohn Institute for Employment Research
    1999   *Economic Conditions and Welfare Reform*. S.H. Danziger, ed. Kalamazoo, MI: W.E. Upjohn Institute for Employment Research.
Wallace, G., and R. Blank
    1999   What goes up must come down? Explaining recent changes in public assistance caseloads. In *Economic Conditions and Welfare Reform*, S. Danziger, ed.. Kalamazoo, MI: Upjohn Institute.

Weinberg, D.H., and S.S. Shipp
    2000   The Survey of Program Dynamics: A Mid-Term Status Report. U.S. Census Bureau. Available: http://www.sipp.census.gov/spd/workpaper/summary10.htm#N_1_

Weiss, C., and B. Bailar
    2001   High response rates for low income populations in in-person surveys. In *Data Collection and Research Issues for Studies of Welfare Populations*. Panel on Data and Methods for Measuring the Effects of Changes in Social Welfare Programs, C.F. Citro, R. Moffitt, and M. Ver Ploeg, eds. Committee on National Statistics. Washington, DC: National Academy Press.

Zedlewski, S.
    1999   *Work Activity and Obstacles to Work Among TANF Recipients.* Working Papers B-2. Washington, DC: Urban Institute.

Ziliak, J., D. Figlio, E. Davis, and L. Connolly
    1997   *Accounting for the Decline in AFDC Caseloads: Welfare Reform or Economic Growth?* DP 1151-97. Madison, WI: Institute for Research on Poverty, University of Wisconsin.

Appendix A

Major Current Welfare-Related Research Sponsored by the U.S. Department of Health and Human Services

This appendix presents two tables that summarize the ongoing research programs of the Office of the Assistant Secretary for Planning and Evaluation (ASPE) and the Administration for Children and Families (ACF). These two agencies within the Department of Health and Human Services (DHHS) support research work on welfare programs and the well-being of the populations they serve. Table A-1 describes ASPE-sponsored studies, and Table A-2 describes ACF-sponsored studies. There is some overlap between the two as several projects are jointly sponsored.

The tables are organized into broad classifications by the type of study: descriptive and monitoring studies; studies of welfare leavers, divertees and related groups; studies that use experimental evaluation methods; implementation and process studies; program description data; other studies that often have multiple purposes (and so do not fit easily into one category); and projects that are focused on data development and providing technical assistance for data or methodological improvements.

TABLE A-1 Major Welfare-Related Research Sponsored by the Office of the Assistant Secretary for Planning and Evaluation

Project Title	Purpose	Jurisdictions Covered
Descriptive and Monitoring Studies		
Contingent Employment Among the Low-Income and Low-Skilled	Use CPS and other relevant data to describe the prevalence of contingent employment among welfare and low-income populations.	All states
Grants and Technical Assistance to Advance States' Child Indicators Initiatives	Promote state efforts to develop and monitor indicators of the health and well-being of children in their states and to institutionalize this monitoring effort in the states.	13 states: AK, DE, FL, GA, HA, ME, MD, MN, NY, RI, UT, VT, WV
Indicators of Welfare Dependence	Annual publication of indicators of dependence on public welfare and cash assistance programs.	All states
Los Angeles Study of Families and Communities (RAND)	ASPE is providing support to this longitudinal survey of families, children and their neighborhoods to collect information on health insurance coverage and health status among children and families.	Los Angeles
Project on Devolution and Urban Change (Manpower Demonstration Research Corporation [MDRC])	ASPE is providing support to this multipurpose and multimethod study.	Cleveland, Miami, Los Angeles, Philadelphia
Transition Events in the Dynamics of Poverty	Describe the dynamics of entry and exit to and from poverty for different populations such as single working-age adults, children, families and the elderly. Also describe the extent to which different events account for exit from and entry to poverty.	All states
Trends in the Demand for Emergency Services Providers	Describe patterns of usage of emergency assistance services (e.g., homeless shelters and food banks) between 1993-2000, during the economic expansion and before and after PRWORA.	Various sites across country

Trends in the Well-Being of Children and Youth	Annual report on trends in indicators of economic well-being of children and youth.	All states
Trends in the Well-Being of Low-Income Americans	Reference book describing trends in income, poverty, and other economic measures of the low income population over time.	All states
Understanding the Declines in the Teen Birth Rate	Use data from National Survey of Family Growth to describe data on sexual activity, partner characteristics and contraceptive use for women who were teens in 1995. Simulation models will try to decipher what factors are associated with teen pregnancy.	National
Welfare Reform, the Economic and Health Status of Immigrants, and the Organizations that Serve Them (Urban Institute)	Study of immigrant families and their communities.	Los Angeles and New York

Studies of Welfare Leavers, Divertees, and Related Groups

Effect of Job Accessibility and Neighborhood Characteristics on the Employment Stability of Welfare Leavers in an Urban Labor Market (Case Western Reserve University)	Examine post-TANF exit employment, earnings and wage trajectories over a 13-month period of women leaving welfare. Includes individual level data, local labor market data, and measures of neighborhood distress.	Cleveland metropolitan area
Employment, Earnings, and Recidivism: How Do Entrants to TANF Differ from Entrants to AFDC (Washington University)	Compare outcomes of five cohorts of welfare recipients. Pre-TANF, early TANF and later TANF cohorts will be examined. Employment stability, earnings, welfare exits and recidivism will be examined. Uses state- and county-level administrative data.	North Carolina
Employment Opportunities for the Welfare-to-Work Target Population in Rural and Small Metropolitan Areas	Studies the impact of welfare leavers on the wages and unemployment levels of welfare leavers in rural and small metropolitan areas between 1993-1998.	11 sites throughout country

continues

TABLE A-1 Continued

Project Title	Purpose	Jurisdictions Covered
MDRC Analysis of Caseload Composition and the Non-Working Welfare Leavers	Examines three groups of low-income populations: (1) working welfare leavers; (2) welfare stayers; and (3) nonworking welfare leavers. Describes and compares characteristics of each group. Uses data from seven evaluation studies (including six experimental studies).	Various sites
South Carolina Welfare Outcomes Grant	Multiyear effort to survey and link administrative data on multiple cohorts of former welfare recipients.	South Carolina
Welfare Outcomes Studies—Fiscal 1998 (Continuation grants also issued for some grantees in fiscal 1999)	Grants to 13 states or counties to track two cohorts of welfare leavers, usually a pre-PRWORA and post-PRWORA cohort with administrative and survey data.	AZ; Cuyahoga County, OH; DC; FL; GA; IL; L.A. County, CA; MA; MO; NY; San Mateo County, Consortia, CA; WA; WI
Welfare Diversion and Leaver Studies fiscal 1999	Grants to seven states and counties to track the outcomes of diverted applicants and potential applicants for TANF. Also includes studies of TANF leavers.	AZ; IL; IA; NY; TX; WA, Contra Costa and Alameda Counties, CA
Welfare Outcomes Grants Results Synthesis	Project will examine the results of all the welfare leaver grant projects and synthesize findings. Project will also use data from as many grantees as possible to conduct further analysis.	Across all 13 leaver grantee locations
Wisconsin, Institute for Research on Poverty Welfare Leaver Project	Follow-up to a previous project that tracked a 1995 cohort of welfare leavers with administrative data. This project will track another cohort of AFDC leavers who left AFDC/TANF in late 1997 in the early stages of implementation of WI-Works.	Wisconsin

Experimental Studies

National Evaluation of Welfare-to-Work Strategies (formerly JOBS program evaluation)	Evaluates alternative welfare-to-work strategies in seven sites. Strategies employed range from work first strategies to human capital development strategies. Impact evaluations, process studies and cost-benefit analyses conducted in each site.	Riverside, CA; Atlanta, GA; Grand Rapids and Detroit, MI; Columbus, OH; Oklahoma City, OK; Portland, OR
Evaluation of the New Jersey Substance Abuse Research Demonstration (joint with ACF)	Compares impacts on randomly assigned participants of two different intervention models that are aimed at improving post-welfare prospects of TANF recipients with substance abuse problems.	Two New Jersey counties
National Evaluation of Welfare-to-Work Strategies Grant Program	Program provides grants to states and communities to develop programs that promote job opportunities and employment preparation for harder to serve TANF recipients. Evaluation uses multiple methods: (1) description of grantees; (2) in-depth process and implementation study; (3) Experimental impact study in some sites.	Various sites across country

Implementation and Process Studies

Implementation of Welfare Reform at the Local Level: Implications for Special Populations	Case studies on how selected agencies, staff and caseworkers treat special populations, particularly those individuals with limited English language abilities.	Five metropolitan areas
Mental Health and Employment Among TANF Recipients	Describe how selected local TANF programs organize and deliver mental health services to clients.	Various local sites
Poor Families with Infants and Toddlers	Examine strategies implemented in states and communities to provide high-quality child care and other support services for welfare and working poor families with infants and toddlers.	Various sites across country
Welfare-to-Work Screening and Assessment Project (joint with ACF)	Describe state and local efforts to screen for and assess the situations of TANF or welfare-to-work recipients with high barriers to employment.	Various sites across country

continues

TABLE A-1 Continued

Project Title	Purpose	Jurisdictions Covered
Other Studies		
Effects of Welfare Reform on Investments in Human Capital and Family Formation (Baruch College)	Examine whether behavior of teens and young adults aged 16-21 has changed as a result of welfare reform. Will examine high school completion, child-bearing, employment and welfare receipt behavior. Uses data from the NLSY79 and NLSY97.	National
The Effects of the Work Pays Demonstration, EITC Expansions, and the Business Cycle on the Labor Market Behavior of the California Caseload	Examine the effect of welfare reform and EITC policy changes as well as changes in the business cycle on employment and earnings. Will use administrative data from welfare, unemployment insurance, and tax systems.	California
Entry, Exit and the Changing Composition of the Caseload (RAND)	Explore caseload dynamics and the effect of the economy in explaining changes in the caseload. Administrative data from 1987-mid 2001.	California
Fragile Families and Welfare Reform (funded jointly with ACF) (Columbia University)	Describe conditions and capabilities of vulnerable mothers and fathers in the first few years of PRWORA. Uses data from Fragile Families survey.	20 large U.S. cities
From Prisons to Home: The Effect of Incarceration on Children, Families, and Low-Income Communities	Project will produce a literature review, commissioned papers, and a conference in order to develop a research and practice baseline on what is known or can be known about this high-risk, high-welfare use population.	National
Linking State TANF Policies to Outcomes	Analyzes and synthesizes information on welfare and related support programs collected through various sources. Also develops characteristics of state programs important for predicting outcomes.	National
How Important is Marriage to Low-Income Family Well-Being (Urban Institute)	Examine the interactions between marital status, household status, and economic well-being. Uses data from the 1997 and 1999 NSAF.	National

How Low-Wage Working Families Cope as Parents and Workers	Exploratory study to examine how low-income families handle work and parenting and the barriers they face to self-sufficiency. Study will frame the issues, provide initial analysis and recommend areas of further research.	12 sites
Integration of Welfare and Workforce Development Systems	Case studies: examines the relationship between TANF and workforce development systems in 12 sites in six states.	Detroit metropolitan area
Mental Health, Substance Abuse, and Domestic Violence Service Utilization by Welfare Recipients (University of Michigan)	Examine impact of spatial proximity to social service providers and impact of individual-level characteristics on service utilization rates for welfare recipients. Uses data from Mother's Well-Being Study and linked data on geographic location of mental health and substance abuse treatment providers.	
Multi-Site Evaluation of Responsible Fatherhood Programs (joint with ACF and Office of Child Support Enforcement)	Implementation and outcomes study of clients of eight Responsible Fatherhood programs.	CO, MA, NW, CA, WI, MO, MD, WA
Research Grants on Welfare Outcomes, Fiscal 1999	Examines caseload dynamics, spatial distribution of economic opportunities, health insurance and health care utilization, use of food stamps, living arrangements, maternal and child health, domestic violence, and quality-of-life issues.	Seven private and university grantees throughout country
Support for the Research Forum on Children, Families, and the New Federalism—Database and Web Site	Supports the project that provides information on welfare reform initiatives and research.	National
TANF and Household Savings (University of Oregon)	Examine savings behavior of TANF recipients. Uses 1989, 1994, 1999 PSID wealth supplements.	National
Working Poor Population: Data Analysis on Definitions, Composition and Outcomes	Data analysis to compare different definitions of the working poor and understanding the composition of working poor population. Uses SIPP data.	National
Young Mothers' Transitions on and off TANF: How Do Child Care Assistance, Job Training, and Social Supports Influence These Decisions	Examine likelihood young mothers will go on or off or stay on TANF given they use child care, job training, and other social services.	Chicago area

continues

TABLE A-1 Continued

Project Title	Purpose	Jurisdictions Covered
Technical Assistance and Data and Methodological Improvement Efforts		
The Feasibility of Replicating the Women's Employment Study	Project will review what is known about barriers to employment and to consider survey designs for finding this information, using commissioned papers, panels of experts and final report.	
Grants to Enhance State Surveys of the Low-Income Population, Fiscal 2000	As part of on-going welfare leavers and outcomes studies, these grants will support further enhancements to existing data collection efforts in state and local areas. Possible enhancements issues include: sample size, the data collection period, data content, and validity and representativeness of data. Grants were made to 5 state and local areas.	Alameda and San Mateo, Counties, CA; MO; IA; WI
Household Definitions	Uses data from SIPP to develop poverty estimates based on a broader definition of unit of analysis. May use other data sets as well.	National
Improving Evaluation Methods and Their Relevance to Policy	A series of meetings with evaluation experts to discuss methods for evaluating public policies when random assignment is not feasible and ways to advance both experimental and nonexperimental methods.	
Measurement of Impacts on Children in Evaluations of State Welfare Reforms (jointly with ACF)	Phase I: Planning phase. Working with states to improve measurement of child outcomes in state welfare evaluations. Phase II: Large scale data collection activities to expand states' abilities to measure and track child outcomes for impact analyses	Phase I: CA, CT, FL, IL, IN, IA, MI, MN, OH, OR, VT, VA Phase II: CT, FL, IN, IA, MN
National Academy of Sciences Panel on Data and Methods for Measuring the Effects of Changes in Social Welfare Programs	Expert panel to review data and methodological needs for measuring the effects of policy changes. Panel will also consider ways to track welfare leavers.	

Policy Implications of Welfare Reform: Technical Assistance to States for Serving People with Disabilities (with Urban Institute and SSA)	Review of state efforts to provide welfare services to those with disabilities; also case study series.	All states
Project on Child Outcomes: Enhancing Measurement of Child Outcomes in State Welfare Evaluations and Other State Data Collections (jointly with ACF and private organizations)	Technical assistance to states collecting data as part of their welfare policy evaluations to improve measurement of child outcomes in these evaluations and data collection efforts.	All states
Reporting of Welfare Benefits in the SIPP Using Matched Administrative Records in California (joint with ACF) (UCLA and RAND)	Examine accuracy of self-reports of program participation in survey data in comparison to matched administrative records from AFDC/TANF, Food Stamps, and Medicaid.	California
Research Design Framework for the Federal Parent Locator Service Data (joint with ACF)	Propose and evaluate designs for longitudinal database for Title IV-A and IV-D program-related research.	Data from all states
Supporting Families after Welfare Reform (joint with ACF and R.W. Johnson Foundation)	Technical assistance to improve eligibility processes and access and retention of Medicaid, Food Stamps and S-CHIP for low income families at a number of sites. Includes site visits and a report on promising practices.	22 sites total (6 federally funded)
Technical Assistance on Researcher Access to Data Sets	Provide technical assistance to 14 FY1998 welfare leaver outcome studies to create public use data sets from the data collected as part of these projects. Will also provide technical assistance to improve comparability of these data sets across areas.	14 welfare leaver grantees for FY1998
Use of Social Security Summary Earnings Records to Assess Welfare Reform Outcomes	Match earnings records obtained from Social Security Administrative Records to a sample of adult recipients from 1996 SIPP, March 1997 CPS and 1997 SPD.	National

continues

TABLE A-1 Continued

Project Title	Purpose	Jurisdictions Covered
Support for Numerous Data Sets and Data Development Efforts	Early Childhood Longitudinal Birth Cohort Study Interagency Forum on Child and Family Statistics Iowa State University Survey of Program Dynamics Project National Survey of Family Growth National Longitudinal Study of Adolescent Health New Immigrant Survey Panel Study of Income Dynamics Conference on Public Policy Applications with the American Community Survey and Administrative Records State and Local Integrated Telephone Survey (SLAITS) for Children with Special Health Care Needs	Various

TABLE A-2 Major Welfare-Related Research Sponsored by the Administration for Children and Families

Project Title	Purpose	Jurisdictions Covered
Descriptive and Monitoring Studies		
National Study of Low-Income Child Care	Monitor status of low-income child care market in 25 communities in 17 states and a substudy in 5 neighborhoods from these communities. Will conduct survey, site visits, and focus groups.	25 communities in 17 states
Welfare to Work: Monitoring the Impact of Welfare Reform on American Indian Families with Children	Monitor demographic, social and economic conditions of American Indian families with children on welfare. Includes implementation study of TANF programs in tribal entities. Use CPS and SIPP, administrative records, in-depth interviews, and site visits.	Arizona American Indians
Program Description Data		
Assessing Enhanced Transitional Employment Programs	Will identify and describe programs that provide transitional employment or work experience to build skills for TANF recipients and others who have high barriers to employment. Will survey programs and conduct site visits.	National
Experience of Tribal TANF Programs: Problems Solutions and Lessons Learned	Describe all TANF programs funded in 1999 serving Native American tribes. Survey about programs and on-site case studies. Will also survey sample of TANF recipients from eight tribes.	All Native American tribes
Support for the Urban Institute's Welfare Rules Database 2000 Collection	Provide funding for collection of program description data on state TANF plans. Funding will cover update of 2000 state TANF plans.	All states
Support for APHSA,WIN, and NGA State TANF Plans Database	Develop and maintain database on state TANF plans. State plans will be updated every 24-27 months.	All states

continues

TABLE A-2 Continued

Project Title	Purpose	Jurisdictions Covered
Experimental Studies		
Child Impact Studies for Welfare Waiver Programs	Assess impact of different welfare reform approaches on child well-being in five states with welfare waivers. Control group under old AFDC policies.	CT, FL, IN, IA, MN (FL and MN have released reports)
Employment Retention and Advancement Project	Initial phase will provide planning grants to states to develop strategies for employment retention and career advancement for welfare recipients. Second phase is grants to experimentally implement these strategies.	Phase I: CA, IL, MD, NJ, NC, OH, RI, SC, TN, TX, VA, WA, WI Phase II: CA-Los Angeles, Riverside; FL, IL, MN, OR, SC, TN, TX, VA
Evaluation of Los Angeles Jobs-First GAIN (MDRC)	Estimates impact of the Los Angeles GAIN program. Includes an implementation study and a cost-benefit study.	Los Angeles, CA
Evaluation of the New Jersey Substance Abuse Research Demonstration (joint with ASPE)	Compares impacts on randomly assigned participants of two different intervention models that are aimed at improving post-welfare prospects of TANF recipients with substance abuse problems.	Two New Jersey counties
Track I Welfare Waiver Studies	Evaluation of state pre-PRWORA waiver demonstration programs that changed rules of prior AFDC programs in states.	AZ, CT, FL, IN, IA, MN, TX, VT, WI (FL, MN, and WI projects are completed)

Study	Description	Sites
Track II Welfare Waiver Studies	Pre-PRWORA waiver demonstrations that were modified after PRWORA. Some are experimental designs. Some include process studies.	CA, IL, IA, MD, MT, NE, NH, NC, ND, OH, SC, VA (IL, ND, SC projects are completed)
Other Studies		
Child Care Research Partnerships	Field-initiated research on child care policies especially for low-income families.	Five research partnership sites
Field Initiated Projects	Many different types of studies conducted throughout the country. Includes experimental studies, implementation studies, monitoring studies and technical assistance provision. Covers populations such as Native Americans, rural welfare recipients and low-income families, and domestic violence victims.	Various sites
Fragile Families and Welfare Reform (jointly with ASPE) (Columbia University)	Describe conditions and capabilities of vulnerable mothers and fathers in the first few years of PRWORA. Uses data from Fragile Families survey.	20 large U.S. cities
Research Synthesis of the Effects of TANF (RAND)	Synthesize research on the effect of TANF on income, earnings, government benefit receipt, family formation and structure. Document areas where further research is needed.	National
Rural Welfare Reform Strategies Project	Purpose is to help rural states develop strategies for serving rural low-income and welfare families. Effort will also develop evaluations of those strategies. Includes implementation grants in four states.	IL, IA, LA, MD, MN, MS, MO, NY, VA, VT, WA
State Welfare Reform Impacts Study (UC Data)	Tests nonexperimental methodologies for examining impacts of TANF and other programs.	California

continues

TABLE A-2 Continued

Project Title	Purpose	Jurisdictions Covered
Testing Nonexperimental Methodologies Using National Evaluation of Welfare to Work Data (MDRC)	Uses data from the experimental NEWWS study to explore the use and validity of nonexperimental data.	NEWWS sites
Implementation and Process Studies		
Front-Line Management and Practice Study (SUNY-Albany)	Examine TANF implementation at local administrative offices to see how budget priorities have changed within and across states and how policy changes have affected budgetary priorities.	Pilot studies in 4 states and full case studies in 13 states.
Welfare to Work Screening and Assessment Project (joint with ASPE)	Describe state and local efforts to screen for and assess the situations of TANF or welfare-to-work recipients with high barriers to employment.	Various sites across country
Technical Assistance and Data and Methodological Improvement Efforts		
Annual Welfare Reform Evaluation Conference	Annual research conference with representatives from all states.	All states
Project on Child Outcomes: Enhancing Measurement of Child Outcomes in State Welfare Evaluations and Other State Data Collections (joint with ASPE and private organizations)	Technical assistance to states collecting data as part of their welfare policy evaluations to improve measurement of child outcomes in these evaluations and data collection efforts.	All states
Reporting of Welfare Benefits in the SIPP Using Matched Administrative Records in California (joint funding with ASPE) (UCLA and RAND)	Examine accuracy of self-reports of program participation in survey data in comparison to matched administrative records from AFDC/TANF, Food Stamps, and Medicaid.	California

Research Design Framework for the Federal Parent Locator Service Data (joint with ASPE)	Propose and evaluate designs for longitudinal database for Titles IV-A and IV-D program-related research.	Data from all states
Supporting Families after Welfare Reform (joint with ASPE and R.W. Johnson Foundation)	Technical assistance to improve eligibility processes and access and retention of Medicaid, Food Stamps and S-CHIP for low income families at a number of sites. Includes site visits and a report on promising practices.	22 sites total (6 federally funded)

NOTES:
ACF, Administration for Children and Families
AFDC, Aid to Families with Dependent Children
APHSA, American Public Human Services Association
ASPE, Assistant Secretary for Planning and Evaluation
CPS, Current Population Survey
EITC, Earned Income Tax Credit
GAIN, Greater Avenues to Independence
MDRC, Manpower Demonstration Research Corporation
NEWWS, National Evaluation of Welfare-to-Work Strategies
NGA, National Governors Association
NLSY, National Longitudinal Survey on Youth
NSAF, National Survey of American Families
PSID, Panel Study of Income Dynamics
PRWORA, Personal Responsibility and Work Opportunity Reconciliation Act
SCHIP, State Children's Health Insurance Program
SSA, Social Security Administration
SIPP, Survey of Income Program Participants
SPD, Survey of Program Dynamics
TANF, Temporary Assistance for Needy Families
WIN, Welfare Information Network

Appendix B

Summary of Current
Welfare Reform Projects

The table is organized according to broad classifications of types of studies: (1) descriptive or monitoring studies; (2) studies of welfare leavers or divertees; (3) studies that employ experimental evaluation designs (these studies may also include components that use other evaluation or data collection methods; (4) studies that use multiple methods of evaluation; (5) implementation or process studies; (6) program description data collection studies; (7) data collection or data development projects; (8) technical assistance for evaluation or data collection; and (9) other studies that cannot be otherwise classified. In many cases, studies may fit in multiple categories, but we have only included them into one primary category.

The information in this appendix comes from the Research Forum's web site (http://www.researchforum.org/), the Wisconsin Department of Workforce Development's Welfare Reform Research Database (http://www.dwd.state.wi.us/dwd/wrr/), Congressional Research Service (2000), and from reviews of web sites of study investigators.

This appendix summarizes current studies (as of this writing) of welfare reform and related welfare policies.

TABLE B-1 Summary of Current Welfare Reform Projects

Project Title	Investigators	Study Description	State/Locality Studied	Data Sources
Descriptive Study/Monitoring				
Assessing Effective Welfare-to-Work Strategies for Domestic Violence Victims and Survivors in the Options/Opciones Project	Center for Impact Research (in partnership with the Illinois Department of Human Services)	Descriptive analysis of assessment and case management of services for victims of domestic violence	Chicago, IL	Administrative data, survey
Assessing the Effects of Welfare Reform on California's Most Precarious Families	Center for Social Services Research, School of Social Welfare, University of California, Berkeley	Descriptive study of well-being of hard-to-serve welfare recipients	Alameda and Los Angeles Counties, CA	Administrative data, direct observations of child interactions, ethnography, focus group, secondary data, survey
Child Care Subsidy Duration Study	D. Schexnayder; Columbia University, Oregon State University	Descriptive study	FL, IL, MD, MA, OR	Linked longitudinal data sets of children receiving subsidies
Devolution, Welfare Reform, and Well-Being Study: New York Social Indicators Survey	Columbia School of Social Work	Tracks individual and family well-being over time	NYC	Administrative data, survey of 2,250 households, structured interviews with 1,000 households
Disaggregating the TANF Child-Only Cases in Three States	Lewin Group	Describes composition and trends in child-only TANF cases	CA, FL, MO	Administrative records and case file records, interviews with state and county staff
The Dynamics of AFDC, Medicaid and Food Stamp Use	Chapin Hall Center for Children, University of Chicago	Description and event-history analysis	IL	State-level administrative data

Effects of Welfare-to-Work Programs in Illinois	Chapin Hall Center for Children, University of Chicago	Descriptive study of welfare employment experiences of AFDC/TANF recipients for 1991-1999	IL	Administrative data
Evaluation of the North Carolina Work First Program	MAXIMUS	Descriptive study, nonexperimental evaluations, implementation/process study	NC	Administrative data, survey of current and former recipients, site visits for implementation data
Evaluation of Washington State's Welfare Reform	Washington State Joint Legislative Audit and Review Committee	Cost-benefit study, descriptive study, implementation/process study	WA	Administrative data, field research, survey, program descriptions and documents
Expanding Medicaid Enrollment Using Tax Data (in development)	New Mexico Human Services Department	N/A	NM	Administrative data from tax records to assess Medicaid eligibility
Georgia Welfare Reform Impact Assessment	Georgia Department of Human Resources	Study of former welfare recipients	GA	Administrative data, survey data
Growing Up in Poverty Project	University of California, Berkeley, and Yale University	Descriptive study to track child development and school readiness for welfare populations	New Haven, CT; San Francisco, CA; Santa Clara, CA; Tampa, FL	Developmental assessments and screenings, field research, focus group, survey
Illinois Families Study	University Consortium on Welfare Reform	Descriptive embedded child outcomes study	Nine counties in IL	Administrative data, longitudinal data survey colllected annually on sample representatives of IL caseloads

continues

TABLE B-1 Continued

Project Title	Investigators	Study Description	State/Locality Studied	Data Sources
Maximizing Job Opportunities for Welfare Recipients Through Expansion of Value-Added Industries in Economically Disadvantaged Rural Areas	Louisiana State University	Descriptive study of small group of welfare recipients and local employers	Rural and remote areas of LA	Focus groups, interviews with employers and recipients
Monitoring the Impact of Welfare Reform on American Indian Families	Washington University School of Social Work	Descriptive and monitoring study, implementation/process study	Within the state of Arizona in-depth interviews will be conducted at three reservations	Administrative data, annual surveys with 400 families with children, focus group, program descriptions, and documents
Nevada Welfare Reform Evaluation	University of Nevada, Reno	Descriptive study	NV	Administrative data, survey
Rural Welfare-to-Work Strategies Project: Iowa	Iowa State University	Descriptive study of transportation needs of rural welfare populations	Lee County, IA	Administrative data, focus group, secondary data, survey
San Bernardino County (CA) TANF Recipients Study	MAXIMUS Longitudinal descriptive study	Study of sample of TANF recipients	San Bernardino County, CA	Administrative data and survey data
The State of the Child	Chapin Hall Center for Children	Monitoring study of child well-being	IL	Multiple data sources
Welfare Reform and Its Impact on Persons with Disabilities	Part of Three-City Study with funding from DHHS/ASPE	Descriptive study	Boston, MA; Chicago, IL; San Antonio, TX	Will be initial part of 5-year longitudinal study

Work First New Jersey Evaluation	Mathematica Policy Research, Inc.	Descriptive study, implementation/process study	NJ	Administrative data, ethnography, focus group, program descriptions and documents, longitudinal survey of 2,000 families over 5 years
Youth Fair Chance Program	Mathematica Policy Research, Inc.	Descriptive study	17 sites in high-poverty areas	Telephone survey of youth in target areas
Welfare Leaver and Diversion Studies				
Illinois Study of Former TANF Clients	University of Illinois	Descriptive study of cohorts of welfare leavers	IL	Administrative data, survey
Illinois TANF Applicant Study	MAXIMUS	Study of 6,000 people who initiate application for TANF but withdraw or are denied	IL	Administrative survey, site visits to offices to observe practices
Impact of Welfare Reform on Women Leaving TANF in Georgia	Georgia State University Applied Research Center	3 cohorts of welfare leavers	GA	Administrative data, longitudinal survey
Iowa Leavers Project	Mathematica Policy Research, Inc.	One cohort of welfare leavers	IA	Administrative data, survey of leavers 8-11 months after leaving
Kentucky Welfare Reform Evaluation	University of Louisville, Kentucky	Descriptive study of welfare leavers. Also develops database for future studies	KY	Survey of 3,225 clients discontinued from TANF subsample for longitudinal follow-up
Missouri Welfare Reform Results Study	Missouri Department of Social Services	Descriptive study of two cohorts welfare leavers	MO	Administrative data, survey

continues

TABLE B-1 Continued

Project Title	Investigators	Study Description	State/Locality Studied	Data Sources
New Mexico TANF Longitudinal Study	MAXIMUS	Longitudinal study of TANF recipients and leavers	NM	Administrative data, survey of 2,500 randomly sampled cases
New York Leavers Project	Nelson A. Rockefeller Institute of Government, New York State Department of Social Services	Descriptive study of two cohorts of welfare leavers	NY	Administrative data, survey
San Mateo County Leavers Project	SPHERE Institute	Descriptive study of cohort of welfare leavers	San Mateo, Santa Cruz, Santa Clara, CA	Administrative data, survey
South Carolina: State Welfare Reform Evaluation Program	South Carolina Department of Social Services, Office of Program Reform, Evaluation and Research	Descriptive study of TANF leavers, Ethnographic study	SC	Administrative data, in-depth interviews, survey of 1,000 former recipients
South Carolina Welfare and Food Stamp Leavers Study	MAXIMUS	Longitudinal descriptive study of TANF leavers and divertees, embedded child outcomes study	SC	Administrative data, ethnography, survey
Survey of Former Family Independence Program Clients	South Carolina Department of Social Services, Office of Program Reform, Evaluation and Research	Descriptive study of former Family Independence (TANF) recipients	SC	Administrative and survey data
Survey of Welfare Recipients Employed or Sanctioned for Noncompliance	Bureau for Business and Economic Research, University of Memphis	Descriptive study of former Families First Program participants	TN	Survey

Study	Organization	Design	Location	Data
Texas Welfare Applicants and Potential Applicants Study	Texas Department of Human Services, and University of Texas at Austin	Descriptive study of cohorts of TANF applicants and potential applicants	TX	Administrative data, survey, in-depth interviews
Tracking Participants and Families Affected by Welfare Reform in Florida	Florida State University	Descriptive study of cohorts of welfare leavers and divertees	Four multicounty regions in FL	Administrative data, survey
Washington State's Families After Welfare	Washington Department of Social and Health Services	Descriptive study of cohorts of welfare leavers, divertees, and stayers	WA	Administrative data, survey data
The Welfare in Transition Project: Consequences for Women, Families, and Communities	Radcliffe Public Policy Institute	Descriptive study of welfare recipients and ex-recipients	Cambridge and Boston, MA	Administrative data, field research, focus group, in-depth interviews
Wisconsin Leavers Project	Institute for Research on Poverty	Descriptive study of a cohorts of welfare leavers	WI	Longitudinal administrative data, base survey of random sample of cohorts of leavers
Experimental Design				
Arizona's EMPOWER Program	Abt Associates, Inc.	Experimental design; random assignment, cost-benefit study	Four cities in AZ	Longitudinal survey of participants, administrative data, focus group, survey
A Better Chance (ABC) Evaluation	Abt Associates, Inc.	Experimental design, implementation/process study, descriptive study	DE	Administrative data, field research, focus group, survey

continues

TABLE B-1 Continued

Project Title	Investigators	Study Description	State/Locality Studied	Data Sources
CAL—Learn Program Evaluation	University of California Data Archive and Technical Assistance (UC Data)	Random assignment; 2-way factorial design of the two program elements	Four counties in CA	Three cohorts of AFDC 4,900 teens
Canada's Self-Sufficiency Project	Social Research and Demonstration Corporation	Implementation/process study, experimental design, descriptive study	British Columbia and New Brunswick, Canada	Administrative data, focus group, program descriptions and documents, survey
Child Outcomes Study of the National Evaluation of Welfare-to-Work Strategies	Child Trends funded through DHHS/ASPE	Experimental design	Atlanta; Columbus, OH; Detroit; Grand Rapids; Oklahoma City; Portland, OR; Riverside, CA	Development assessments, direct observation, surveys of mothers
Connecticut's Jobs First Program: Welfare Reform Evaluation Project	Manpower Demonstration Research Corporation	Experimental design, implementation/process study, cost-benefit study, descriptive study	New Haven and Manchester, CT	Administrative data, field research, survey
Employment Retention and Advancement Project—Impact Evaluations	Manpower Demonstration Research Corporation	Experimental design cost-benefit analysis, implementation/process study	Los Angeles and Riverside Counties, CA; FL; IL; MN; OR; SC; TN; TX; VA	Administrative and survey data
Indiana Welfare Reform Evaluation	Abt Associates, Inc.	Experimental design, implementation/process study, cost-benefit study	IN	Administrative data, keep interviews w/office staff, child outcomes survey, client follow-up survey

Program	Organization	Study Design	Location	Data
Minnesota Family Investment Program	Manpower Demonstration Research Corporation	Experimental design, implementation/process study, cost-benefit study, descriptive study	Eight counties in MN	Administrative data, field research, survey
Moving to Opportunities for Fair Housing Demonstration Project	Abt Associates with U.S. HUD funding	Experimental design of program to measure public impact of housing and Section 8 voucher program	Baltimore, Boston, Chicago, LA, NYC	Administrative data, survey, qualitative data
National Evaluation of Welfare-to-Work Strategies and Child Outcome Component	Manpower Demonstration Research Corporation and Child Trends	Implementation/process study, experimental design, cost-benefit study	Seven sites nationwide	Administrative data, developmental assessments, screenings/direct observations of child interactions, field research, survey
Nebraska Employment First Program Evaluation	Nebraska Department of Health and Human Services	Experimental design, implementation/process study, cost-benefit study	Lincoln and Omaha, NE	Administrative data, focus group, program descriptions and documents, survey
New Visions Evaluation	Abt Associates, Inc.	Experimental design, implementation/process study	Riverside County, CA	Administrative data, field research, survey
Oregon's Evaluation of Welfare-to-Work program	Manpower Demonstration Research Corporation	Experimental design	OR	Administrative data on 5,547 single parent AFDC applicants and recipients aged 21+ who attended orientation between 10/93 and 10/94

continues

TABLE B-1 Continued

Project Title	Investigators	Study Description	State/Locality Studied	Data Sources
Parent's Fair Share Demonstration	Manpower Demonstration Research Corporation	Experimental design, implementation/process study of program to increase involvement of noncustodial parents with children	Seven counties across country	Administrative data, survey data, qualitative data, key informant interviews, and site visits
Texas Achieving Change for Texans (ACT) Welfare Reform Waiver Evaluation	Texas Department of Human Services, University of Texas at Austin	Experimental design, implementation/process study	Various sites in TX	Administrative data, site observations, staff and client interviews, sample of leavers and divertees
Vermont's Welfare Restructuring Project	Manpower Demonstration Research Corporation	Experimental design, implementation/process study, cost-benefit study	Six districts in VT	Administrative data, focus group, survey
Wisconsin Works Child Support Waiver Demonstration	Institute for Research on Poverty	Experimental design, implementation/process study	WI	Administrative and survey data, ethnography, field research, program descriptions and documents, survey
Multimethod Study				
Assessing the New Federalism	Child Trends, Urban Institute, and Westat, Inc.	Descriptive/analytical study, implementation/process study, impact study	AL, CA, CO, FL, MA, MI, MN, MS, NJ, NY, TX, WA, WI	Administrative data, survey, state indicators
California: Welfare Reform's Impact on Legal Immigrants' Access to Health Care	Latino Issues Forum	Cost-benefit study, descriptive study, non-experimental impact study	CA	Administrative data, developmental assessments screenings, survey, program descriptions and documents

Program	Organization	Study Type	Sites	Data Sources
CASAWORKS for Families	Treatment Research Institute, Inc., M. Gephart Associates	Implementation/process study, descriptive analysis and non-experimental analysis of substance abuse policies for welfare recipients	Sites in CA, MD, MO, NC, NY, OH, OK, PA, TN	Administrative data, structured interviews with 1,100 welfare recipients
Comprehensive Evaluation of Welfare Reform in New York State	New York State Office of Temporary and Disability Assistance	Implementation/process study, nonexperimental/pre-post cohort design, descriptive study	NY (specific sites to be determined)	Not yet available
Evaluating CalWORKS in Los Angeles County	Los Angeles County Department of Public Social Services	Descriptive and monitoring study, process and implementation	Los Angeles County, CA	Focus groups, survey of recipients and caseworkers
Evaluation of Wisconsin Works Child Support Demonstration	Institute for Research on Poverty, University of Wisconsin	Nonexperimental impact evaluation, implementation/process study	WI	
Family Well-Being and Welfare Reform in Iowa	Iowa State University	In-depth interviews with recipients, case studies of communities	Nine sites in IA	Administrative data, ethnography, field research, focus group, program descriptions and documents
Jobs-Plus Community Revitalization Initiative for Public Housing Families—Employment Demonstration Program	Manpower Demonstration Research Corporation	Implementation/process study, nonexperimental design	Public housing developments in seven cities	Administrative data, field research, survey
Maryland Family Investment Program (FIP) Evaluation	Maryland Department of Human Resources	Implementation/process study, Nonexperimental impact study, descriptive study	MD	Administrative data, focus group, survey

continues

TABLE B-1 Continued

Project Title	Investigators	Study Description	State/Locality Studied	Data Sources
Project on Devolution and Urban Change	Manpower Demonstration Research Corporation	Implementation/process study, descriptive study, multiple cohort non-experimental design, ethnographic study	Los Angeles, Miami, Cleveland, Philadelphia	Administrative data, field research, survey focus groups and in-depth interviews
Rural Welfare Reform Project: Does Welfare Reform Work in Rural America?	Ohio University	Descriptive study, ethnographic study, implementation/process study	29 Appalachian Ohio counties	Administrative data, field research, focus group, program descriptions and documents, survey, in-depth interviews, employer interviews
Statewide CalWORKS Evaluation	RAND under contract with CA DHHS	Nonexperimental impact evaluation, cost-benefit study, descriptive study, implementation/process study	Certain research activites will examine statewide trends in California, while others will concentrate on six focus counties	Administrative data, program descriptions and documents, survey
Welfare Children and Families: A Three-City Study	Johns Hopkins University, University of Chicago, University of North Carolina at Chapel Hill, Pennsylvania State University, University of Texas at Austin, University of Illinois, Brandeis University, Harvard University	Descriptive study, implementation/process study, ethnographic study, embedded child development study	Boston, Chicago, and San Antonio	Longitudinal survey of low-income households, key informant interviews, direct observations, site visits

Implementation/Process Study

Study	Organization	Description	Location	Methods
Examining Customer Pathways and Assessment Practices	University of Maryland, School of Social Work, Welfare and Child Support Research and Training Unit	Process analysis of Maryland's welfare program which is state supervised, locally administered	MD	In-person staff interviews, site visits, case record review, observation of worker-customer interactions
Expanding Health Insurance Coverage for Low-Income People: Experiments in Five States	Mathematica Policy Research, Inc., with Urban Institute	Implementation study	HA, MD, OK, RI, TN	Current Population Survey; interviews with local and state officials, managed care reps, health care providers, consumers; focus groups with consumers and providers
Finding Common Ground in the Era of Welfare Reform	Center for Population and Family Health, Columbia University	Study health outcomes of controls on maternal behavior	All 50 states, Washington, DC, and Puerto Rico	Administrative data, field research, focus group, program descriptions and documents, survey of state directors of social service programs
Front-Line Management and Impact Study	Rockefeller Institute of Government	Implementation/process study, program description of how TANF programs operate on front lines	11 local welfare offices in GA, MT, NY, TX	Structured observations of caseworker/client interaction, interviews with office staff, program description data
The Impact of Welfare Reform on Families	Institute for Research on Poverty, University of Wisconsin	Study of applicants, divertees, and enrollees	Milwaukee, WI	Survey with follow-ups

continues

TABLE B-1 Continued

Project Title	Investigators	Study Description	State/Locality Studied	Data Sources
Impact of Welfare Reform on Social Services Agencies in New York City	Hunter College School of Social Work	Process study	Social service agencies in the New York Metropolitan area (Manhattan, Bronx, Brooklyn, Queens, and Staten Island)	Survey with purposive sample of senior staff at nonprofit service providers
State Capacity Study and Implementing PRWORA	Rockefeller Institute of Government Federalism Research Group, SUNY Albany	Implementation/process study	20 sample states	Field research, program descriptions and documents
State Case Studies of Policy and Programs	Urban Institute: Assessing the New Federalism	Document development and implementation of state policies	AL, CA, CO, FL, MA, MI, MN, MS, NJ, NY, TX, WA, WI	Collecting data in base year (1996) and in following years
Program Description Data				
Child Support and Data Analysis Project	Center for Law and Social Policy	Describe child support programs and financing decisions in states	National	Administrative data, survey
State Case Studies of Policy and Programs	Urban Institute: Assessing the New Federalism	Document development and implementation of state policies	AL, CA, CO, FL, MA, MI, MN, MS, NJ, NY, TX, WA, WI	Collecting data in base year (1996) and in following years
State Policy Documentation Project	Center for Law and Social Policy and Center for Budget and Policy Priorities	Collect and summarize program description data	National	Monitor, document, and analyze state welfare, health, and family support programs

continues

Summaries of Selected Elements of State Programs for Temporary Assistance for Needy Families (TANF)	National Governors Association	Program description	All states	Keeping track of state welfare policies
Summary of State Welfare-to-Work plans	National Governors Association	Program description	States with welfare-to-work programs	Summarizes state plans
Welfare Policy Typology Project	Urban Institute with funding from DHHS/ASPE	Program description	All 50 states	Develop characteristics of state welfare policies to use in evaluation research
Welfare Rules Database	Urban Institute	Collects state policy and program description data	National	Reviews state program plans and caseworker manuals. Interviews with staff administrators to supplement reviews

Data Collection and Data Development

California Health Interview Survey	UCLA Center for Health Policy Research, and CA Department of Health and Human Services, Public Health Institute	Survey data collection	Statewide and includes local level data for counties with at least 40,000 people	Interviews 55,000 households in 2-year cycles; data collection began in November 2000; collects data on health status of adults and children, health insurance coverage, care access, and eligibility and participation in Medi-Cal and Healthy Families Program

TABLE B-1 Continued

Project Title	Investigators	Study Description	State/Locality Studied	Data Sources
CA Work Pays Demonstration Project	University of California Data Archive & Technical Assistance (with California Department of Social Services Research)	Data development	CA	State-level administrative records for AFDC, Medi-Cal, UI, other state and federal assistance programs, and employment tax files; county-level administrative records for AFDC and food stamp programs; nonautomated client records at county welfare offices; and telephone interviews with AFDC recipients
Dynamic Employer-Household Data and Social Data Infrastructure	Based at Cornell University, funding from Census Bureau and NSF	Data linkages and data access for research purposes	U.S., broad project includes other countries	Links social and economic data from surveys with administrative data from employers and employment related sources; also has a confidentiality and data access development function
Fragile Families and Child Well-Being Study	Columbia University and Princeton University	Survey data collection for later analysis	20 cities randomly selected from all cities over 200,000	Surveys of 4,800 families; initial interviews with mothers at birth of child, follow-up interviews with both parents when child is 12, 30, and 48 months, child assessment at 48 months

Integrated Data Base on Children's Services	Chapin Hall Center for Children	Developed linked data sets	IL	Administrative data from child welfare, TANF, Medicaid, food stamps, special education, corrections, and mental health
Iowa Survey of Program Dynamics	Iowa State University and Census Bureau	Survey data collection	IA	Modified SPD survey instrument implemented with Iowa sample
Los Angeles Study of Families and Communities (LASFC)	RAND	Longitudinal/household study with child outcomes collection	Los Angeles County, CA	Administrative data, developmental assessments/ screenings for children, longitudinal survey of 3,250 households
Massachusetts Longitudinal Database for Research on Child Support Enforcement and Social Service Agencies	Chapin Hall Center for Children	Developing outcome indicators	MA	Constructing a longitudinal database of administrative data from TANF, Medicaid, food stamps, child enforcement, wage reporting, and new hires
Michigan Women's Employment Survey			An urban county in MI	Simple random sample of 753 single mothers with children who received cash assistance in Feb. 1997; face-to-face interviews; in total, 3 waves of data to be collected

continues

TABLE B-1 Continued

Project Title	Investigators	Study Description	State/Locality Studied	Data Sources
National Longitudinal Study of Children and Families in the Child Welfare System	DHHS/ASPE	Data collection	National	Longitudinal survey data; sample representative of children and families who enter the child welfare system; over 6,000 children; first interview in spring 1999; three annual follow-up rounds planned
National Survey of America's Families	Urban Institute: Assessing the New Federalism	Data collections and descriptive/monitoring study of well-being of 3 cross-sections	AL, CA, CO, FL, MA, MI, MN, MS, NJ, NY, TX, WA, WI	Survey of over 40,000 households in 1997; second cross-section in 1999; third cross-section in 2002
New Immigrant Study	NYU, RAND, University of Pennsylvania	Multiple cohort longitudinal survey of new immigrants	National	Administrative data, survey
Survey of Program Dynamics	Census Bureau	Survey data collection	Nationally representative sample	Longitudinal survey. Includes module on child and adolescent well-being
National Neighborhood Indicators Project	Urban Institute and local partners	Data development	12 U.S. cities	Will assist other communities in developing neighborhood level information systems for policy making
Women's Employment Survey	University of Michigan Poverty Research and Training Center	Data collection and descriptive reporting	Urban MI county	4-wave panel study of 753 current and former welfare recipients

Technical Assistance for Evaluation or Data Collection

Measurement of Impacts on Children in Evaluations of State Welfare Reforms	DHHS, ASPE, ACF, Child Trends, and Chapin Hall Center for Children	Technical assistance to states to develop data collection ability	Phase I: CA, CT, FL, IL, IN, IA, MI, MN, OH, OR, VT, VA; Phase II: CT, FL, IN, IA, MN	Phase I: Planning phase; Phase II: Large-scale data collection activities to expand states' abilities to measure and track child outcomes for impact analyses
Other				
Analysis of the Determinants of AFDC Caseload Growth	Lewin Group	Models effects of changes in demographics, the economy, and programs to changes in the caseload, participants and expenditures per case	All 50 states and DC	Quarterly state-level data for 1979-1994
Cross-State Study of Time-Limited Welfare	Manpower Demonstration Research Corporation	Synthesizes findings of evaluations of time limits in state welfare programs	Various states	Data and results from previous evaluations
Effects of Child Care Subsidy on Transition from Welfare to Work Among Welfare Mothers	National Center for Child Poverty, David Stevens, Anne Witte, Chapin Hall Center for Children, with funding from DHHS	Caseload dynamics of use of child care subsidy and welfare use; program entry cohorts	IL, MD, MA	Linked administrative data on child care subsidies, welfare and employment data
Research Forum on Children, Families and the New Federalism	National Center for Children in Poverty, Columbia University	Welfare program research clearinghouse. Promote monitoring and evaluation research; promote collaboration among key	National	

continues

TABLE B-1 Continued

Project Title	Investigators	Study Description	State/Locality Studied	Data Sources
		stake-holders; information exchange that includes a clearinghouse for welfare research projects		
State Efforts to Track and Follow-Up on Welfare Recipients	American Public Human Services Association and National Conference of State Legislatures	Tracks welfare leaver studies	All states	APHSA and NCSL with the National Governors Association is keeping track of leaver studies
Welfare Reform Research Database	WI Department of Workforce Development	Documents past and current research on welfare reform related topics	Nationwide	Not applicable
Urban Welfare-to-Work Transitions	Consortium of collaborators headed by the University of Baltimore funded by the Department of Labor	Dynamics of work and welfare	Atlanta, Baltimore, Chicago, Ft.. Lauderdale, Houston, Kansas City	Linked administrative data

SOURCES: Data from the Research Forum's web site (http://www.researchforum.org/); the Wisconsin Department of Workforce Development's Welfare Reform Research Database (http://www.dwd.state.wi.us/dwd/wrr/); and Monitoring the effects of pre- and post-TANF welfare reform initiatives, *2000 Green Book*. Washington, DC: U.S. Department of Health and Human Service (2000). Sources also have other information on welfare-related topics.

NOTES:

ACF, Administration for Children and Families
AFDC, Aid to Families with Dependent Children
APHSA, American Public Human Services Association
ASPE, Assistant Secretary for Planning and Evaluation
DHHS, Department of Health and Human Services
HUD, Housing and Urban Development
MDRC, Manpower Demonstration Research Corporation
PRWORA, Personal Responsibility and Work Opportunity Reconciliation Act
TANF, Temporary Assistance for Needy Families

Appendix C

The Statistical Power of National Data to Evaluate Welfare Reform

John Adams and V. Joseph Hotz

As discussed in Chapter 4, a common form of analysis for assessing welfare reform is to use cross-state (as well as over time) variation to identify the overall effects as well as specific components of welfare reforms that have occurred over the last 20 years. As summarized in Chapter 2, a number of recent studies have used the cross-state variation in waivers granted to states in their administration of the AFDC program to assess the extent to which these particular reforms could account for the decline in the AFDC caseloads that occurred during the 1990s, as well as trends in labor force participation, earnings and poverty rates among welfare-prone groups in the population (see, e.g., Bartik and Eberts, 1999; Blank, 1997, 1999; Council of Economic Advisers, 1997; Figlio et al., 2000; Moffitt, 1999; Schoeni and Blank, 2000; Ziliak and Figlio, 2000; Ziliak et al., 2000). This approach takes as the unit of analysis a state in a given year. For example, the dependent variable might be the AFDC caseload in a state for a particular year. The independent variables could be state indicators, time trends, measures of a state's economic conditions, as well as measures of the particular components of a state's AFDC program granted under the waiver process.

A key question that must be addressed in evaluating the results of such analyses is the statistical power of such analyses to detect the effect: whether an indicator variable for a feature of a state's welfare policy (or any other state-specific provision) has a statistically significant effect on a particular outcome being analyzed. Typically these analyses are conducted using regression analyses, either ordinary regression models, logistic regression models, or Poisson regression models. The question of statistical power for regression models is whether there is sufficient information to determine if a regression coefficient is different from zero. The regression coefficients of greatest policy relevance are for the indicator variables describing state policy. The simplest form of this analysis would be a single indicator variable for the state having welfare reform in place.

In this paper, we examine the statistical power of analyses to detect the effects of these indicators of state-level welfare policy reforms that are associated with alternative types of statistical analyses. Mirroring the existing literature, we examine the effects of state-level AFDC waivers on several different outcome measures with data for the pre-PRWORA era. These analyses will have the flavor of post-hoc power analysis, which researchers sometimes do after developing a regression model. But we also intend these analyses to serve as examples, or given the relatively large effects, optimistic estimates of the potential of this type of analysis to detect the effects of future changes.

THE MODELS CONSIDERED

The most widely circulated study in this genre is a 1997 report by the Council of Economic Advisers (CEA) (Council of Economic Advisers, 1997). This report used the aggregate state level AFDC caseload rate as the outcome variable. The unemployment rate and state waiver activity were used as independent variables. In this paper we focus on a variant of the CEA analysis, using data from various waves of the Current Population Surveys (CPS) as implemented in Moffitt (1999). The extensions in Moffitt (1999) make it easy to explore some refinements and more thoroughly capture the range of models used by analysts.

Moffitt (1999) implements the CEA model using CPS data. The advantage of this approach is that the CPS data can be subdivided to finer subsets of the population. For example, the data on outcomes can be disaggregated by age and education status. Furthermore, the CPS data includes alternative outcome variables, such as weeks worked and earnings. Although the future pattern of welfare reform is unknown, we believe that the power of these future analyses to measure the effects will probably be similar.

The outcome variables we consider (as in Moffitt, 1999) are AFDC caseload, annual weeks worked, annual hours worked, annual earnings, and weekly earnings. The focal independent variable was whether there was any waiver in place in the state in a given year. This variable was coded 0 or 1. If the waivers were in place for a fraction of the year, the variable was set to that fraction. Other dependent variables include the unemployment rate, the lagged unemployment rate, state indicators, and state trends to account for other factors that may explain the cross-state and temporal variation in outcomes. The substate demographic cell versions of these models also included education status, age, and waiver by education interaction terms. These variables were binned and entered as indicator variables (see Moffitt, 1999).

For the power calculations, all we require from these analyses are the effect size estimates and their standard errors. These statistics appear in Table C-1. The CEA analyses use log AFDC caseload rate as the outcome variable. In the log scale the effect estimates have a percentage interpretation. The CPS analyses for the AFDC participation rates do not use a log transformation. These effects were reported in the Council of Economic Advisers (1997) and Moffitt (1999) papers as rates. Here, the corresponding estimates are converted to percentages to

TABLE C-1 Models and Effect Sizes

Model	Outcome	Focal Independent Variable	Effect Estimate[a]	Standard Error Estimate
CEA	Log(AFDC rate)	Any waiver	−5.751	2.6
CEA	Log(AFDC rate)	JOBS sanctions	−2.043	5.641
CEA	Log(AFDC rate)	JOBS exemptions	5.733	4.695
CEA	Log(AFDC rate)	Termination time limits	−6.79	7
CEA	Log(AFDC rate)	Work requirement time limits	−9.211	5.6
CEA	Log(AFDC rate)	Family cap	−10.58	4.751
CEA	Log(AFDC rate)	Earnings disregard	−4.569	4.318
CPS	AFDC rate	Any waiver	−1.007	0.3673
CPS Doubled[b]	AFDC rate	Any waiver	−1.007	0.2597
CPS-Disaggregated	AFDC rate	Waiver by education < 12 interaction	−1.67	0.6064
CPS-Disaggregated	AFDC rate	Waiver by education = 12 interaction	−0.947	0.6064
CPS-Disaggregated	AFDC rate	Waiver by education = 13–15 interaction	−0.662	0.6064
CPS-Disaggregated	AFDC rate	Waiver by education = 16+ interaction	−0.751	0.6065
CPS	Annual Weeks Worked	Any waiver	9.837662	8.766234
CPS	Annual Hours Worked	Any waiver	13.72197	10.49327
CPS	Annual Earnings	Any waiver	27.68749	16.33189
CPS	Weekly Earnings	Any waiver	16.84836	11.89296

[a]Due to different definitions of the dependent variable CEA and CPS AFDC effect estimates are not directly comparable; see discussion for details.

[b]The effect estimate is taken from the same analysis as the CPS row. The standard error estimate is the CPS row standard error estimate divided by $\sqrt{2}$ to approximate the effect of doubling the sample size on standard errors. In future analyses, perhaps a figure greater than the somewhat conservative $\sqrt{2}$ should be used since an expansion of sample size should enable considerable unclustering of the sample and increase efficiency even more.

facilitate comparison to the CEA analyses. The CPS analyses were done at the state level and at the disaggregated level where the state was disaggregated by women's age and educational attainment. In addition, other CPS based models for other outcome variables are included.

AN INTRODUCTION TO REGRESSION POWER CALCULATIONS

Statistical power is the probability of detecting an effect of a certain size if that effect does exist. To perform power calculations, one needs an estimate of effect size[1] and an estimate of the variance or standard error of the effect. Power calculations for regressions require an estimate of the regression coefficient of interest (β), an estimate of the variance of the error (σ), and an estimate of the variance-covariance matrix of the independent variables. Using these quantities, an estimate of the variance of a regression coefficient vector is

$$\hat{VAR}(\hat{\beta}) = \hat{\sigma}^2 (X'X)^{-1}.$$

It is usually only possible to perform regression power calculations if a similar regression is available, as we have in the analyses considered here.

Note that all of the quantities involved can affect the power. Larger regression coefficients are easier to detect. Incorporating important variables can reduce the estimated variance. Less obviously, the correlations between the independent variables can reduce power. In this paper we condition on the observed values of the variance estimates and independent variables. We then explore the power over plausible ranges of effect sizes and total sample sizes.[2]

THE POWER OF CEA MODELS TO DETECT WAIVER EFFECTS AND COMPONENT EFFECTS ON AFDC CASELOADS

The CEA models use the log of the AFDC case rate as the dependent variable. The rate is defined as the AFDC caseload divided by the state population. The log transformation gives the coefficient estimates in Table C-1 a convenient percent change interpretation. For example, the –5.75 in the first "any waiver" row corresponds to a decrease of 5.75 percent in caseload if a state has a waiver.

The CEA effect estimates in Table C-1 come from two models. The first model has an indicator for the state's waiver status in a given year. We label these as "any waiver" models. The second model replaces this waiver indicator

---

[1]Some discussions of power use effect size to refer to the ratio of the quantity of interest to its standard error. Here we use the term to refer only to the quantity of interest. This is more consistent with the use of effect size in the welfare evaluation literature.

[2]For any given effect size power = $\Phi(\dfrac{\beta}{\hat{\sigma}_\beta} - Z_{a/2})$, where Φ is the standard normal cumulative distribution function, β is the hypothesized effect size, $\hat{\sigma}_\beta$ is the estimated standard error from the regression, and $Z_{a/2}$ is the critical value from the normal distribution for a two sided test of size α. All of the power calculations presented in this appendix use an α of 5 percent.

with a collection of indicators describing the particular components of a state's AFDC program. These included: (1) whether a state imposed sanctions for failure of AFDC recipients to participate in the state's Job Opportunity and Basic Skills (JOBS) program; (2) whether a state exempted various groups from the JOBS program; (3) whether a state imposed time limits on receipt of cash assistance from the AFDC program; (4) whether a state had time limits on the work requirements of AFDC recipients; (5) whether the state imposed a family cap on an assistance unit's monthly AFDC benefit; and (6) whether the state disregarded some amount of earnings of an assistance unit when calculating the AFDC monthly cash benefit. In addition to an indicator for waiver status or a collection of component indictors as independent variables, the models include state indicators and trends, unemployment rate and lagged unemployment rate, and the log of the maximum AFDC benefit for a family of three.

Figure C-1 presents power curves for the CEA models. Each curve shows the power of the models to detect an effect over a range of potential effect sizes.

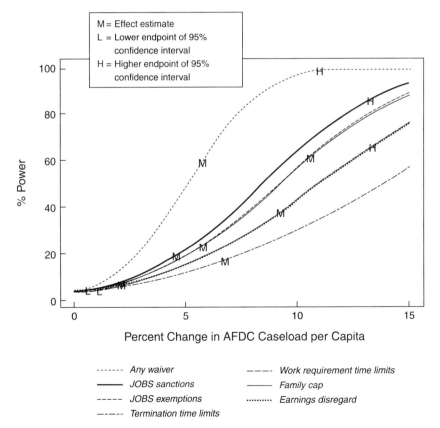

FIGURE C-1 Power for the CEA models.

All power curves in this figure use the absolute value of the effect size. For reference, each curve has been labeled with estimates of the effect sizes from the CEA models. The "M" corresponds to the effect estimate. The "L" and "H" correspond to the lower and upper endpoints of a 95 percent confidence interval for the effect size. Note that the L and H may not appear on some curves if they are out of the range of the figure. In particular, effects that were not significantly different from zero will have lower bounds below zero.

For the CEA models, only the any waiver effect has substantial power for this observed effect size, sample size, state sample allocation, and pattern of waivers across the states and over time. The roughly 60 percent power at the observed effect size (5.75) suggests that an effect of this size could be detected in 6 out of 10 similar situations. This is not a very encouraging power for one of the larger welfare reforms in recent history. The power to detect component effects is typically smaller. The exception is the family cap indicator, which has a somewhat larger power than the any waiver indicator. A decomposition of a bundle of features can have larger power for some or even all of the components if the components have substantial effect sizes and are not too correlated with each other.

The usefulness of Figure C-1 goes beyond simply assessing the statistical power associated with the observed effects. The figure can also be used to understand the power to detect other effect sizes with a similar pattern of state "roll out" over time. Consider a reform hypothesized to have a similar roll out pattern but only half the any waiver effect size: the Figure C-1 suggests that the power to detect this effect would be only 20 percent.

THE POWER OF CPS MODELS TO DETECT WAIVER EFFECTS ON AFDC CASELOADS AND CASELOADS IN SUBSETS OF THE POPULATION

In his paper, Moffitt (1999) modifies the CEA analysis by using CPS data in place of the size of state caseloads in a given year. There are two motivations for this modification. The first motivation is to move below the state level of aggregation and explore the effects of reform in subsets of the population. Here, we focus on the disaggregation by educational attainment. The second motivation is to capitalize on the availability of other outcome measures in the CPS. We address these other outcome measures in the next section.

In the CPS analyses, the definition of the dependent variable is different from the definition used in the CEA analyses in three ways. First, the denominator (population) definition in the AFDC case rate calculation is changed to women age 16 to 54. Second, the caseload is estimated from the CPS rather than the CEA estimates. Third, no log transformations of outcome measures are used. An effect in the CPS models is the percent change in women aged 16-54 on AFDC. The models in the original work reported results as rates. Here we have multiplied the rates by 100 to yield percentage. Note that these percentage are of women aged 16-54, not percentage changes in caseload.

Figure C-2 presents power curves for a model with a single any waiver indicator and a model that replaces the any waiver indicator by the indicators for the interactions of any waiver with different levels of educational attainment. Additional independent variables are state indicators and trends, unemployment rate, lagged unemployment rate, and the log of the maximum AFDC benefit for a family of three.

As in Figure C-1, each curve has been labeled with estimates of the effect sizes from the CEA models. The "M" corresponds to the observed effect estimate. The "L" and "H" correspond to the lower and upper endpoints of a 95 percent confidence interval for the effect size. Note that the L and H may not appear on some curves if they are out of the range of the figure. In particular effects that were not significantly different from zero will have lower bounds below zero.

The any waiver curve in Figure C-2 shows the larger power, approximately 80 percent, at the observed effect size than the CEA model. We speculate that this is due to the combination of the more targeted population (women aged 16-64) for which the outcome is assessed and the disaggregation of the model into age and education cells. After disaggregation, there are 15,504 cells, quadrupling the number of cells. Since this disaggregation almost certainly reduces bias, this is a more defensible and a more powerful model. The power curves for the any

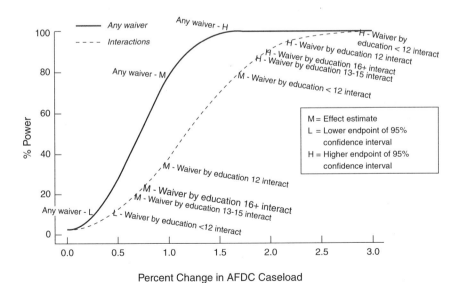

FIGURE C-2 Power for models with CPS data.

waiver by educational attainment interactions are all superimposed in Figure C-2. This is a consequence of the model's having the same structure for each education group. Note that the least educated group has the largest observed effect size. Despite the lower power curves for the population subsets this larger effect size results in more power at the observed effect size than the any waiver model. This result illustrates the valuable power consequences of finding an appropriate desegregation of the data. It is possible for the average effect in the aggregate data to be the result of a more pronounced result in a subset of the data averaged with smaller effects.

As discussed for Figure C-1, these curves provide information on more than just the statistical power for the observed effects. The figure also helps one to understand the power to detect other effect sizes with a similar pattern of state roll out over time. The interaction curves should be of particular interest to anyone trying to understand the power to evaluate interventions that focus on a subset of the eligible population.

THE POWER OF CPS MODELS TO DETECT WAIVER EFFECTS ON OTHER OUTCOME MEASURES

Another advantage of the use of CPS data rather than aggregate caseload size is the availability of other outcome measures of welfare reform. Using the same model specification as the any waiver CPS model presented in the previous section, Moffitt considered four other outcome measures: annual weeks worked, annual hours worked, annual earnings, and weekly earnings. Figure C-3 presents power curves for these other outcomes. Note that the units are different for the different outcome measures and that none of the observed effect sizes have a power of more than 50 percent. The lower powers here are a consequence of the higher error variance for these outcomes. This result suggests that these outcome measures would be difficult to use for welfare reform evaluation unless the reform was expected to have a substantially larger effect on these measures than waivers or a larger data set was available.

OBTAINING MORE POWER

Despite the seemingly important changes that waivers brought to the welfare system, the above analyses imply that the basic CEA analysis barely has enough statistical power to detect an effect of waivers on the size of state AFDC caseloads. Clearly, more statistical power is needed to maximize the usefulness of this type of analysis to inform future welfare policy issues. The analyses presented above suggest two possible methods for obtaining more power—improved modeling and increased sample size.

Improved modeling is the most economical way to improve statistical power. Moffitt's success in getting more power out of the same policy shift is exemplary.

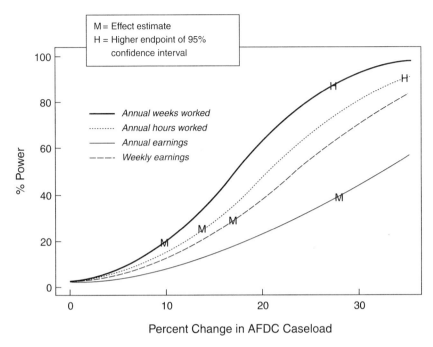

FIGURE C-3 Power for CPS models of additional outcomes.

More detailed modeling, if there are data to support the additional detail, can improve power with no increase in data collection costs. Further disaggregation also appears to be a promising direction. Perhaps more geographical detail (e.g., urban versus rural) could be obtained. Similarly, more detailed decomposition of the features of reform hold the promise of additional power potential.

The other key driver of statistical power is total sample size. In Figure C-4, we present an additional power curve for a hypothetical doubling of the size of the CPS samples in every state. The power for the observed effect size increases to approximately 95 percent. In study design problems, one frequently sees power curves where doubling the sample size increases the power from inadequate to slightly less inadequate. This is not the case here. A doubling of the CPS sample size would add substantially to the ability to measure the effects of welfare reform. However, a simple doubling of the sample sizes for each state is not necessarily the optimal way to allocate a doubling of sample size. Although the optimal allocation depends on the pattern of reform roll out in a future evaluation, it is likely that the best use of resources is to more than double sample sizes in the smaller states at the expense of less than doubling them in the larger states.

Several caveats should be made when interpreting the power analyses we have presented in this paper. First, a different pattern of roll out for the waivers

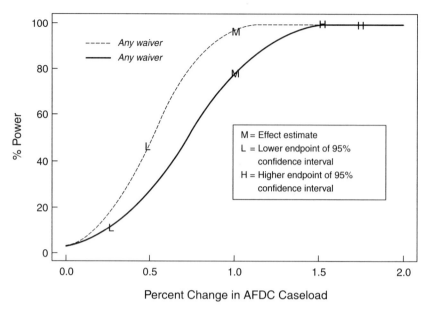

FIGURE C-4 Power for the CPS model if sample sizes are doubled.

could result in a different power. Second, the other variables in the model (e.g., unemployment rate) can affect power as well. Different patterns in the future could confound with changes, reducing power. Third, there are other functional forms (e.g., first differences) that could have better or worse power. Fourth, we have not incorporated any elaborate error structure in the modeling herein. Correlated errors could further reduce power.

One of the advantages of this style of analysis is that it does fit one model for the entire United States. Models of this type can set the context for other analyses of more limited scope. With further improvements in disaggregation and increased sample sizes, this style of analysis could increase its contribution to the reform analysis portfolio of methods.

REFERENCES

Bartik, Timothy, and Randall Eberts
    1999   Examining the effect of industry trends and structure on Welfare caseloads. Pp.119-157
            in *Economic Conditions and Welfare Reform*. Sheldon Danziger, ed. Kalamazoo, MI:
            Upjohn Institute.
Blank, Rebecca M.
    1997   What Causes Public Assistance Caseloads to Grow? Working Paper #2, Joint Center for
            Poverty Research, University of Chicago and Northwestern University.

1999 What Goes Up Must Come Down? Explaining Recent Changes in Public Assistance Caseloads. Working Paper # 78, (March). Joint Center for Poverty Research, University of Chicago and Northwestern University.

Council of Economic Advisers
1997 *Technical Report: Explaining the Decline in Welfare Receipt, 1993-1996.* Washington, DC: U.S. Government Printing Office.

Figlio, David, Craig Gundersen, and James Ziliak
2000 The effects of the macroeconomy and welfare reform on food stamp caseloads. *American Journal of Agricultural Economics*, Forthcoming.

Moffitt, Robert
1998 The effect of pre-PRWORA waivers on AFDC caseloads and female earnings, income and labor force behavior. Pp. 91-118 in *Economic Conditions and Welfare Reform*, Sheldon Danziger, ed. Kalamazoo, MI: Upjohn Institute.

Schoeni, Robert F., and Rebecca M. Blank
1999 What has Welfare Reform Accomplished? Impacts on Welfare Participation, Employment, Income, Poverty, and Family Structure. Working Paper No. W7627, National Bureau of Economics Research (March).

Ziliak, James P., and David N. Figlio
2000 Geographic Differences in AFDC and Food Stamp Caseloads in the Welfare Reform Era. Working Paper # 180, Joint Center for Poverty Research, University of Chicago and Northwestern University (May).

Ziliak, James P., David N. Figlio, Elizabeth Davis, and Laura Connolly
2000 Accounting for the decline in AFDC caseloads: Welfare reform or the economy? *The Journal of Human Resources* 35(3):570-586.

Appendix D

Summaries of National-Level Survey Data Sets Relevant to Welfare Monitoring and Evaluation

DECENNIAL LONG FORM

2000 Census Long Form

The 2000 census, like every census since 1960, included a long-form questionnaire that is administered to a sample of households. The long form includes the short-form questions that are asked of all households with additional questions that are included only on the long form. The added questions include ones on total income and income from seven different sources (e.g., wages, Social Security, and public assistance or welfare benefits, etc.) for the previous calendar year for each household member aged 15 or older. Both the short-form and long-form census questionnaires are mandatory.

The *sample design* for the 2000 census long form was similar to the design used in the 1990 census with some modification. In 1990 the overall sampling rate was about 1 in 6, producing a sample of about 18 million occupied housing units. In 2000, the overall sampling rate was again be about 1 in 6, producing a sample of about 18 million housing units.

Data collection in the census is mainly by self-enumeration, whereby a respondent for each household fills out a questionnaire received in the mail.

NOTE: Descriptions of the census long form, the American Community Survey, the March Current Population Survey, and the Survey of Income and Program Participation in this appendix are based on National Research Council (2000).

Enumerators follow up those households that fail to return a questionnaire and collect the information through direct interviews. *Response rates* to the census mailout have declined since 1970, when mailout-mailback techniques were first used. In 1990 approximately 60 percent of U.S. households mailed back their long form questionnaires; in 2000 approximately 54 percent mailed back their questionnaires.

As in all censuses, there were uncounted people in 1990; there were also duplications and other erroneous enumerations. The net undercount in 1990 (gross undercount minus gross overcount) was estimated at 1.8 percent for the total population, but there were substantial differences among population groups. For example, the net undercount was estimated at 5.7 percent for blacks and 1.3 percent for nonblacks. The net undercount also varied significantly by age: almost two-thirds of the estimated omitted population consisted of children under age 10 and men aged 25-39 (Robinson et al., 1993:13).

Item nonresponse rates in 1990 were generally higher for income than for most other items. When household income information is missing, the Census Bureau uses statistical techniques to impute data on the basis of nearby households with similar characteristics. On average, 19 percent of aggregate household income was imputed for 1990 (National Research Council, 1995:387).

Processing and release of the long-form sample data will be provided for areas as small as census tracts and school districts. Typically, long-form data products are released beginning in year 2 and continuing through year 3 after the census year.

Additional information can be found at The Census Bureau website for the census: (http://www.census.gov/dmd/www/2khome.htm).

AMERICAN COMMUNITY SURVEY

The American Community Survey is planned to be a large-scale, continuing monthly sample survey of housing units in the United States, conducted primarily by mail. It will include content similar to that of the decennial census long-form sample, including questions on income and its sources and on participation in public assistance programs, such as cash assistance and noncash assistance such as food stamps, and rental subsidies. The income and assistance receipt questions will refer to the 12 months preceding the interview month. It is planned that the ACS will be mandatory, like the census, rather than a voluntary survey. If the ACS is successfully implemented, there will likely be no long form in the 2010 and subsequent censuses.

Development of the ACS began in 1996 when the survey was tested in four sites, in 1997-1998 it was tested in eight states. Beginning in 1999 and extending through 2001, the ACS will be conducted in 31 sites, chosen to facilitate comparison with the 2000 census long-form data for census tracts and other areas. In

25 of the 31 sites, about 0.4 percent of housing units will be sampled each month, which will generate a sample of about 5 percent of housing units for each of the 3 years, or 15 percent for the 3-year period. (For budgetary reasons, the 3-year sample will be about 9 percent in five sites and 3 percent in one site.) Also, for each year from 2000 to 2002, there will be a nationwide survey, using the ACS questionnaire, of about 700,000 housing units.

Beginning in 2003, the *full ACS sample* will be 250,000 housing units each month for the rest of the decade, for an annual sample size of about 3 million housing units spread across all counties in the nation. Over a 5-year period, the addresses selected for the ACS sample will cumulate to about 15 million housing units, similar to but somewhat smaller than the 2000 census long-form sample size of about 18 million housing units.

Each month's ACS sample will be drawn from the Census Bureau's Master Address File (MAF) for the entire nation. The MAF is a comprehensive residential address list developed for the 2000 census that the Census Bureau intends to update on a continuous basis following the census. The current design calls for the ACS to use a sample design similar to that of the 2000 census long form, with higher sampling rates for small governmental units and lower sampling rates for large census tracts. The sampling rates would be applied by systematic sampling from the MAF.

Data collection in the ACS will be conducted by mailing a questionnaire similar to the census long form to all households in the sample. A replacement questionnaire will be mailed to nonresponding households about 3 weeks later. Then, after about another 3 weeks, nonresponding households will be contacted to the extent possible by the use of computer-assisted telephone interviewing (CATI). In the final stage of follow-up, a one-third sample of the remaining nonrespondent households will be drawn, and field representatives will be sent to interview these households in person, using computer-assisted personal interviewing (CAPI) techniques.

Responses were obtained from about 78 percent of the originally designated sample for the four initial ACS test sites—61 percent of occupied housing units responded by mail, another 8 percent responded to the telephone follow-up, and 9 percent responded to the personal follow-up. Because of subsampling at the final stage of follow-up, the weighted response rate in the four initial ACS test sites was over 95 percent.

Item nonresponse rates may be lower in the ACS than in the 1990 census, at least for some items, based on preliminary results from the 1996 ACS test sites (Salvo and Lobo, 1997: Tersine, 1998). On the other hand, the ACS, like other household surveys, may cover the population less well than the census, based on one analysis that found more small households and fewer large households in the 1996 ACS than in the 1990 census. This result could indicate that the ACS is missing a larger proportion of people in interviewed households than are missed in the census (Ferrari, 1998).[1]

Publication plans for the ACS, once it is fully implemented, call for the Census Bureau to issue annual reports containing yearly averages of the monthly data for areas with 65,000 or more people. The Census Bureau also plans each year to publish 3-year averages for areas with 20,000-65,000 people and 5-year averages for areas with fewer than 20,000 people.

Although delivery schedules are not known with certainty, yearly averages from the full ACS should be available beginning within a year after the ACS is fully implemented in 2003 (i.e., in 2004). However, 3-year averages will not be available until 2006 at the earliest, and 5-year averages will not be available until 2008 at the earliest. Once sufficient years of data are cumulated to provide 1-, 2-, 3- or 5-year averages as appropriate, each set of averages will be updated yearly. The production goal is to deliver averages within 6 months after the close of a calendar year.

Additional information can be found at The Census Bureau website for the ACS: (http://www.census.gov/acs/www/).

MARCH CPS

The Current Population Survey is a voluntary monthly labor force participation survey, begun in the 1940s, that includes supplemental questions in many months. For the annual March income supplement, the CPS asks household respondents about income received during the previous calendar year, including income received from public cash assistance programs. The questionnaire also asks about noncash benefit receipt, including Medicaid coverage for household members, food stamps receipt and amount of benefits, energy assistance benefit receipt and amount, free and reduced priced school lunch program benefits for children in the household, and whether the household lives in public housing or receives a housing subsidy.

The monthly CPS *sample,* beginning in 1996, included about 50,000 households, or 1 in 2,000—a reduction in sample size of about 17 percent from the early 1990s. Part of the CPS sample is changed each month: in the rotation plan—under which each sampled address is in the survey for 4 months, out of the survey for 8 months, and in the survey for another 4 months—three-fourths of the sample addresses are common from one month to the next, and one-half are common for the same month a year earlier.

The CPS uses a multistage probability sample design, which is revised after

---

[1]In addition to within-household undercoverage, which occurs when some but not all household members are listed in the interview, there is undercoverage due to whole household misses, which this study did not address.

each decennial census. A design based on the 1990 census was phased in between April 1994 and July 1995: it included 792 sample areas consisting of about
1,300 counties, chosen to represent all 3,143 counties and independent cities in
the 50 states and the District of Columbia.[2]

The CPS has a state-representative design, which results in larger states
generally having larger CPS sample sizes, but with the largest states having CPS
sample sizes that are smaller than their proportionate share of the U.S. population
and the smallest states having proportionately larger sample sizes. For example,
California, with 12.2 percent of the U.S. population, has 9.9 percent of the CPS
sample; Wyoming, with 0.18 percent of the U.S. population, has 1.3 percent of
the CPS sample. This sample design means that income and program participation estimates in large states are generally more precise than those in smaller
states. The largest states, however, have larger relative errors due to sampling
variability than would be expected if the CPS sample were allocated to the states
in proportion to their population; the reverse holds true for smaller states.[3] In fall
1999 the Census Bureau received an appropriation to adjust the March CPS
sample size and design so that reliable annual estimates at the state level could be
provided of the numbers of low-income children lacking health insurance coverage by family income, age, and race or ethnicity.

Data collection for the CPS is carried out by permanent, experienced interviewers. The first interview and fifth interviews at an address are usually conducted in person; the other six interviews at an address are usually conducted by
telephone; CAPI and CATI are used. One household member who is aged 15 or
older is allowed to respond for other members.

Response rates in the CPS are high, typically about 94-95 percent of households respond, though they declined by 1-2 percentage points beginning in 1997.
each month. However, some interviewed households do not provide information
for all members—for this reason, there is little data beyond basic demographic
characteristics for about 9 percent of members of interviewed households. In
addition, some people who respond to the basic CPS labor force questionnaire do
not respond to the March income supplement. To adjust for whole household
nonresponse to the basic CPS, the Census Bureau increases the weights of similar
responding households. To adjust for person nonresponse to the basic CPS, it
imputes a complete data record for another person with similar demographic
characteristics.

Like other household surveys, the CPS exhibits population undercoverage at

---

[2]In January 1996 the number of sample areas was reduced from 792 to 754.

[3]To meet national-level reliability criteria for the unemployment rate, the sample size in a few
large states (e.g., California, Florida, New York, Texas) is somewhat longer than what would be
required by a state-based design (see the joint Bureau of Labor Statistics and Bureau of the Census
CPS website: www.bls.census.gov/cps/mdocmain.html).

higher rates than the census. For March 1994, the ratio of the CPS estimated population to the census-based population control total (all ages) was 92 percent; for black men aged 30-44 years, the coverage ratios were as low as 67-68 percent (U.S. Census Bureau, 1996:Table D-2). It is estimated that about two-thirds of CPS undercoverage is due to missed people in otherwise interviewed households (i.e., people whose existence, let alone any information about them, is not known to the interviewer); the remainder is due to missed housing units because the address was not included in the sampling frame. CPS undercoverage is corrected by ratio adjustments to the survey weights that bring the CPS estimates of population in line with updated national population controls by age, race, sex, and Hispanic origin. Beginning with the March 1994 CPS, the population controls for survey weights reflect an adjustment for the undercount in the census itself. However, the ratio adjustments do not correct for other characteristics, such as income, on which the undercovered population might be expected to differ from the covered population in each adjustment cell.

There is substantial item nonresponse in the March income supplement. About 20 percent of aggregate household income is imputed (about the same percentage as in the census; see National Research Council, 1993:Table 3-6). Imputation techniques are used to provide values for people who fail to respond to the income supplement entirely, as well as for people who fail to answer one or more questions on the supplement.

Publication of detailed official income and poverty estimates from the CPS for the nation as a whole and population groups occurs each year about 6 months after data collection in March. Limited statistics are also published for states on the basis of 3-year averages.

Additional information can be found at The Census Bureau website for the CPS (http://www.bls.census.gov/cps/ads/adsmain.htm).

SURVEY OF INCOME AND PROGRAM PARTICIPATION

SIPP is a continuing voluntary panel survey begun in 1983. From 1983 to 1993, a new sample (panel) of households was introduced each February. Adult members of originally sampled households in each panel were followed and interviewed every 4 months for 32 months, although some panels had fewer than eight interview waves because of budget restrictions, and the 1992 and 1993 panels had ten waves and nine waves, respectively. The 1996 panel, begun in April, followed original sample adults every 4 months for 4 years. A new two-wave panel began in 2000, and a new 3-year panel will begin in 2001.

SIPP is focused on income measurement. The core questionnaire, administered at each interview wave, obtains monthly information on detailed sources and amounts of income from earnings and public and private transfer payments and information for the 4-month period on income from assets. In total, about 56 separate sources of cash income are identified together with benefits from 7 in-kind programs. Additional detail on program participation and related topics (e.g., child care, health) is collected in various supplements (topical modules).

The SIPP *sample* covers the U.S. civilian noninstitutionalized population and members of the armed forces living off post or with their families on post. Sample sizes for the 1983-1993 panels varied from 12,500 to 23,500 originally sampled households per panel. The sample size for the 1996 panel was 37,000 originally sampled households; it included households in all states but was not designed to provide reliable estimates at the state level. The sample size for the two-wave 2000 panel was 11,000 households. The sample size for the 3-year 2001 panel is 37,000 households; another larger sized panel will begin in 2004. The 1996 sample included an oversample of addresses in which the residents had family incomes below 150 percent of the poverty level in 1989, based on information from the 1990 census. Proxy characteristics, such as housing tenure and family type, were used for oversampling addresses for which only short-form census information was available. In rural areas, some addresses were oversampled on the basis of 1990 census poverty-related characteristics for the census block in which they were located.

Data collection for SIPP is carried out by permanent, experienced interviewers. The first and second interviews and one interview in each subsequent year of a panel are conducted in person, using CAPI (computer-assisted personal interviewing). Other interviews are conducted by telephone, using CATI (computer-assisted telephone interviewing). Household members aged 15 or older are supposed to respond for themselves, but proxy responses from other householders are accepted. About 35 percent of interviews for adults in each wave are by proxy; over the life of a panel, 60-65 percent of adult sample members have at least one proxy interview (U.S. Census Bureau, 1998).

Response rates to the first wave of a SIPP panel are somewhat lower than CPS response rates: about 5-8 percent of eligible households in the 1983-1991 SIPP panels did not respond to the first interview wave and were dropped from the sample. The first wave nonresponse rate for households in the 1992 and 1993 panels was 9 percent. It was 8 percent for the 1996 panel. By wave 8, the cumulative household nonresponse rate in the 1983-1991 panels was 21-22 percent; in the 1992 and 1993 panels it was 25 percent. By wave 6 of the 1996 panel, the cumulative nonresponse rate was 27 percent. About three-quarters of household nonresponse is due to refusals, and one-quarter is due to losing track of sample household members who move (U.S. Census Bureau, 1998).

People who drop out of SIPP tend to differ from those who stay in the survey: attrition is more likely to occur among young adults, males, minority groups, never-married people, poor people, and people with lower educational attainment (see, e.g., Lamas et al., 1994). There is also evidence that the current noninterview weighting adjustments do not fully compensate for differential attrition across population groups (see, e.g., King et al., 1990).

Like the CPS and other household surveys, SIPP covers the population less well than the census. Coverage ratios (survey population estimates divided by census-based population estimates) are similar for the CPS and SIPP. SIPP has lower item nonresponse rates than the March CPS: overall, only 11 percent of total regular money income obtained for calendar year 1984 from the first four waves of the 1984 SIPP panel was imputed, compared with 20 percent in the March 1985 CPS. The SIPP and March CPS imputation rates for 1984 for earnings were 10 percent and 19 percent, respectively; for public and private transfers, 12 percent and 21 percent, respectively; and for property income, 24 percent and 32 percent, respectively (Jabine et al., 1990:Table 10.8; see also National Research Council, 1993:Tables 3-4, 3-5).

Data processing for SIPP involves complex operations, particularly to produce calendar-year and longitudinal panel files. Historically, this has often resulted in delays of 1, 2, or more years between collection of data from an interview wave or all waves in a panel and release of data files and publications. There is no regular publication series for SIPP; publications are released on topics of interest, such as program participation, and include estimates for population groups for the nation as a whole.

Additional information can be found at The Census Bureau website for SIPP (http://www.sipp.census.gov/sipp/).

SURVEY OF PROGRAM DYNAMICS

The Survey of Program Dynamics (SPD) is a voluntary study being conducted by the Census Bureau under a requirement of the 1996 PRWORA legislation. The purpose of the SPD is to collect longitudinal data on the demographic, social, and economic characteristics of a nationally representative sample of the U.S. population so that overall evaluations of welfare reforms can be conducted. Congress mandated that the 1992 and 1993 SIPP panels continue to be followed so that the prereform characteristics and well-being of families would be understood. The data from the 1992 and 1993 SIPP panels give 3 years of a longitudinal baseline before the reforms in 1996 (1992-1994 for half the sample and 1993-1994 for the other half; no longitudinal data from 1995 were collected). SPD will follow the 1992 and 1993 panels of SIPP participants over the years 1996-2001, meaning that, combined, SIPP and SPD will provide 9 years of panel data.

In 1997 there was the SPD Bridge Survey, based on a modified version of the March 1997 CPS questionnaire. A new core SPD questionnaire was developed for the 1998 survey (with the assistance of Child Trends, Inc.). The 1998 survey included a self-administered adolescent questionnaire and retrospective questions on the core topics of jobs, income, and program participation for all persons over the age of 15. The 1999 SPD included a module on child well-being, and the 2000 SPD included a children's residential history module. Both the adolescent and child well-being questionnaire modules will be included in the 2002 SPD.

The SPD *sample* consists of all sample persons in the almost 38,000 households that completed all waves of the 1992-1993 SIPP panels (76% of the two original SIPP samples). The sample size for the 1998 SPD was reduced to approximately 18,500 because of budget constraints. In subsampling the original households, the Census Bureau kept more low-income households and low income households with and without children in the survey than high-income households with and without children.

The SPD data collection is carried out by permanent, experienced interviewers. Computer-assisted interviews, by telephone and in person, are conducted for the questionnaire once a year in May and June. The adolescent questionnaire is a self-administered questionnaire.

Response rates for the Bridge Survey were about 82 percent (about 30,000). The 1998 SPD interviewed 89 percent of eligible households, and the 1999 survey had a response rate of 86 percent. The cumulative attrition rate is high: the beginning 1992 and 1993 SIPP panels had already lost 27 percent of the original SIPP panels, and through the 1999 SPD, the rate is approaching 50 percent. The Census Bureau is planning several steps to address the attrition problem, including interviewing a targeted sample of SIPP and SPD Bridge survey nonrespondents and offering cash incentives to these nonrespondents for completing a survey. Plans to link Social Security Administrative earnings records to SPD households to assess any effects of attrition and to look at employer-side variables have also been made. The Office of the Assistant Secretary for Planning and Evaluation is contributing funds for the Social Security records and SPD/SIPP analysis.

The Census Bureau has explored the degree to which reported data from the SPD differs from data reported from the March CPS, particularly information on program benefit receipt, income, and earnings. There are some statistical differences in measures of these items between these two surveys (Weinberg and Shipp, 2000).

Data from the 1997 survey and preliminary data from the 1998 survey are currently available. A longitudinal file with data from 1992 through the 1998 survey is scheduled to be released in the summer of 2001.

Additional information can be found at The Census Bureau website for SIPP (http://www.sipp.census.gov/spd/).

THE NATIONAL SURVEY OF AMERICA'S FAMILIES

The National Survey of America's Families (NSAF) is part of the Urban Institute's New Federalism Project, which is analyzing the devolution of responsibility for social programs from the federal government to the states. The survey is voluntary and is designed to document the well-being of children, their families, and adults under the age of 65 within and across states, as well as changes in the well-being of these populations over time. The survey questions collect data on many benefits programs, including AFDC; Social Security Insurance (SSI); food stamps; Women, Infants, and Children (WIC); and school lunches. The initial survey was conducted from February to November 1997, and the second-round survey was fielded from February to October 1999. A third round is planned for 2002.

The NSAF sample includes approximately 1,800 families with children under age 18 in each of 13 states (Alabama, California, Colorado, Florida, Massachusetts, Michigan, Minnesota, Mississippi, New Jersey, New York, Texas, Washington, and Wisconsin) where intensive case studies of policies and implementation will be conducted, as well as a sample drawn from the balance of the nation. Together, the 13 states encompass more than half of the nation's population and represent a broad range of fiscal capacity, child well-being, and approaches to government programs. About 950 families with incomes below 200 percent of poverty are included from each of the 13 states. These low-income households are oversampled because it is anticipated that the policy changes will most affect them. The sample also includes about 1,200 households without children under age 18 in each state. There is overlap between the 1997 and 1999 samples designed to reduce the variance of estimates. Because of the focus on low-income families, the sample includes families without telephones and uses a dual-frame design consisting of a random-digit-dialing component for telephone households and an area sample for households without telephones.

NSAF data collection is conducted primarily by telephone survey using CATI. The interviews average 25 minutes in length for a household without children and 40 minutes for a household with children. Questions are asked about one or two focal children per household, one under the age of 6 and the other between the ages of 6 and 17 years old. The respondent is the household member who is most knowledgeable about the selected children. In households without children under age 18, the respondent is randomly selected from among the adults under the age of 65.

The data collected in 1997 serve as a baseline against which changes can be measured from the 1999 data. In 1997, detailed information was obtained for more than 75,000 adults and 34,000 children in more than 44,000 households. The response rate in 1997 was 70 percent. In 1999, detailed information was obtained for more than 73,000 adults under age 65 and almost 36,000 children in more than 42,000 households.

Data from both the 1997 and 1999 surveys have been published, and data files from both survey rounds are accessible for public use. The Urban Institute has issued a report of the initial results from both rounds of the survey.

Additional information can be found at the Urban Institute's website for this project (http://newfederalism.urban.org/nsaf/index.htm.)

THE PANEL STUDY OF INCOME DYNAMICS

The Panel Study of Income Dynamics (PSID) has been conducted since 1968 as a longitudinal survey of a representative sample of U.S. men, women, and children and their family units. PSID is conducted at the Survey Research Center (SRC) of the University of Michigan's Institute for Social Research. The survey is voluntary and emphasizes the dynamic aspects of economic and demographic behavior. Questions are asked regarding many benefit programs, including AFDC, SSI, food stamps, low income health services, and housing subsidies.

The sample for PSID has grown from 4,800 families in 1968 to 6,434 families in 1999, and is projected to grow to almost 7,400 in 2005. In 1968, it consisted of two independent samples—a cross-sectional sample and a national sample of low-income families. The cross-sectional sample was drawn by SRC as an equal probability sample of households from the 48 contiguous states designed to result in approximately 3,000 completed interviews. The second sample consisted of 2,000 low-income families who had responded to the Census Bureau's Survey of Economic Opportunity (SEO). The SRC and SEO samples were combined to yield the PSID core sample. In 1990, 2,000 Latino families originally from Mexico, Puerto Rico, and Cuba were added.

Every year from 1968 through 1996, PSID interviewed and reinterviewed individuals from families in the core sample. In 1997, the interview schedule became biennial and the sample was changed in two major ways to keep the study representative of the U.S. population. First, the core sample was reduced from 8,500 families in 1996 to approximately 6,168 in 1997 by reducing the SEO subsample by two-thirds. However, 609 families headed by at least one African American and containing at least one child aged 12 or under were added back into the sample. Second, a refresher sample of post-1968 immigrant families and their adult children was introduced. The Latino sample of 2,000 families that had been added in 1990 was dropped after 1995, and a more representative sample of 441 immigrant families was added in 1997.

In 1997 a Child Development Supplement was added to the core data collection. The supplement interviewed children and parents of children aged 0-12 on a variety of topics concerning the cognitive, behavioral, and health status of the children, as well as measures of the children's time use and the parents' or caregivers' time spent with the children.

From 1968 through 1972, data collection was conducted in face-to-face interviews with paper-and-pencil questionnaires. Since then, the majority of interviews have been completed by telephone. In 1993, PSID started using CATI; in 1999, 97.5 percent of the interviews were conducted by phone, all used CATI. As of 1997, PSID had collected information about more than 60,000 individuals, spanning as much as 30 years of their lives.

In 1968, 76 percent of sampled families were successfully interviewed. The response rate in 1969 was 88.5 percent, but interviews were attempted only with the heads of family units containing adults who were members of families interviewed in 1968. With a minor exception in 1990, no attempt has been made to recontact people who had been lost by attrition from previous years. Since 1969, annual response rates have ranged from 96.9 to 98.5 percent. However, when attrition is taken into account, the response rate for individuals who lived in the original 1968 households was 56.1 percent as of 1988.

The PSID Data Center is one of the main sources of data dissemination for this survey. As of November 2000, the most recent data available through the PSID Data Center are 1997 early release data (see http://stat0.isr.umich.edu/psid/data-center/data-center.html). The most recent final release data available are from the 1993 survey. In February 2000, the 1999 data were added to the 1984, 1989, 1994, and 1999 wealth files, but as of November 2000 the most recent data in the other PSID supplemental data files are from the 1997 survey (see http://www.isr.umich.edu/src/psid/suppdata.html).

Additional information can be found at the PSID website (http://www.isr.umich.edu/src/psid/).

THE NATIONAL LONGITUDINAL SURVEYS OF YOUTH

The National Longitudinal Survey of Youth 1979 cohort (NLSY79) is one of a set of surveys of cohorts initiated by the U.S. Department of Labor to analyze the sources of variation in the labor market experience of the U.S. population. The first set of surveys, initiated in 1966, consisted of four cohorts, referred to as the older men, mature women, young men, and young women and are known collectively as the NLS original cohorts. The NSLY79 cohort is the fifth cohort. The NLSY79 is a voluntary longitudinal survey of men and women representative of all Americans born in the late 1950s and early 1960s.

NLSY79 gathers data in an event history format, collecting dates for the beginning and ending of important life events, such as employment, marital status, and participation in government assistance programs, including AFDC, food stamps, and cash assistance. It is conducted by the National Opinion Research Center for the Ohio State University Center for Human Resource Research under a contract with the Bureau of Labor Statistics.

The NLSY79 sample is nationally representative of men and women who were born in the years 1957 to 1964 and were living in the United States when the sample was selected in 1978. It does not represent people who were born in the years 1957-1964 and immigrated to the United States after 1978. Three independent probability samples were drawn to represent this population: (1) a cross-sectional sample designed to be representative of the noninstitutionalized civilian population of youth; (2) a supplemental sample that oversamples civilian Hispanic, black, and economically disadvantaged non-Hispanic, nonblack youth and, (3) a military sample designed to represent the population aged 18-21 serving in the military as of September 30, 1978. The original sample included 12,686 young men and women. The oversample of youth enlisted in the military was discontinued after 1984, and the oversample of economically disadvantaged whites was discontinued after 1990. With these two subsamples removed, 9,964 respondents remain eligible for interview. Hispanics and blacks have continued to be oversampled. In 1986, the NLSY79 was expanded to include surveys of the children born to women in that cohort. The child survey is given on a biennial basis to all children born to NSLY79 mothers and includes cognitive, socio-emotional, and physiological assessments of each child. Demographic and development information are also collected for each child from either the mother or child.

Data collection for NLSY79 was annual until 1994, and biennial starting in 1996. Interviews were conducted in person or by telephone. Some data are collected for the respondent's spouse as well as the respondent. The response rate for each round of the survey has been over 84 percent.

In 1997, a new cohort of young people aged 12 to 16 as of December 31, 1996, were surveyed. This new cohort of about 9,000 youth is the National Longitudinal Survey of Youth 1997 (NLSY97). The initial round of the annual longitudinal survey interviewed both the youth and the youth's parent.

NLSY79 data publication occurs biennially. As of November 2000, the most recent data available were from the survey administered in 1998 (see http://stats.bls.gov/nlsdata.htm). Data from the first round of the NLSY97 were released in January 1999, data from the second round were released in May 2000, and data from the third round are scheduled to be released in May 2001.

Additional information can be found at the website of the Bureau of Labor Statistics (http://stats.bls.gov/nlshome.htm).

REFERENCES

Ferrari, P.
  1998 1996 American Community Survey vs. 1990 Decennial Census–Household Size and Characteristics by Response Mode. Paper prepared for the American Community Survey Symposium. Bureau of the Census, U.S. Department of Commerce, Washington, DC.
Jabine, T.B., K.E. King, and R.J. Petroni
  1990 *Survey of Income and Program Participation: Quality Profile.* Washington, DC: U.S. Department of Commerce.
King, K.E., S. Chou, M.K. McCormick, and R.J. Petroni
  1990 Investigations of the SIPP's cross-sectional noninterview adjustment method and variables. In *Proceedings of the Survey Research Methods Section.* Alexandria, VA: American Statistical Association.
Lamas, E., J. Tin, and J. Eargle
  1994 The Effect of Attrition on Income and Poverty Estimates from the Survey of Income and Program Participation (SIPP). SIPP Working Paper Number 190. Available at www.sipp.census.gov/sipp/wp190
National Research Council
  1993 *The Future of the Survey of Income and Program Participation.* Panel to Evaluate the Survey of Income and Program Participation. C.F. Citro and G. Kalton, eds. Washington, DC: National Academy Press.
  1995 *Measuring Poverty: A New Approach.* Panel on Poverty and Family Assistance: Concepts, Information Needs, and Measurement Methods. C.F. Citro and R.T. Michael, eds. Committee on National Statistics. Washington, DC: National Academy Press.

2000   *Small-Area Income and Poverty Estimates: Priorities for 2000 and Beyond.* Panel on Estimates of Poverty for Small Geographic Areas. C.F. Citro and G. Kalton, eds. Committee on National Statistics. Washington, DC: National Academy Press.

Robinson, J.G., B. Ahmed, P. Das Gupta, and K. Woodrow
1993   Estimation of population coverage in the 1990 U.S. based on demographic analysis. *Journal of the American Statistical Association* 88(423):1061-1079.

Salvo, J.J., and A.P. Lobo
1997   The American Community Survey: Nonresponse Follow-up in the Rockland County Test Site. Paper prepared for the American Community Survey Symposium. Population Division, Department of City Planning, New York, NY. (March).

Tersine, A.
1998   Item Nonresponse: 1996 American Community Survey. Paper prepared for the American Community Survey Symposium. Bureau of the Census, U.S. Department of Commerce, Washington, DC.

U.S. Census Bureau
1996   *Poverty in the United States: 1995.* Current Population Reports, Series P60-194. Washington, D.C.: U.S. Department of Commerce
1998   *Survey of Income and Program Participation Quality Profile 1998, 3rd Edition.* Washington, DC: U.S. Department of Commerce.

Weinberg, D.H., and S.S. Shipp
2000   The Survey of Program Dynamics: A Mid-Term Status Report. U.S. Census Bureau. Available: http://www.sipp.census.gov/spd/workpaper/summary10.htm#N_1_

Biographical Sketches of
Panel Members and Staff

ROBERT A. MOFFITT *(Chair)* is a professor in the Department of Economics and the Department of Population Dynamics at Johns Hopkins University. He is an affiliate of the Institute for Research on Poverty at the University of Wisconsin and a senior associate and member of the External Advisory Committee for the Northwestern University/University of Chicago Joint Center on Poverty Research. He is a member of the American Economic Association, the Econometric Society, the Population Association of America, and the Association of Public Policy Analysis and Management. He has published extensively in his field, particularly in the areas of labor economics, econometrics, public economics, and population economics. He received a B.A. in economics from Rice University and master's and Ph.D. degrees in economics from Brown University.

JOHN L. ADAMS is a senior statistician and head of the Statistical Consulting Service of the Statistics Group at RAND. Previously, he was a statistician for the Center for Urban and Regional Affairs and a research associate for the Management Information Division at the University of Minnesota. His research interests include statistical computing, data analysis, experimental design, and forecasting. He is a member of the American Statistical Association and received a Ph.D. in statistics from the University of Minnesota.

CONSTANCE F. CITRO is a senior staff member of the staff of the Committee on National Statistics. She is a former vice president and deputy director of Mathematica Policy Research, Inc., and was an American Statistical Association/ National Science Foundation research fellow at the Bureau of the Census. For the committee, she has served as study director for numerous panels, including the Panel on Poverty and Family Assistance, the Panel to Evaluate the Survey of Income and Program Participation, the Panel to Evaluate Microsimulation Models for Social Welfare Programs, and the Panel on Decennial Census Methodology. Her research has focused on the quality and accessibility of large, complex microdata files, as well as analysis related to income and poverty measurement. She is a fellow of the American Statistical Association. She received a B.A. degree from the University of Rochester and M.A. and Ph.D. degrees in political science from Yale University.

THOMAS CORBETT is associate director of the Institute for Research on Poverty and senior scientist at the University of Wisconsin, Madison. He has been involved at all levels of government in policy analysis and the development and evaluation of social welfare programs for over two decades. His research activities have focused on program administration and implementation and on the historical evolution of welfare issues, policies, and strategies in the United States. He received a Ph.D. in social welfare from the University of Wisconsin, Madison.

JOHN L. CZAJKA is a senior sociologist at Mathematica Policy Research, Inc. Much of his research has focused on statistical uses of administrative records and the design and analysis of longitudinal data. He is a member of the American Statistical Association, the Population Association of America, and the Washington Statistical Society. Czajka received a B.A. in government from Harvard University and a Ph.D. in sociology from the University of Michigan.

KATHRYN EDIN is an associate professor of the Department of Sociology and the Institute for Policy Research at Northwestern University. Before joining the university, she was associate professor of the Department of Sociology and the Population Studies Center at the University of Pennsylvania, an assistant professor of the Department of Sociology and the Center for Urban Policy Research at Rutgers University, and a visiting scholar at the Russell Sage Foundation. Her research interests include qualitative methods, social policy, gender, race, family studies, and urban sociology. Edin is also an associate fellow of the Institute for Research on Poverty at the University of Wisconsin, Madison, and of the Joint Center for Poverty Research at Northwestern University/University of Chicago. She received M.A. and Ph.D. degrees in sociology from Northwestern University.

IRWIN GARFINKEL is the Mitchell I. Ginsburg professor of contemporary urban problems at Columbia University School of Social Work. Previous positions held include professor and director of the school of social work and research member and director of the Institute for Research on Poverty at the University of

Wisconsin, Madison. He is also an affiliate of the Institute for Research on Poverty at the University of Wisconsin and a senior affiliate of the Northwestern University/University of Chicago Joint Center for Poverty Research. His research interests include social policy, child support, and single-parent families, and he has published extensively in these fields. He received a Ph.D. in social work and economics from the University of Michigan.

ROBERT M. GOERGE, associate director and research fellow at the Chapin Hall Center for Children at the University of Chicago, analyzes the experiences of children and families in the human service system in order to affect policy and program development at the state and national levels. His primary goal has been to describe these experiences over time and across the range of services, so that the complete experience of the child or family is understood. In order to do this, he developed the Integrated Database on Children and Family Services in Illinois, which makes use of computerized administrative data gathered by public agencies. This work is being replicated in other states with Chapin Hall's assistance. Dr. Goerge also co-led the development of the Multistate Foster Care Data Archive, which described the foster care histories of nearly two-thirds of the children in the United States. His recent and current work includes a study of the effect of teenage childbearing on child maltreatment and foster care, and an analysis of how children's need for human services is affected by welfare reform. He received master's and Ph.D. degrees in social policy from the University of Chicago.

ERIC A. HANUSHEK is the Paul and Jean Hanna Senior Fellow at the Hoover Institution of Stanford University. Previously he was a professor of economics and of public policy and director of the W. Allen Wallis Institute of Political Economy at the University of Rochester. He was formerly deputy director of the Congressional Budget Office and is a past president of the Association for Public Policy Analysis and Management. He previously held academic appointments at Yale University and the U.S. Air Force Academy and governmental appointments at the Cost of Living Council and the Council of Economic Advisers. He is an associate of the Institute for Research on Poverty at the University of Wisconsin, Madison. His research involves applied public finance and public policy analysis with special emphasis on education issues. He has also investigated the determination of individual incomes and wages, retirement income security, housing policy, social experimentation, statistical methodology, and the economics of discrimination. He received a Ph.D. in economics from the Massachusetts Institute of Technology.

V. JOSEPH HOTZ is a professor and chair of the Department of Economics at UCLA. He is a national research associate of the Northwestern University/University of Chicago Joint Center for Poverty Research and chaired the center's

Advisory Panel for Research Uses of Administrative Data. He is a research associate of the National Bureau of Economic Research, a member of the Board of Overseers of the Panel Study of Income Dynamics and chair of the Oversight Board of California Census Research Data Center. His research focuses on the economics of the family, applied econometrics, and the evaluation of social programs. He received a Ph.D. in economics from the University of Wisconsin, Madison.

RICHARD A. KULKA is senior research vice president of statistics, health, and social policy at the Research Triangle Institute. Prior to his current appointment, he was senior vice president for survey research at the National Opinion Research Center. He has been involved in the design, conduct, and analysis of numerous statistical surveys on health, mental health, and other social policy issues for over two decades, while also conducting a broad range of applied research on survey research methods in these areas. Kulka is a member of several professional associations, including the American Statistical Association, the American Association for Public Opinion Research, and the American Public Health Association. He received a Ph.D. in social psychology from the University of Michigan.

REBECCA A. MAYNARD is trustee professor of education and social policy at the University of Pennsylvania. Prior to her appointment, she served as senior vice president and director of research at Mathematica Policy Research, Inc. While at Mathematica, she spent over 18 years designing and evaluating education, employment, and welfare policies and programs. She has served as a consultant to the U.S. Department of Health and Human Services on welfare reform and to the U.S. General Accounting Office and the Rockefeller Foundation on various social welfare projects. She received a Ph.D. in economics from the University of Wisconsin, Madison.

SUZANNE M. RANDOLPH is an associate professor of family studies at the University of Maryland, College Park. In addition, she is co-project director of the Head Start Violence Prevention Project at the university, and a co-principal investigator on the NICHD Study of Early Child Care and Youth Development and the Johns Hopkins University study on the ecology of African American children's development. Her research interests include the normative development of African American infants, toddlers, and preschoolers and culturally responsive evaluation of community-based programs for African American families and other families of color. Randolph is a member of the Society for Research in Child Development and received a B.S. degree in psychology from Howard University and master's and Ph.D. degrees in developmental psychology from the University of Michigan at Ann Arbor.

WERNER SCHINK recently retired as the chief of research for the California Department of Social Services, where he was responsible for California's extensive welfare reform demonstration projects. In addition, his responsibilities included oversight of the evaluations that are being conducted by the University of California, Los Angeles, and the University of California, Berkeley. Previously, Schink held positions as chief of California's $325 million Job Training Partnership Act program and chief economist for California's Employment Development Department. Schink is a member and past president of the National Association for Welfare Research and Statistics, an organization comprised of researchers and statisticians from state and local social services agencies. He received an M.A. from the University of California, Davis.

MICHELE VER PLOEG is a member of the staff of the Committee on National Statistics and serves as study director for this panel. Her research interests include the effects of social policies on families and children, the outcomes of children who experience poverty and changes in family composition, and individuals' education attainment choices. She received a B.A. in economics from Central College and an M.S. and a Ph.D. in consumer economics and housing from Cornell University.

Index